When the People Speak

When the People Speak

Deliberative Democracy and
Public Consultation

James S. Fishkin

OXFORD
UNIVERSITY PRESS

OXFORD

UNIVERSITY PRESS

Great Clarendon Street, Oxford OX2 6DP

Oxford University Press is a department of the University of Oxford.
It furthers the University's objective of excellence in research, scholarship,
and education by publishing worldwide in

Oxford New York

Auckland Cape Town Dar es Salaam Hong Kong Karachi
Kuala Lumpur Madrid Melbourne Mexico City Nairobi
New Delhi Shanghai Taipei Toronto

With offices in

Argentina Austria Brazil Chile Czech Republic France Greece
Guatemala Hungary Italy Japan Poland Portugal Singapore
South Korea Switzerland Thailand Turkey Ukraine Vietnam

Oxford is a registered trade mark of Oxford University Press
in the UK and in certain other countries

Published in the United States
by Oxford University Press Inc., New York

First published 2009
First published in paperback 2011

British Library Cataloguing in Publication Data
Data available
Library of Congress Cataloging in Publication Data
Data available

Typeset by SPI Publisher Services, Pondicherry, India
Printed in Great Britain
on acid-free paper by
Clays Ltd, St Ives plc

ISBN 978-0-19-957210-6 (hbk)
      978-0-19-960443-2 (pbk)

1 3 5 7 9 10 8 6 4 2

This book is dedicated to the memory of my parents,
Joseph and Fannie Fishkin, who made it all possible

Contents

Contents

Preface to Paperback Edition

There are thousands of polls that show what the public is thinking—usually when it is not thinking very much or paying much attention. The Deliberative Poll attempts to show what the public would think—under transparently good conditions for considering an issue in depth. There seems to be a need around the world for this sort of consultation. Since this book was finished, Deliberative Polling has continued to find new applications in places such as Japan, Brazil, Argentina the United Kingdom, and on a European wide basis as well as in the US.

The first Japanese project in Kanagawa was notable for the extraordinary complexity of the topic—the possibility of a change to the Doshu system. Since then there have been two projects in Fujisawa, notable because they were an explicit part of the town planning process. The first national DP in Japan, on policy options to reform the pension system, has just been completed as this edition goes to press.

Brazil's first Deliberative Poll took place in Porto Alegre, the home of the famous "participatory budgeting." For a statewide project, the DP had the advantage that it could scientifically represent the entire state of Rio Grande du Sol. The topic was the contentious issue of career reform of the civil service. This project offered a useful contrast between self selected forums and random sampling and led to some actual legislation being passed. A similarly useful project took place soon after in Argentina, in La Plata, the capital of the state of Buenos Aires. It focused on specific changes to transportation policy, with many of the results being implemented.

In the United Kingdom, *Power 2010* used an online crowd-sourcing suggestion process to generate possible reforms of the political system. An advisory group boiled down the suggestions to 59 proposals. Those fifty nine proposals were evaluated by a national sample that met for a weekend in a Deliberative Poll in London. This project was notable for the way it involved the public in setting the agenda and for the way it combined cyberspace with face to face deliberations over a weekend.

In Brussels the *Europolis* project convened the second European wide Deliberative Poll. The first one, described in this book, showed that a European wide public sphere was possible involving ordinary citizens. A microcosm of all 27 countries speaking 22 languages was once again gathered in Brussels. Instead of the French just talking to the French and the Germans to the Germans, all 27 countries in microcosm could discuss European issues together. The novelty of the second European wide Deliberative Poll was that it occurred soon before the European Parliamentary Elections. And for the first time, a European wide deliberation was combined with the question of voting intention. As the microcosm of European voters came to support more ambitious action on climate change they also came to adopt higher support for the Greens. As they became more tolerant of immigration, they moved somewhat against the conservative party block. Their changes in policy coherently connected with their changes in voting intention.

In the United States the most notable development was the application of the Deliberative Poll to statewide issues. It was applied to the economic future of Michigan, a state hard hit by the recession. A statewide sample was gathered in the capital, Lansing, for deliberations entitled "Hard Times, Hard Choices." The public had dramatic changes of opinion after deliberation, supporting rises in taxes whose pain they felt directly (sales and income taxes) and supporting decreases in taxes whose pain they would not directly feel—business taxes, presumably to stimulate jobs. A one hour documentary was broadcast throughout the state on PBS stations and a detailed report is available (see http://cdd.stanford.edu for details on this project and all the others mentioned above).

The basic picture of deliberative processes offered in this book continues to hold true. It is eminently practical to gather scientific samples, demonstrably representative in attitudes and demographics, to deliberate on complex policy questions. They often show many significant changes in opinion after completing the process. Participants also become more informed on the issues. Lastly public policymakers often have strong incentives to take the public deliberations seriously and implement some or all of the results. Deliberative democracy is not a utopian ideal just for abstract theorizing. It can be implemented via practical methods for public consultation. The public consistently shows that it is smart and worth listening to listening to listening to listening to listening to.

James S. Fishkin

Stanford, CA
February, 2011

Acknowledgments

This is a short book with a long history. It is the result of many deliberations—normative, empirical, and practical.

On the normative side I want to thank some key teachers and colleagues. Robert Dahl first inspired me to think about democratic theory. Bruce Ackerman and I have had a dialogue now over three decades, a dialogue which led to our book *Deliberation Day*. The late Peter Laslett, with whom I coedited some volumes of *Philosophy, Politics and Society*, set an inspiring example for how to make political theory practical. He was also a key adviser in my effort to bring the first Deliberative Poll (DP) to reality, during my year as a Visiting Fellow Commoner at Trinity College, Cambridge. Other moral, political, and social theorists who were notably helpful at various stages included the late Bernard Williams, Doug Rae, William Galston, Charles E. Lindblom, Robert Goodin, Cass Sunstein, Brian Barry, Carole Pateman, Sandy Levinson, Philippe Van Parijs, Philippe Schmitter, Claus Offe, Albena Azmanova, Jane Mansbridge, T.K. Seung, Dan Wikler, Dan Brock, David Miller, Beth Noveck, and the late Iris Young. Larry Lessig has been very helpful in thinking about new technology and deliberative democracy. I am also grateful to Josiah Ober, with whom I have been teaching a seminar at Stanford on "Models of Democracy." The dialogue in that class allowed me to test out many of the ideas of this book and I have also learned much more about Athenian institutions from the experience.

On the empirical side, I owe most to my longtime collaborator Robert Luskin. He and I are preparing a systematic empirical book on these issues. In addition, he and I are coauthors, with a number of other collaborators, on various scholarly papers. These papers, many of which are either in press or in the "revise and resubmit" stage, are all referred to in the book with web links. I have left all the actual analyses to be presented in the papers and the later book as they are all the fruit of collaborative research. My intellectual debts to Luskin are too numerous to mention but they are evident throughout this work, not just where I refer to our empirical work, but also on the normative theory side.

In addition, I would like to thank Norman Bradburn and Roger Jowell for their crucial collaborations on the early British and American DPs. They are both inspiring researchers to work with. I would also like to thank Don Green, Cynthia Farrar, Christian List, Kasper Moeller Hanson, Pam Ryan, Tessa Tan-Torres, Viroj Tangcharoensathien, Vijj Kasemsup, Stephen Boucher, Henri Monceau, Pierangelo Isernia, John Panaretos, Evdokia Xekalaki, Baogang He, Gabor Toka, Doug Rivers, and Shanto Iyengar for the inspiring and creative work we have done together.

Phil Converse deserves special thanks for chairing the Technical Review Committee of the first National Issues Convention (NIC). Norman Bradburn equally deserves thanks for chairing the Committee for the second NIC. Results from both are reported here. Henry Brady and the Berkeley Survey Research Center were extraordinary partners in the second NIC just as NORC was in the first.

The Deliberative Poll was born in 1987 when I was a Fellow at the Center for Advanced Study in the Behavioral Sciences at Stanford. I want to thank the Center and its staff for creating such a congenial place. The Center also played a key role in DP research when I returned years later with a group project on Deliberative Public Opinion in 2001/2. At that point, Luskin and I were joined by Jane Mansbridge, Bruce Ackerman, Henry Brady, David Brady, as well as Stanford faculty such as Shanto Iyengar and Paul Sniderman for a year-long dialogue.

The origins of the idea came in 1987 as I prepared to introduce another Fellow at the Center, Larry Bartels, for his talk about the presidential primary process. I asked myself, as a political theorist how I would change the primary system in the best of all possible worlds. The idea of the DP came into my mind as I was thinking about the dynamics and irrationalities of the process he described so well. I am forever indebted to Larry for providing me with the occasion, not just because of his excellent book but because of the problem it posed

When I thought of the idea, I immediately consulted two Fellows I especially trusted for advice, Bob and Nan Keohane. They raised enough interesting and tough questions that I continued to pursue it. Soon after that, I published it in the *Atlantic* (August 1988). But it only became practical when I met with Max Kampelman and Jeff Kampelman in Washington and we realized that it could be piloted by a television program on PBS. The idea for what became the "National Issues Convention" was born at that time.

The National Issues Convention, and then the many DPs in the United States that followed, would not have happened were it not for two extraordinary persons: Dan Werner, Executive Producer, MacNeil/Lehrer Productions, and Charls E. Walker, who taught me, more than anyone else, how an idea could be turned into reality. I also want to thank David Lloyd, Commissioning Editor, Channel Four, who made the British projects happen and who supervised them with care and vision. Andreas Whittam Smith, Founder and Editor of *The Independent*, was also a key partner in making the first DP happen. The five British DPs on Channel Four were also successful because of superb talent at Granada Television such as Sheena MacDonald, Charles Tremayne, Dorothy Byrne, and the late Sarah Mainwaring-White.

The various "energy" DPs were based on an insight of Dennis Thomas, a former Chairman of the Texas PUC. Along with Will Guild, Ron Lehrer, and Robert Luskin, we went on to work together on all the projects discussed here on energy choices. The Rome project was an initiative of Giancarlo Bosetti, publisher of *Reset*. The Chinese projects are based on the insight and initiative of our collaborator Baogang He. Deliberative Polling was brought to Bulgaria by the Centre for Liberal Strategies headed by Ivan Krastev working with the Open Society Institute. George Soros, Andre Wilkins, Darius Cuplinskas, and Jerzy Celichowski have all been extremely helpful over the years. Smita Singh of the Hewlett Foundation and Chris Kwak and Kara Carlisle of Kellogg proved to be enlightened program officers.

Kasper Moeller Hansen and Vibeke N. Andersen deserve credit for initiating the Danish project on the Euro with *Monday Morning*. All the Australian projects are due to the leadership of Pam Ryan and the organization she created, Issues Deliberation Australia. I also want to thank Gyorgy Lengyel for our recent Hungarian project. David Russell and Ian O'Flynn get primary credit for the Northern Ireland project. They are responsible for the idea of applying the DP to a deeply divided society—our thanks to the vision of Atlantic Philanthropies for making that possible.

Joyce Ichinose is a splendid Manager of the Center for Deliberative Democracy at Stanford. Alice Siu, whose work is reported on here, has completed an important Stanford dissertation and is now Associate Director of the Center. Other graduate students, past and present, have made important contributions including Dennis Plane, Mike Weiksner, Kyu Hahn, Jennifer McGrady, Neil Malhotra, Gaurov Sood, Rui Wang, and Nuri Kim.

Acknowledgments

The European-wide DP *Tomorrow's Europe* is based on the work of two extraordinary collaborators, Stephen Boucher and Henri Monceau, both from Notre Europe at the time. They created a European-wide deliberation for the planning and implementation of a project whose scope had never been realized before. They surmounted every daunting challenge superbly.

The video which accompanies this book, "Europe in One Room," is the work of Emmy Award winning London documentary makers Paladin Invision (PITV). My thanks to Bill Cran, Clive Syddall , Anne Tyerman, and all those at PITV who turned out to do such superb work, not only in coordinating the television coverage of the weekend but also in producing a compelling narrative.

There are too many other collaborators and supporters to list here but many are mentioned in the text. I do, however, want to especially thank Shanto Iyengar for conceiving of the idea that I could move my research program to Stanford and establish the Center for Deliberative Democracy. In addition, then Dean Sharon Long and then Associate Dean Karen Cook deserve special thanks. Two visionaries in the foundation world, Paul Brest of the William and Flora Hewlett Foundation and Sterling Speirn of the W.K. Kellogg Foundation, have been instrumental in making it possible for the Center to thrive and develop thus far. Their support has been central to the work reported on here.

Lastly I want to thank my wife, Shelley, my two sons, Bobby and Joey, my mother-in-law, Carol Plaine Fisher, and most especially my late father-in-law, Milton Fisher. They have not only tolerated my quest for deliberative democracy, but on many occasions they have joined me in the effort and done a great deal to make it all possible.

Charts

1

Democratic Aspirations

Introduction

Democracy gives voice to "we the people." We think it should include "all" the people. And we think it should provide a basis for "the people" thinking about the issues they decide. These two presumptions about democracy are often unstated. While most people would admit they are essential conditions for democracy, the difficulty of realizing them in combination is largely unexamined. How to do so is the subject of this book.

Our subject is how to achieve *deliberative democracy*: how to include everyone under conditions where they are effectively motivated to really think about the issues. This is the problem of how to fulfill two fundamental values—political equality and deliberation.

We live in an age of democratic experimentation—both in our official institutions and in the many informal ways in which the public is consulted. Many methods and technologies can be used to give voice to the public will. But some give a picture of public opinion as if through a fun house mirror. They muffle or distort, providing a platform for special interests to *impersonate* the public will—to mobilize letters or phone calls, emails, text messages, or Internet tabulations of opinion that appear to be representative of the general public, but are really only from specific and well-organized interest groups.[1] In those cases, "grass roots" are synthetically transformed into what lobbyists call "astro turf." And mass phoning to policymakers may represent about as much citizen autonomy as if they were "robocalls." Ostensibly open democratic practices provide an opportunity for "capture" by those who are well enough organized. These are distortions in how public views are expressed. There are also distortions in how they are shaped. Elites and interest groups attempt to mold public opinion by using focus-group-tested messages in order later to invoke those same opinions as a democratic mandate.[2] From the standpoint of some democratic theories these practices are entirely appropriate. They are just part of the terms of political competition between parties and between organized interests.[3] But from the perspective outlined here—deliberative democracy—they detour democracy from the dual aspiration to realize political equality and deliberation. And at least for some issues some of the time, there ought to be ways to represent the views of the people equally under conditions in which they can think and come to a considered judgment.

Why is it difficult to achieve both inclusion and thoughtfulness, both political equality and deliberation? Consider some of the limitations of mass opinion as we routinely find it in modern developed societies. We can then ponder the problem of how those limitations might be overcome in a way that, in some appropriate sense, includes everyone.

First, it is difficult to effectively motivate citizens in mass society to become informed. Levels of information about most political or policy questions are routinely low. Social scientists have an explanation—"rational ignorance."[4] If I have one opinion in millions why should I take the time and trouble to become really informed about politics or policy? My individual views will have only negligible effects. From the standpoint of many ideals of citizenship, we would like the situation to be otherwise. We would like citizens to be able to cast informed votes and have enough information to evaluate competing arguments. But most of us have other demands on our time. A democracy in which we all had substantive information would seem to take too many meetings.

Second, the public has fewer "opinions" deserving of the name than are routinely reported in polls. Respondents to polls do not like to admit that they "don't know" so they will choose an option, virtually at random, rather than respond that they have never thought about the issue. George Bishop found that people responded with apparent opinions to survey questions about the so-called Public Affairs Act of 1975 even though it was fictional. And when the *Washington Post* celebrated the twentieth un-anniversary of the nonexistent Public Affairs Act of 1975 by asking about its repeal, respondents seemed to have views about that as well, even though it never existed in the first place.[5] Of course on many issues the public does have views, but some of them are very much "top of the head," vague impressions of sound bites and headlines, highly malleable and open to the techniques of impression management perfected by the persuasion industry. A democracy in which we all had substantive opinions would also seem to take too many meetings.

A third limitation is that even when people discuss politics or policy they do so mostly with people like themselves—those from similar backgrounds, social locations, and outlooks. And if one knows someone with sharply contrasting political viewpoints, it is usually far easier to talk about the weather than to talk about the political issues one disagrees about.[6] Why put your relationships at risk by raising flashpoints of conflict? In a highly partisan environment, having a mutually respectful conversation with those one disagrees with takes work and the right social context. Actually talking—and listening to others—across the boundaries of political disagreement would seem to take too much effort and too many (potentially unpleasant) meetings.[7]

Perhaps, it might be argued, the Internet makes up for our limitations in conversation. We can so easily consult almost any viewpoint. In theory, the information available is almost limitless. And technologies, such as the multichannel cable environment, podcasts, Tivo, Kindle, satellite radio, all make it so easy to hear or see what we want, precisely when we want it. J.S. Mill argued in his classic *On Liberty* that freedom of thought, expression, and association would facilitate exposure to diverse points of view allowing us to achieve, or approach achieving, "individuality" (his word for our thinking for ourselves and living lives which are, in substantial part, self-chosen).[8]

Yet, suppose we exercise this liberty, with all its technological enhancements, not to engage with contrasting points of view but rather to read, watch, listen to, and converse with the like-minded. Suppose increasing freedom and ease of choice simply facilitate our exposure to comforting and confirming points of view. To the extent this is the case, the technological expansion of our ease of choice backfires on the presumptions of a liberal/democratic society. Liberty allows us to choose less diversity and to self-impose a dialogue (to the extent we have one at all) mostly with ourselves or people like ourselves. There is no reason to presume that technology will counterbalance the tendency of face-to-face political conversation toward self-selection among the like-minded. There is a plausible case that it may make it worse.[9]

A fourth limitation of public opinion as we routinely find it in mass societies is its vulnerability to manipulation. A disengaged and uninformed public is more easily manipulated than one that has firm opinions based on extended thought and discussion. Such opinions are more manipulable, first, because they are more volatile at the individual level.

They may be just "top of the head" impressions of sound bites and headlines or they may even be close to non-attitudes or phantom opinions. Second, public opinion in mass society may be open to manipulation because of the public's low information levels. If people have little background information, then foregrounding particular facts may be persuasive when people have no idea of the broader context. Clean coal advocates make a powerful case for the benefits of clean coal compared to dirty coal, but the mass public has little idea that clean coal is much dirtier than natural gas (as well as other alternatives like renewable energy). Selective invocation of true facts (such as that clean coal is cleaner than dirty coal) without a context where those facts can be compared to others (how clean coal compares to other energy alternatives) can allow advocates to manipulate opinion.[10] Third, when people have little information they may easily fall prey to misinformation. Even when contrary information was in the public domain, assertions that Iraq was responsible for 9/11 apparently carried weight when it was shrouded in the protective glare of national security. Fourth, a strategy of manipulation that is probably more common than misinformation is strategically incomplete but misleading information. If one argument based on true but misleadingly incomplete information has high visibility through expensive advertising and the counter to it never gets an effective audience, then the public can be seriously misled. Fifth, another key strategy of manipulation is to "prime" one aspect of a policy, making that dimension so salient that it overwhelms other considerations. In effect, a candidate or policy advocate changes the terms of evaluation so that the issue on which his or her side does best becomes the one that is decisive.[11]

The strategic use of priming to change the terms of competition can sometimes depend on a true incident magnified many times when taken out of context by ads, by campaigns, by campaign surrogates, or apparently independent commentators or groups (Willie Horton for Dukakis; sighing in the presidential debate for Gore; Giuliani taking a cell phone call from his wife during a speech), or a false claim asserted intensely (Swift Boats for Kerry), or even an outsider intervening with the intention of influencing the election (a plausible interpretation of Bin Laden appearing in video just before the 2004 presidential election). By priming a dimension, whether crime or character or national security, the incident can be intentionally employed to change (or further emphasize) the terms of evaluation to the neglect of other issues.[12] As campaigns (and outside actors) compete to reshape the playing field, the result is literally MAD or what might be termed *mutually assured distraction*.

The enormous growth in financing of campaign ads in the United States from legally independent groups (527 groups named after a section of the IRS code) adds many more opportunities for the manipulation of public opinion. Normally the disincentive to attack an opponent or a policy proposal is that a candidate can be held responsible for going negative or, worse, for misleading or distorting the records of opponents. But under the miasma of legal independence, there is a new form of what is called, in the national security context, *asymmetrical warfare.* Just as terrorists can attack a country but offer only a shadowy return address for retaliation or deterrence, 527s can attack a candidate but offer only a shadowy return address—giving the candidate who benefits plausible deniability. For example, even when a presidential candidate is supported by a 527 started by a paid staff member, he can disavow all connection.[13]

Asymmetrical (campaign) warfare and MAD combine in the use of campaign surrogates and nominally independent commentators to prime issues, reshape the debate and crowd out less sensational topics from the airspace. In 2004, did John Kerry insult Dick Cheney's daughter when he alluded in a presidential debate to the fact that she was lesbian? Some commentators took up a lot of air time claiming that he did. In 2008, did Hillary Clinton insult or demean the memory of Martin Luther King when she said President Johnson was necessary to realize the dream? Again, crucial days of public discussion in the middle of the primary campaign went to such an "issue" ignited by commentators and surrogates with plausible deniability by candidates.

In addition, changing technology makes it difficult to limit the public dialogue to stories that can be filtered through the judgment of editors. The mere fact that someone asserts something can make it news. So a shadowy group such as "Vietnam Veterans Against McCain" can make claims about his war record during the primary season, claims reminiscent of the Swift Boat efforts against Kerry, and such assertions become part of the public dialogue. The Internet can spread misinformation, such as claims that Senator Obama is a Muslim, and this information spreads virally in emails. Text messages that spread from an anonymous or fake source tell Obama voters to vote Wednesday due to long lines when the election is Tuesday.[14] Asymmetrical (campaign) warfare can come from anywhere and the result can be manipulative even on the eve of elections.[15]

Our US system began with an aspiration for deliberation—for representatives to "refine and enlarge" or "filter" the public voice, as

James Madison theorized. But the technology of the persuasion industry has made it possible for elites to shape opinion and then invoke those opinions in the name of democracy. Techniques of persuasion tested in focus groups and measured by people meters have been developed for commercial purposes to sell us products ranging from detergents to automobiles. The same techniques are routinely employed to sell candidates and policies or to mobilize or demobilize voting. As our political process is colonized by the persuasion industry, as our public dialogue is voiced increasingly in advertising, our system has undertaken a long journey from Madison to Madison Avenue.

Efforts to manipulate public opinion work best with an inattentive and/or uninformed public. If the public is inattentive, then it may not take much to persuade and it may be easy to prime. If it is uninformed, it may be manipulated even if it is highly engaged or even emotionally gripped by an issue. In that case, it may be easily misled through misinformation or primed to consider only certain dimensions of an issue.

One might ask what is the difference between manipulation and persuasion. Democracy needs to preserve ample room for freedom of thought and expression and persuasion is a natural activity within that protected space. Manipulation can be expected to take place in that space as well. But to the extent freedom of thought and expression are used to manipulate public opinion, this will fall far short of deliberation. *A person has been manipulated by a communication when she has been exposed to a message intended to change her views in a way she would not accept if she were to think about it on the basis of good conditions—and in fact she does change her views in the manner that was intended.* So if she is fooled by misinformation and changes her views on that basis, then she has been manipulated. If she had good information instead, then on this definition, her views would not have changed. In all these cases, the definition of manipulation turns in part on the alternative of good conditions and good information we are hypothesizing as a benchmark for comparison. Those good conditions are, in fact, a good part of what we will mean by deliberation as we develop the concept here.

By hypothesizing what people would think under good conditions as a point of comparison, we are not asserting that whenever people are not deliberating they are being manipulated. Others must actually intend to manipulate opinion in a given direction for the opinions to be manipulated. And the good conditions defined by deliberation are just a benchmark for comparison—a way of clarifying what is shortcut by manipulation. Perhaps manipulators want me to think X. Perhaps I would in fact think X if I deliberated on the issue (if I considered the competing arguments and had good information about them). On the definition offered here, I have not been manipulated if that is the case and I do think X.[16]

These are only some of the limitations of public opinion as we find it in mass society. But even with this incomplete list, we can see the difficulty of achieving both inclusion and thoughtfulness. Most people are not effectively motivated to get information, to form opinions, or to discuss issues with those who have different points of view. Each citizen has only one vote or voice in millions and most have other pressing demands on their time. The production of informed, considered opinions for politics and policy is a public good. And the logic of collective action for public goods dictates that motivating large numbers to produce a public good requires selective incentives (incentives that apply just to those who produce them) otherwise there will be a failure to provide them.[17] Barring some transformation of preferences in which people valued forming informed and considered judgments for its own sake (maybe after some transformative form of civic education[18]) there is every reason to believe that a large-scale public opinion with the limitations just sketched will be the norm. The bulk of the public will lack information, often lack opinions about specific policy issues on the elite agenda, and will limit its conversations and sources to those from similar social locations and viewpoints. It will also be vulnerable to manipulation (largely as a consequence of the first three limitations). In short, we can expect an under-informed and nondeliberative mass public. In that case, if we include everyone, it seems that we are unlikely to get a thoughtful public input from our democratic institutions. We might, if we somehow selected only elites or opinion leaders, but then we would be risking violations of political equality. A democracy of elites or opinion leaders would at best be a democracy *for the people*, but not one in any significant sense *by the people*. Our continuing focus here will be on prospects of involving ordinary citizens in a manner that is both representative and deliberative.

The picture of the mass public just sketched is widely accepted. In most modern developed societies, it is the "street level epistemology" of public opinion in the large-scale nation-state.[19] However, there are some counterarguments about the significance of this picture. First, some have argued that even if the public is not well informed, it does not much matter because ordinary citizens, as a by-product of their daily lives, pick up bits of information (cues or shortcuts) that can inform them about what they really need to know in a democracy. For example, I need not know the details of a referendum proposition if I know who is for it and who is against it. I can then follow the endorsements and express my views and interests without going to too many meetings or spending too much time.

Of course, knowing who endorses the yes or no side is itself information that is often scarce.[20] But for many contested issues, there may be different cues whose significance deserves deliberation and competing arguments engaging the elites that ordinary citizens might find compelling if only they focused on them. We found in a referendum in Australia and in a general election in Britain that when a scientific sample became more informed and really discussed the issues, it changed its voting intentions significantly.[21] Hence, in at least some cases, deliberation makes a considerable difference and the uninformed do not simply reach the same result.

A second line of counterargument is that we can make do without a public that is generally well informed by dividing up the electorate into "issue publics." Farmers may be very concerned about agricultural policy. Jews may be especially interested in Middle East policy. And Cuban-Americans may be especially interested in policy about Cuba. For those issues, the relevant issue publics may in fact become well informed. If I do not care about farm policy I can just leave it to the farmers (or so the argument goes). But from the standpoint of democratic theory, the worry is that farmers have special interests. And all the other issue publics have their own distinct interests and values. To what extent do we want to delegate policy to the relevant issue publics? As Robert Dahl noted years ago, leaving policy to those especially interested leads to a pattern not of majority rule but of "minorities rule."[22] While such a picture may have plausibility as an interpretation of how our system actually works, it does not fare well if the aspiration is to realize both political equality and deliberation. There is little reason to think that the minorities who self-select to become engaged in their areas of special interest would approximate the views of the rest of the electorate.[23] However, if the minority deliberating were a random sample of the whole public, rather than a self-selected group with special interests (farmers, Cuban-Americans, etc.), then it might be plausible for a representative microcosm to combine both political equality and deliberation. However, issue publics are special; they are not representative of the broader public. That is part of what makes them distinctive. A solution to our problem must depend on institutional designs intended to bring about representativeness as well as thoughtfulness.

From Athens to Athens

On a crisp summer morning in June 2006, a scientific sample of 160 randomly chosen citizens gathered in a suburb of Athens to select a candidate for mayor. The question was who would be the official candidate representing one of Greece's two major parties, the left-center party PASOK. George Papandreou, the national party leader, had decided to employ Deliberative Polling,[24] rather than a decision by party elites or a mass primary, to officially select its candidate in Marousi, the portion of the Athens metropolitan area which hosted the Olympics.[25]

In an essay in the *International Herald Tribune*, Papandreou outlined his reasoning for this bold step. "Democracy is less credible if the choices on the electoral ballot are not determined by truly democratic means." But each of the alternative methods seemed to have difficulties. The main means of democratizing was the mass primary which has "low and unrepresentative turnout" and opinions often formed from "name recognition and a superficial impression of sound bites." So what is the alternative? "In most countries, parties that do not use the mass primary usually leave the nomination of candidates to party elites." This dilemma suggested a challenge for which Athenian history provided a solution:

> Is there a way to include an informed and representative public voice in the nomination process? A solution can be found in the practices of ancient Athens, where hundreds of citizens chosen by lot would regularly deliberate together and make important public decisions.[26]

Before the day's deliberations, a party committee had narrowed down the candidates to six finalists. Then, a scientific random sample of voters had responded to a survey on the candidates and issues. The survey respondents were invited to a day of deliberation both among themselves and with the candidates. When the sample arrived, participants spent the day discussing nineteen local issues and questioning the six candidates about their positions. At the end of ten hours of deliberation, they filled out the same questionnaire as on first contact and then went to a polling booth to cast a secret ballot to select the nominee.

Panos Alexandris, a local lawyer who had been the least well known among the six candidates at the start, led the first round of balloting that evening. As the ballots were counted, the voters went to dinner. Since no candidate got a clear majority, a second round to choose among the two finalists was held. Alexandris emerged with a clear majority. For the first time in 2,400 years, a random sample of citizens had been convened in Athens to deliberate and then officially make an important public decision.

The process fit the pattern of other Deliberative Polls: first a random sample of a population (in this case eligible voters) responded to a telephone survey, then they were convened together for many hours of deliberation, both in small groups and plenary sessions, directing questions developed in small groups to competing candidates, experts, or policymakers in the plenaries, and then, at the end of the process, they filled out the same questionnaire as the one they had been given when they were first contacted in their homes. In this case, the questionnaires were supplemented by a secret ballot in a separate polling booth because the process was more than a poll. It was an official decision.

The Italian newspaper *La Repubblica* described the plenary session with the candidates, following hours of small group discussion:

> When, on Sunday afternoon, the six candidates—four men and two women—faced the hall full of people, it was a dramatic moment. They knew they were facing people who had thought about the issues. The questions which came—on the environment, on the big debt which the city had run up, on the dirt in the streets—were sharp and detailed, demanding good answers to be convincing. And because they were so precise, it became clear very soon which of the candidates were themselves knowledgeable on the issues, and which were not.[27]

The sample became more informed during the process (according to an index of knowledge questions about local issues) and its voting intentions changed dramatically. Alexandris, for example, gained fifteen points (from 24% to 39% from first contact until the final survey). He also gained another sixteen points in the runoff between the two finalists. And, as in other Deliberative Polls, it was the people who became more informed who also changed their views.[28] The changes of opinion were driven by information, and not just perceptions of candidate personality.[29]

For the party this project brought a substantive form of democracy to candidate selection while at the same time opening up the pathways to candidate recruitment. While one cannot infer too much from the first case, it is instructive that the least well-known candidate at the start was the one who got the nomination. Afterward, party leader Papandreou concluded that this process "strengthened democratic procedures." He added: "We want to transfer this experience to many parts of the world ... and to use it in other cities (of the country) and for different issues."[30]

This project brought to life a modern version of an ancient political life-form, one that was the distinctive practice in ancient Athens. In the fifth and fourth centuries BC, Athenian citizens chosen by lot would gather together for a day, and sometimes much longer, to make important public decisions. There were citizen juries of 500 or more, whose purview was far broader than that of law courts in the modern era. In addition, there were other distinctive institutions. Legislative commissions chosen by lot (*nomothetai*) would make the final decisions on legislation by the fourth century. There was a special procedure (the *graphe paranomon*) in which someone who made an illegal or irresponsible proposal in the Assembly could be brought to trial before a randomly chosen jury of 500 delib-erators. Anticipation of such a possible trial made people more careful about what they might say in the Assembly. And most importantly, the Council of 500 was randomly chosen and met for the entire year, setting the agenda for meetings of the Assembly and alternating in groups of fifty for periods of more than a month to take administrative responsibility for much of the government.

The Athenian practices were unique in combining two key elements—deliberation and random sampling. That combination provided a distinc-tive solution to the problem social scale poses to deliberative democracy (a term we are reserving for the *combination* of political equality and deliberation). In a deliberative democracy everyone's views are considered equally under good conditions for the participants to arrive at their views. The process is deliberative in that it provides informative and mutually respectful discussion in which people consider the issue on its merits. The process is democratic in that it requires the equal counting of everyone's views as we will see below.[31]

Of course, a great deal will depend on what we mean by "good con-ditions" for the participants to arrive at their views. But for the moment notice how this aspiration to combine deliberation with political equality is affected by the problem of social scale.

While ordinary citizens are subject to the incentives for rational ignorance, those chosen in the microcosm face an entirely different situation—once they are chosen. They are all part of a smaller group whose members do, individually, have influence. Each participant in what we call a Deliberative Poll has the influence of one person's voice in a small group of fifteen or so and one person's responses in a few hun-dred in the final questionnaire or balloting. Once selected, the corrosive calculations of rational ignorance no longer apply to members of the microcosm. Within the microcosm, democracy is reframed on a human scale where individual voices can seem important enough to effectively motivate individual effort.

One might think that ancient Athens presented a different situation, one that was free of this problem of social scale. It is often discussed as a city-state where everyone could gather together in the Assembly.[32] But depending on the period and on some competing calculations, the citizenry ranged from 30,000 to 60,000.[33] And the Pnyx, the hill where the Assembly met, could only hold between 6,000 and 8,000 (the latter after it was enlarged).[34] Hence, ancient Athens had the same fundamental problem. Everyone could not gather together to discuss the issues and each person's share of direct democracy would be vanishingly small.

But direct democracy in the Assembly, open to all citizens, was only one way to involve the public. Random sampling or the process of selection by lot, which was conducted from a citizen list of willing participants with a machine called a Kleroterion, offered a form of representative democracy that provided strong incentives for ordinary citizens to pay attention once selected. Just as an individual citizen in modern times may have only the faintest reason to follow the details of a jury trial if one is not a juror, but great reason to pay attention if one has been selected to be a juror, the individuals empanelled by lottery had every reason to focus on the merits of the issues presented. One difference is that with ancient juries or groups of deliberators of several hundred, the whole microcosm was large enough to be representative of the total population of citizens. Modern juries of twelve, whose sampling is interfered with on many grounds (peremptory challenges, advice of jury consultants, etc.), cannot make comparable claims of representativeness. They are too small and there are too many strategic decisions involved in their selection in our adversary legal system.

Ancient Athenian democracy should not be idealized. Notoriously, a citizens' jury chosen by lottery or random sampling convicted Socrates and set the cause of democracy back almost two and half millennia (although modern investigations have shown how he probably manipulated, indeed goaded, them into such a verdict).[35] And the one-day deliberations of most Athenian institutions, unlike the Council of 500, lacked any small group or face-to-face discussion as 500 people or so would sit in an amphitheater and hear opposing arguments. There were also obvious limitations in the application of random sampling. Only those who put themselves forward ("those who were willing") were on the list in the first place. In addition, the definition of citizenship, determining those who were eligible, was extremely limited. Females, slaves, and metics (resident aliens) were all left out. Still, the Athenians had an idea that provided deliberative democracy for its citizenry on a human scale. And it was a scale that was not limited in size to the city-state.

These Athenian practices were distinctive for combining two key ideas—random sampling and deliberation. Both have since lost their prominence in the design of democratic institutions (although random sampling has been embedded in our unofficial political life through conventional public opinion polling). And the idea of combining random sampling with deliberation was largely lost throughout the history of democratic practice.[36] Interest in the combination is a recent phenomenon, part of the revival of interest in deliberative democracy.[37] Let us situate this combination in the range of possible strategies for public consultation. Then we will turn to further clarification of the values and democratic theories at issue in these different practices.

Consulting the public

Who speaks for the people? There are many democratic mechanisms for giving voice to public opinion. Let us explore a range of them from the standpoint of achieving the values of deliberation and political equality.

In our democratic experience thus far, the design (and possible reform) of democratic processes has confronted a recurring choice between institutions, on the one hand, that express what the public actually thinks but usually under debilitated conditions for it to think about the issues in question, as contrasted with institutions, on the other hand, that express more deliberative public opinion—what the public *would* think about an issue if it were to experience better conditions for thinking about it. The hard choice, in other words, is between debilitated but actual opinion, on the one hand, and deliberative but counterfactual opinion, on the other. One sort of institution offers a snapshot of public opinion as it is, even though the people are usually not thinking very much. The public is usually not very informed, engaged, or attentive.

Another sort of institution (at its best) gives expression to what the public would think about an issue if it were more informed, engaged, and attentive—even though this more thoughtful opinion is usually counterfactual in that it is not actually widely shared. The only way out of this dilemma would be to somehow create more informed, engaged, and attentive public opinion that was *also* generally shared by the entire mass public. Later, we will consider this challenging possibility.

Deliberative or "refined" public opinion (I take the term "refined" from Madison's famous phrase in *Federalist* No. 10 referring to representatives serving to "refine and enlarge the public views") can be thought of as opinion, after it has been tested by the consideration of competing arguments and information conscientiously offered by others who hold contrasting views. I will refer to opinion as "raw" when it has not been subjected to such a process. A basic distinction among democratic institutions is between institutions designed to express refined public opinion and those that would merely reflect opinion in its raw form.

Raw public opinion is routinely voiced by all the established institutions of mass democracy—initiatives, referenda, public opinion polls, focus groups.[38] Moves to more direct consultation in the United States, say, through direct election of senators rather than the original indirect method, were also moves in the direction of more mass democracy in that they gave more weight to raw public opinion. The transformation of the Electoral College into a vote aggregation mechanism, as opposed to the original vision (which was that, state by state, it should function as a deliberative body) is a similar move in the direction of mass democracy empowering raw public opinion. In the same way, the dramatic increase in the use of the direct primary for presidential candidate selection, particularly after the McGovern–Fraser reforms in the 1970s, has been a move toward more mass democracy. In the United States, the national party conventions were once institutions of elite deliberation, engaged in multiple ballots for candidate selection and serious discussion of party platforms and issues facing the country. Now they are media extravaganzas, staged for their effects on mass public opinion with candidate selection having been determined beforehand by mass democracy—through direct primaries.

Our most common encounter with refined public opinion is through representative institutions that seek, as Madison said, to "refine and enlarge the public views by passing them through the medium of a chosen body of citizens." At their best, such institutions are sensitive not just to what constituents actually think, but also to what they would think if they were better informed.

This distinction between two forms of public opinion, raw and refined, corresponds roughly, but does not overlap perfectly, with the seemingly parallel distinction between direct and representative democracy. For example, one of the most influential institutions of mass democracy, an institution that depicts the current state of public opinion as it is, with all its limitations, is the public opinion poll. While polls are closely aligned with direct democracy (and were originally offered by George Gallup as a proxy for direct democracy—even to the point that they were first called "sampling referenda"[39]) polls employ statistical samples to stand for, or represent, the rest of the public. The members of such a "representative" sample are selected by a random scientific process rather than by an election. But they are still "representative" of the mass public; they are a small body that stands for the rest, the much larger electorate of mass society.

One way of stating the dilemma of institutional design is that we face a forced choice between forms of opinion that are debilitated but actual or those that are more deliberative but (usually) counterfactual. Actual opinion will be debilitated for the four reasons noted earlier. But actual opinion has more weight in real political processes than a representation of what people would think—even if the latter has some recommending force. Exploring the contexts in which what people would think has consequence will be a main subject in Chapter 5.

Corresponding to each of these notions of public opinion, there is a common image of how democratic institutions work. The American Founders relied on the metaphor of the *filter*. Representative institutions were supposed to refine public opinion through deliberation. Opponents of elite filtering, beginning with the Anti-Federalists, relied on a different notion of representation. Representatives were to come as close as possible to serving as a "mirror" of the public and its actual opinions. The "filter" creates counterfactual but deliberative representations of public opinion. The "mirror" offers a picture of public opinion just as it is, even if it is debilitated or inattentive. The conflicting images suggest a hard choice between the *reflective* opinion of the filter and the *reflected* opinion of the mirror.

The filter and the mirror

American democracy is a palimpsest of political possibilities. As with a painting layered over previous ones, images from an earlier vision sometimes show through. But those bits and pieces of the earlier picture are hard for most Americans to make sense of. Why do we have an Electoral College? Why is the Senate so much smaller than the House? Why do we privilege the idea of a "convention"—for constitution making and ratification, and even in our national party nominating processes?

15

In fact, the earlier vision has coherence and sometimes is foregrounded by events that make it shine through the layers of more recent reforms. The Senate was originally designed to be an indirectly elected and small deliberative body. Too large a body would produce only the "confusions of a multitude" (*Federalist* No. 55). The Electoral College was originally intended as a deliberative body (for each state) in which the Electors would be free to choose the most qualified candidate. The preferred mode of decision on constitutional matters was the "convention"—the constitutional convention and the ratifying conventions for each state. Later party practices picked up this notion of the convention as a deliberative body in the rise of the national party conventions. However, those conventions are usually not much more like a deliberative body than the Electoral College in its current form. Their outcomes are fully as predictable once the delegates (or the electors) are selected. Bringing power to the people, laudable as that may be, takes effective decision-making away from elite deliberative bodies. Our long-standing patterns of democratic reform dramatize the conflict between elite deliberation and mass participation.

As Madison reported on his own position in his notes on the Constitutional Convention, he was "an advocate for the policy of refining the popular appointments by successive filtrations."[40] Famously, he argued in *Federalist* No. 10, that the effect of representation was "to refine and enlarge the public views by passing them through the medium of a chosen body of citizens.... Under such a regulation it may well happen that the public voice, pronounced by the representatives of the people, will be more consonant to the public good than if pronounced by the people themselves, if convened for the purpose." Running throughout Madison's thinking is the distinction between "refined" public opinion, the considered judgments that can result from the deliberations of a small representative body, on the one hand, and the "temporary errors and delusions" of public opinion that may be found outside this deliberative process, on the other. It is only through the deliberations of a small face-to-face representative body that one can arrive at the "the cool and deliberate sense of the community" (*Federalist* No. 63). This was a principal motivation for the Senate, which was intended to resist the passions and interests that might divert the public into majority tyranny.

The founders were sensitive to the social conditions that would make deliberation possible. For example, large meetings of citizens were thought to be dangerous because they were too large to be deliberative, no matter how thoughtful or virtuous the citizenry might be. As Madison said in *Federalist* No. 55, "had every Athenian citizen been a Socrates, every Athenian assembly would still have been a mob." A key desideratum in the Founders' project of constitutional design was the creation of conditions where the formulation and expression of deliberative public opinion would be possible.

The filter can be thought of as the process of deliberation through which representatives, in face-to-face discussion, may come to considered judgments about public issues. For our purposes, we can specify a working notion of deliberation: face-to-face discussion by which participants conscientiously raise, and respond to, competing arguments so as to arrive at considered judgments about the solutions to public problems.[41] The danger is that if the social context involves too many people, or if the motivations of the participants are distracted by the kinds of passions or interests that would motivate factions, then deliberative democracy will not be possible. It is clear that from the Founders' perspective, the social conditions we are familiar with in mass or referendum democracy would be far from appropriate for deliberation.

Reflecting the people as they are

As Jack Rakove has noted, the one widely shared desideratum in the American notion of representation at the time of the founding was that a representative assembly should, to use John Adams's phrase, be "in miniature an exact portrait of the people at large."[42] In the hands of the Anti-Federalists, this notion became a basis for objecting to the apparent elitism of the filtering metaphor because only the educated upper classes were expected to do the refining in small elite assemblies. The mirror notion of representation was an expression of fairness and equality. As the "Federal Farmer" put it: "A fair and equal representation is that in which the interests, feelings, opinions and views of the people are collected, in such manner as they would be were the people all assembled."[43] As Melancton Smith, who opposed the Constitution at the New York ratification convention, argued, representatives "should be a true picture of the people, possess a knowledge of their circumstances and their wants, sympathize in all their distresses, and be disposed to seek their true interests." In line with the mirror theory of representation, Anti-Federalists sought frequent elections, term limits, and any measures that would increase the closeness of resemblance between representatives and those they represented.

"The people all assembled" is exactly the kind of gathering the Federalists believed would give only an inferior rendering of the public good. Recall Madison's claim that a small representative group would give a better account of the public good than would the "people themselves if convened for the purpose" (*Federalist* No. 10). The mirror is a picture of public opinion as it is; the deliberative filter provides a counterfactual picture of public opinion as it would be, were it "refined and enlarged."

The Framers were clearly haunted by the possibility that factions aroused by passions or interests adverse to the rights of others could do bad things. The image they feared seems to be some combination of the Athenian mob and Shays's rebellion. Part of the case for deliberative public opinion is that the "cool and deliberate sense of the community" (*Federalist* No. 63) would be insulated from the passions and interests that might motivate factions. The founders believed that public opinion, when filtered by deliberative processes, would more likely serve the public good and avoid mob-like behavior of the kind that threatens tyranny of the majority (see section below on "Avoiding Tyranny of the Majority").

Deliberative versus mass democracy: An early skirmish

From the standpoint of the founders, the problem of the conflict between the two forms of public opinion—and the institutions that would express them—was soon dramatized by the Rhode Island referendum, the only effort to consult the people directly about the ratification of the Constitution. Rhode Island was a hotbed of paper money and, from the Federalist standpoint, irresponsible government and fiscal mismanagement. An Anti-Federalist stronghold, "Rogue Island" lived up to the Founders' image of a place where the passions of the public, unfiltered by deliberation, might lead to dangerous results.

The Anti-Federalists sparked a thoroughgoing debate over the proper method of consulting the people—one that dramatized the long conflict that followed between mass and deliberative institutions. Referendum advocates held that "submitting it to every Individual Freeholder of the state was the only Mode in which the true Sentiments of the people could be collected."[44] However, the Federalists objected that a referendum would not provide a discussion of the issues in which the arguments could really be joined. The referendum was objected to, in other words, on the grounds that it would produce defective deliberation. By holding the referendum in town meetings scattered throughout the state, different arguments would be offered in each place, and there would not be any shared sense of how the arguments offered in one place might be answered in another.

> The sea-port towns cannot hear and examine the arguments of their brethren in the country on this subject, nor can they in return be possessed of our views thereof . . . each separate interest will act under an impression of private and local motives only, uninformed of those reasons and arguments which might lead to measures of common utility and public good.[45]

Federalists held that only in a convention could representatives of the entire state meet together, voice their concerns, and have them answered by those with different views so as to arrive at some collective solution for the common good. The very idea of the convention as a basis for ratification was an important innovation motivated by the need for deliberation. Direct consultation of the mass public might reflect public opinion, but it would not provide for the kind of coherent and balanced consideration of the issues required for deliberation.

Federalists also noted another defect—lack of information:

> [E]very individual Freeman ought to investigate these great questions to some good degree in order to decide on this Constitution: the time therefore to be spent in this business would prove a great tax on the freemen to be assembled in Town-meetings, which must be kept open not only three days but three months or more, in preparation as the people at large have more or less information.

While representatives chosen for a convention might acquire the appropriate information in a reasonable time, it would take an extraordinary amount of time to similarly prepare the "people at large."

Of course, what happened in the end is that the referendum was held; it was boycotted by the Federalists; and the Constitution was voted down. Rhode Island, under threat of embargo and even of dismemberment (Connecticut threatening to invade from one side and Massachusetts from the other) capitulated and held the required state convention to eventually approve the Constitution.

This incident was an early American salvo in a long war of competing conceptions of democracy. In the long run, the Federalist emphasis on deliberation and discussion may well have lost out to a form of democracy, embodied in referenda and other institutions of mass democracy that mirror public opinion as it is, with all its defects. Of course, democratic institutions typically will offer a mix of deliberative and mass democracy, a mix of the filter and the mirror, but over the last two centuries of democratic experience in America (and indeed in most developed democracies) the balance has shifted toward far greater mass influence in the mix—far greater deference toward raw public opinion (as opposed to refined or more deliberative views).

In the United States, consider what has happened to the Electoral College (intended as a place for deliberating electors), the election of senators (once conducted by state legislatures), the presidential nomination system (once dominated by party elites), the development and transformation of the national party conventions (now preordained in their results), the rise of referenda (where plebiscitary institutions supplant elite decisions) and the pervasiveness of public opinion polling. Many aspects of Madisonian "filtration" have disappeared in a system that increasingly "mirrors" public opinion constrained by rational ignorance. In these and many other ways, there has been a steadily increasing role for the "reflected" public opinion of the mirror rather than the "reflective" public opinion of the filter.

The same dilemma faced by the Federalists and Anti-Federalists at the birth of the US Constitution has resonances with current efforts to build a new constitutional structure for the European Union (EU). Just as only one state voted directly by referendum on the US Constitution, Rhode Island, turning it down, only one state voted directly by referendum on the Lisbon Treaty, Ireland, and also turned it down. The impasse has not been resolved at this writing but it shows the fundamental dilemma: elite deliberation continues to be widely viewed as undemocratic (hence the EU's famous "democratic deficit") while direct mass consultation connects with "top of the head" opinion that may well be uninformed. High gas prices very likely had more to do with the EU treaty being defeated than the merits of the proposed reform. In recent years, constitutional change or reform of the EU oscillates between elite processes (a "convention" which gave birth to a failed new "constitution") and defeat by referenda, whether in Denmark, France, the Netherlands, or Ireland.

Whether the issue is constitutional change or public policy, combining political equality and deliberation continues to pose the problem: how to obtain the consent of the people under conditions when the people can also be informed about what they are consenting to.

Eight methods of public consultation

Consider two fundamental questions: what and who? The first has to do with what form of public opinion is being assessed and the second has to do with whose opinion it is that is being assessed. For the first, we can say that an institution will predominantly offer public opinion that is *raw* or *refined*. The second distinction is concerned with *whose* opinion is being consulted. While the classifications I will focus on do not exhaust all the possibilities, they cover the principal practical alternatives. The people consulted can be self-selected; they can be selected by some method of sampling that attempts to be representative without probability sampling; they can be chosen by random sampling; they can be elected; or they can constitute virtually all voters (or members of the group being consulted). When these two dimensions are combined, the eight possibilities in Chart I emerge.

The first category, 1A, is common whenever open meetings are called or whenever self-selected opinions are solicited by broadcasters or Internet sites. Norman Bradburn of the University of Chicago has coined the acronym SLOP for "self-selected listener opinion poll." Before the Internet, radio call-in shows would commonly ask for responses by telephone to some topic. The respondents to SLOPs are not selected by scientific random sampling. Instead, they simply select themselves. They are predominantly those who feel more intensely or feel especially motivated. Sometimes, they are organized.

A good example of the dangers of SLOPs came with the world consultation that *Time* magazine organized about the "person of the century." *Time* asked for votes in several categories, including greatest thinker, greatest statesman, greatest entertainer, and greatest captain of industry. Strangely, one person got by far the most votes in every category, and it turned out to be the same person. Who was this person who towered above all rivals in every category? Ataturk. The people of Turkey organized

Chart I. Forms of consultation

Public opinion	Method of selection			
	1. Self-selection	2. Nonrandom sample	3. Random sample	4. "Everyone"
A. Raw	1A SLOPs	2A Some polls	3A Most polls	4A Referendum democracy
B. Refined	1B Discussion groups	2B Citizens juries, etc.	3B Deliberative Polls	4B "Deliberation Day"

to vote, by postcard, on the Internet, by fax, and produced millions more votes as a matter of national pride than the rest of the world could muster for any candidate, just through individual, unorganized voting.[46]

Media organizations routinely conduct SLOPs on the Internet on a wide range of political or social matters. A SLOP involves visitors in a web site, gives people a sense of empowerment (they are registering their opinions), but it produces data that are misleading, that offer only a distorted picture of public opinion. Those feeling most intensely make the effort to register their views, sometimes more than once. In the 2008 presidential race, Ron Paul "demolished" the opposition in online polls "leading all the Republican candidates by a comfortable margin" just before the Iowa caucuses—even though he barely registered in polls with scientific samples at the same time.[47] And technological innovations such as web-based social networking have been used to expand the reach of SLOPs. ABC News combined with Facebook in 2008 to solicit self-selected reactions to its New Hampshire presidential debate and the overwhelming victor in the question about who was most "presidential" among Republicans was, again, Ron Paul.[48]

This is a well-trodden path. Alan Keyes had similar self-selected success in SLOPs in his 1996 presidential run. His supporters felt strongly and voted over and over. And the effort to impeach Clinton showed large majorities in favor in SLOPs at the time, while representative samples showed a completely different picture. When Senator Conrad Burns was criticized for his connections to lobbyist Jack Abramoff, his supporters were mobilized to vote over and over in polls in the local paper to indicate that they were not concerned about the connection. When Microsoft wanted to demonstrate the attractiveness of its .net software as an alternative to Java, it mobilized large-scale voting in a media SLOP for computer users. And American celebrity commentator Stephen Colbert entered the Internet contest which the government of Hungary organized to name a new bridge. By appealing on the air, Colbert got a number of votes larger than the population of Hungary to have the bridge named after him. When the organizers claimed that the winner had to speak Hungarian, he demonstrated the effect of his Hungarian lessons on the air. Only when told that the winner had to be dead did he drop out of the contest. SLOPs are open to capture across almost all boundaries of geography and interest.

It is often thought that technology might facilitate the better realization of ancient forms of democracy. But SLOPs hark back to the practices of ancient Sparta, not ancient Athens. In Sparta there was a practice called the Shout, where candidates could pack the hall and the one who got the most applause was the one elected.[49] Later we will turn to a different category that realizes Athenian rather than Spartan democracy.

The difficulty with Category 1A is that it offers a picture of public opinion that is neither representative nor deliberative. It offers a picture of raw opinion that is distorted and partial in whom it includes. SLOPs achieve neither of the two values we are discussing here.

An alternative to the SLOPs of Category 1A is the possibility of serious deliberation among a self-selected group. Discussion groups fill out Category 1B. If the discussion groups offer the opportunity to weigh the main alternative arguments that fellow citizens want raised on an issue, then they can achieve a measure of deliberation on an issue even if the participants are not a good mirror of the entire population. The Kettering Foundation supports a large network of "National Issues Forums" (NIF) in the United States and in several other countries, in which thousands of self-selected participants deliberate conscientiously and sincerely with briefing materials that offer a balanced and accurate basis for discussion.[50] These participants meet in churches, schools, neighborhood venues, and spend hours in serious consideration of the alternatives. However, their conclusions, while filtered or deliberative, are not representative of the views of the entire public. And it is an important, if as yet not fully explored, empirical question whether self-selected groups, limited in their diversity, can fully live up to the value of deliberation. If, for example, a group is mostly middle class and mostly highly educated and mostly fairly homogeneous ideologically, then it is limited in the competing arguments it will raise on many policy issues. The lack of diversity among those deliberating can, in itself, be a limitation to the quality of deliberation.[51] Nevertheless, self-selected discussion groups serve the value of democratic deliberation to some considerable degree. And if there is an infrastructure of balanced discussion with good information, for example, briefing materials and moderators, then the lack of diversity among participants can, to some extent, be compensated for. Yet such groups clearly fall short of achieving both basic values.

Category 2A combines raw public opinion with methods of selection attempting to achieve some degree of representativeness—but without employing probability sampling. Some public opinion polls fall into this category. Those employing quota sampling, a practice still common in many democratic countries outside the United States, justify their method as an attempt to approximate probability sampling. Some spectacular failures, such as the 1948 Dewey/Truman debacle and the 1992 British

General Election, have been blamed at least in part on the use of quota sampling.[52]

Category 2B employs nonrandom methods of selection with attempts to arrive at more deliberative public opinion. There are a variety of methods of public consultation that fit this category. So-called citizens juries use quota samples to select small numbers of participants (typically twelve or eighteen) to deliberate for several days or even weeks on public issues. Consensus Conferences begin with self-selection (soliciting respondents through newspaper ads) and then use quotas to attempt to approximate representativeness. These methods often suffer from the same problem noted above. They begin with self-selection and then employ such small numbers that any claims to representativeness cannot be credibly established.[53]

Category 3A, combining probability samples with raw opinion, is exemplified, of course, by the public opinion poll. In its most developed form, it offers a better "mirror" than anything foreseen by the Anti-Federalists and it avoids the distorted representativeness of SLOPs as well as the more modest distortions of nonrandom sampling in 2B.

Such public opinion polling reflecting raw public opinion offers only a thin "top of the head" expression of the public voice. However, in its initial launch, the aspiration was that it might actually combine deliberation with political equality, or in the images we have been invoking here, combine the filter with the mirror.

George Gallup effectively launched the public opinion poll in US national politics by better predicting the 1936 presidential election than did a rival, a giant SLOP sponsored by the *Literary Digest* magazine. After this initial triumph, Gallup argued that the combination of mass media and scientific sampling could bring the democracy of the New England town meeting to the large-scale nation-state:

> Today, the New England town meeting idea has, in a sense, been restored. The wide distribution of daily newspapers reporting the views of statesmen on issues of the day, the almost universal ownership of radios which bring the whole nation within the hearing of any voice, and now the advent of the sampling referendum which produces a means of determining quickly the response of the public to debate on issues of the day, have in effect created a town meeting on a national scale.[54]

Gallup offered a version of the "mirror" of representation that, by using scientific sampling techniques, offered a better microcosm of the public than anything ever envisaged by the Anti-Federalists. But his achievement only dramatized one horn of the dilemma of democratic reform we have been exploring. He thought that the media would, in effect, put the whole country in one room and the poll would allow for an assessment of the resulting informed opinion. But if the whole country was in one room, he neglected to realize the effects of "rational ignorance"—the room was so big that no one was paying much attention. Instead of the democracy of the New England town meeting, he got the inattentive and often disengaged democracy of modern mass society. Instead of informed and deliberative public opinion, he got the kind of debilitated public opinion based on a casual impression of sound bites and headlines that is common in mass democracy throughout the world. Instead of reflective or "refined" opinion, he only got a reflection of "raw" opinion. Technology helped create a new form of democracy, but it was not one that realized the values of the town meeting. The town meeting, after all, offers the potential of combining deliberation with a consideration of everyone's views.[55] But the trick, in democratic reform, is to pay enough attention to the social context that might really motivate thoughtful and informed public opinion and then to combine the realization of that social context with a process for selecting or counting the views of the participants equally.

Deliberative Polling, which fits in our Category 3B, was developed explicitly to combine random sampling with deliberation. Deliberative Polling attempts to employ social science to uncover what deliberative public opinion would be on an issue by conducting a social science effort, ideally a quasi-experiment, and then it inserts those deliberative conclusions into the actual public dialogue, or, in some cases, the actual policy process.

Deliberative Polling begins with a concern about the defects likely to be found in ordinary public opinion—the incentives for rational ignorance applying to the mass public and the tendency for sample surveys to turn up non-attitudes or phantom opinions (as well as very much "top of the head" opinions that approach being non-attitudes) on many public questions. These worries are not different in spirit from the founders' concerns about mass public opinion, at least as contrasted to the kinds of opinion that might result from the filtering process of deliberation.

At best, ordinary polls offer a snapshot of public opinion as it is, even when the public has little information, attention, or interest in the issue. Such polls are, of course, the modern embodiment of the mirror theory of representation, perfected to a degree never contemplated by the Anti-Federalists. But Deliberative Polling is an explicit attempt to combine the mirror with the filter. The participants turned up by random sampling, who begin as a mirror of the population, are subjected to the filter of a deliberative experience.

Every aspect of the process is designed to facilitate informed and balanced discussion. After taking an initial survey, participants are invited for a weekend of face-to-face deliberation; they are given carefully balanced and vetted briefing materials to provide an initial basis for dialogue. They are randomly assigned to small groups for discussions with trained moderators, and encouraged to ask questions arising from the small group discussions to competing experts and politicians in larger plenary sessions. The moderators attempt to establish an atmosphere where participants listen to each other in a safe public space and no one is permitted to dominate the discussion. At the end of the weekend, participants take the same confidential questionnaire as on first contact and the resulting judgments in the final questionnaire are usually broadcast along with edited proceedings of the discussions throughout the weekend.[56] The weekend microcosm has usually been highly representative, both attitudinally and demographically, as compared to the entire baseline survey and to census data about the population. Furthermore, it is routine to find large and statistically significant changes of opinion over the weekend. Considered judgments are usually different from the "top of the head" attitudes solicited by conventional polls.

But what do the results represent? Our respondents are able to overcome the incentives for rational ignorance normally applying to the mass public. Instead of one vote in millions, they have, in effect, one vote in a few hundred in the weekend sample, and one voice in fifteen or so in the small group discussions. The weekend is organized so as to make credible the claim that their voice matters. They overcome apathy, disconnection, inattention, and initial lack of information. Participants from all social locations change in the deliberation. From knowing that someone is educated or not, economically advantaged or not, one cannot predict change in the deliberations. We do know, however, from knowledge items, that becoming informed on the issues predicts change on the policy attitudes. In that sense, the resulting deliberative public opinion is both informed and representative. As a result, it is also, almost inevitably, counterfactual. The public will rarely, if ever, be motivated to become as informed and engaged as our weekend microcosms.

The idea is that if a counterfactual situation is morally relevant, why not do a serious social science experiment—rather than merely engage in informal inference or armchair empiricism—to determine what the appropriate counterfactual situation might actually look like? And if that counterfactual situation is both discoverable and normatively relevant, why not then let the rest of the world know about it? Just as John Rawls's original position can be thought of as having a kind of recommending force, the counterfactual representation of public opinion identified by the Deliberative Poll also recommends to the rest of the population some conclusions that they ought to take seriously.[57] They ought to take the conclusions seriously because the process represents everyone under conditions where they could think.

The idea may seem unusual in that it melds normative theory with an empirical agenda—to use social science to create quasi-experiments that will uncover deliberative public opinion. But most social science experiments are aimed at creating a counterfactual representation—the effect of the treatment condition. In this effort to fuse normative and empirical research agendas, the trick is to identify a treatment condition that embodies the appropriate normative relevance.

Two general questions can be raised about all research designs—questions of internal and external validity.[58] Sample surveys are relatively high on external validity: we can be fairly confident about generalizing the results to larger populations. By contrast, most social science experiments done in laboratory settings are high in internal validity: we can be fairly confident that the apparent effects are, indeed, the result of the experimental treatments. However, experiments done with college students, for example, lack a basis for external validity if the aim is to find out something about the general population.

If a social science experiment were to have relatively high *internal validity* where we could be confident that the effects resulted from the normatively desirable treatment, and if it were also to have relatively high *external validity* where we could be confident about its generalizability to the entire citizen population, then the combination of those two properties would permit us to generalize the consequences of the normatively desirable property to the entire citizenry. We could be confident in the picture of a counterfactual public reaching its conclusions under normatively desirable conditions. In other words, if an experiment with deliberation were high on internal validity, then we could be confident that the conclusions were the result of deliberation (and related factors such as information). And if such an experiment were high on external validity, then we could be confident about generalizing it to the relevant public of, say, all eligible voters. When it can make a claim to both kinds of validity, Deliberative Polling has a strong basis for representing the considered judgments of the people. We attempt to use social science in the service of democracy—to give credibility to the claim that the refined but counterfactual opinion is representative not of actual debilitated opinion but of the deliberative opinion the public would have under good conditions.

However, even in the best case for realizing Category 3B there is a limitation to what is accomplished. Deliberative Polling involves only a scientific random sample of the population. The thoughtful and informed views created in the experiment are not widely shared because the bulk of the public is still, in all likelihood, disengaged and inattentive precisely because it is subject to all of the four limitations discussed earlier, limitations that routinely apply to the opinions of citizens in the large-scale nation-state. Deliberative Polling overcomes those conditions, at least for a time, for a microcosm, but leaves the rest of the population largely untouched (we say largely since the rest of the population may well witness the process through the media). Deliberative Polling, like the conventional polling of Category 3A, achieves inclusion through political equality, through an equal counting of those randomly sampled—effectively offering each person in the population sampled a theoretically equal chance of being the decisive voter. But political equality is not the only form of inclusion. Another method of inclusion is mass participation. And that method is employed in our last two categories.

Categories 4A and 4B parallel the previous ones, except that when ideally realized, they would offer the full realization of the kind of result represented by scientific sampling in 3A and 3B. If everyone somehow participated in mass consultations such as voting or referendum democracy, then 4A would represent the same views as those offered by public opinion polls in 3A. Of course, one problem with referendum democracy and other forms of mass consultation that attempt to involve the bulk of the mass public is that turnout is often so defective that only a portion of the public participates. Sometimes the participation in referenda or national elections is so low, in fact, that the distinction between mass democracy and self-selected samples in SLOPs becomes difficult to draw. Of course, there are possible institutional remedies for low turnout. Australia has a long tradition of effective compulsory voting, fining nonvoters. Australia achieves one of the highest turnouts in the world in national elections. However, it is well established that compulsory voting has done little or nothing to improve the level of knowledge or engagement among voters, as opposed to the level of participation.

Australian elections show as much raw partisanship and strategic manipulation as those in other mass democracies. Near universal turnout does not raise the level of discourse or provide anything like what we are calling "refined" preferences. The Australian Progressives idealistically advocated compulsory voting on the grounds that if citizens only knew they had to vote they would do the hard work to prepare. However, the result has been to force voters with low information levels to the polls. Hence compulsory voting has certainly not served to significantly raise the level of knowledge (and the likelihood of deliberative preferences) in elections. One might even argue that it has lowered it.

The last possibility, 4B, is the most ambitious. Bruce Ackerman and I developed it to start a dialogue about how to bring deliberative public opinion to the mass scale—how to make the deliberative public opinion we see in the Deliberative Poll an actual reality rather than a representation of the more informed and engaged public that we do not now have.

Conventional polling (3A) uses a randomly selected microcosm to show what (usually) nondeliberative public opinion is like for the whole society. Deliberative Polling (3B) uses a randomly selected microcosm to show what more deliberative public opinion would be like for the whole society. And in the case of 4B the idea is to actually bring it about when it would matter most—in the context of an election. How could such a counterfactual possibility be realized?

Our proposal is simple but ambitious. We call it "Deliberation Day."[59] The problem for the Deliberative Poll was to motivate a microcosm of the entire population to overcome the incentives for rational ignorance and to engage in enough substantive face-to-face discussion to arrive at informed judgments—informed about the issues and the main competing arguments about them that other citizens would offer. But it is one thing to imagine doing this for a microcosm, and quite another to imagine doing it for the entire population. Gallup's vision of the mass media turning the entire country into one great room foundered, as we saw earlier, on the lack of a social context that would encourage small group deliberation. If everyone is in "one great room" in the large-scale nation-state, the room is so big that no one is listening. A different, more decentralized strategy is required.

Our idea is simply to have a national holiday in which all voters would be invited and incentivized to participate in local, randomly assigned discussion groups as a preparation to the voting process a week later.

Candidates for the major parties would make presentations transmitted by national media and local small group discussions would identify key questions that would be directed to local party representatives in relatively small-scale town meetings held simultaneously all over the country. A key point is that incentives would be paid for each citizen to participate in this full day's work of citizenship. The cost ($150 per person), while significant, would make democracy far more meaningful as it would provide for an input from the public that involved most people and that also led to a large mass of citizens becoming informed on the issues and the competing arguments. As shown by Deliberative Polls, some of which are as short as one day, even one day's serious discussion can have a dramatic effect on ordinary citizens becoming more informed and changing their preferences in significant ways.

The result would make real the counterfactual deliberative opinion represented by the Deliberative Polls. Candidate behavior and advertising would have to adjust to the fact that millions of voters would have actually become more informed on the issues. The strategic anticipation of such a more deliberative public could do a great deal to transform the rest of the public dialogue. Candidates will know that on "D Day" the public will be better informed. They will want to tailor their proposals and their appeals accordingly.

The Deliberation Day proposal may not be the only way to get a more deliberative public but it is the first *institutional* proposal intended to regularly produce deliberative opinion on a mass scale before elections. As Ackerman himself has argued, there may have been times in American history when a great crisis produced such a large-scale public dialogue that there was a "constitutional moment."[60] But such crises cannot reliably be made part of an institutional design. And they are rare (the Founding, Reconstruction, the New Deal, etc.). Most of the time we are left with "normal politics" dominated by the competitive and nondeliberative politics of impression management.

There are two categories in our scheme that achieve both values— political equality and deliberation. These two categories are 3B and 4B— categories exemplified by Deliberative Polling and Deliberation Day. The former is a practical and realizable ideal for a microcosm, the latter is enormous in the scale of its ambition, but could realistically apply to the entire society provided we have the political will to make it so. Both have the merit that they give voice to public views representing everyone under conditions where they can think. For the foreseeable future, microcosmic experiments like the Deliberative Poll offer the most practical opportunity for overcoming the limitations of mass democracy and giving voice to the public's considered judgments under good conditions. However, these possibilities, and the scheme within which they are placed, are offered not as solutions, but as a contribution to the continuing dialogue about how to better realize core democratic values.

2

The Trilemma of Democratic Reform

How am I included?

So far we have focused on prospects for achieving political equality and deliberation. But we began with the root notions of inclusion and thoughtfulness. And political equality is not the only approach to inclusion. Another venerable tradition would marry inclusion to the value of mass participation. The Deliberative Poll "includes" people through random sampling. I am included when I am one of the people who has an equal chance of being chosen. But some democratic reformers would insist on actual mass participation as a form of inclusion—perhaps best combined with political equality. I am included when I vote (or perhaps when I have the same opportunity to vote as anyone else). From this perspective we have three core values, not just the two discussed so far—political equality, deliberation, and mass participation. Why not attempt to achieve all three? If one is aspiring to achieve inclusion, political equality would seem important since it requires inclusion on an equal basis—equal counting of ones' views. But the equal counting is not explicitly linked to individual behavior. For that reason it does not seem to be a proxy for any kind of actual mass consent. If I do not participate, but am rather one of the people who had a random chance of being chosen, there is a sense in which I do not individually feel included. The indications of inclusion, while perhaps as effective as from actual mass participation, are nevertheless not very tangible.

Of course, if the sample is a good microcosm, then people *like* me will be included. The arguments I would make will likely be made by them. The concerns I would raise will likely be raised by them. But if I actually voted or participated, then there is a sense that my actual actions offered an indication of my say. Whether my side prevails, I can feel that I had my chance. Without mass participation the sense in which I have a say is thinner and more theoretical. By contrast, actual mass participation is a token for actual mass consent.

Mass participation and political equality would, ideally, work best together. Institutions of mass participation that fail to count opinions equally seem suspect from the standpoint of political equality, arbitrarily privileging some citizens while arbitrarily limiting the influence of others. Of course, this kind of political inequality is exactly the objection to many of our US institutions that are based on geographically defined divisions that receive unequal weight per person. The Senate gives two senators each to California and Wyoming. The Electoral College apportions electors with a substantial bonus to the small states (because it is distorted by the distribution of US senators since Electoral College votes correspond to a state's total representation in Congress). The sequential nature of the presidential primary system gives dramatically disproportionate influence in the process to voters in certain small and unrepresentative states which go first (Iowa and New Hampshire). And while the first official nominating event, the Iowa Caucuses, has some deliberative elements (in the Democratic caucuses voters express their views in public voting rather than secret ballots, which may incentivize greater seriousness[1]) the number of delegates per precinct is determined by the Democratic vote in the last two elections. There can be large differences in the number of delegates per precinct and hence in the number of voters per delegate.[2] Geographical divisions (precincts) combined with a historically based apportionment of delegates play havoc with political equality. These are all examples of how familiar institutions of mass democracy, while encouraging participation, can routinely violate political equality. But these violations are remediable. It is possible to institutionalize equal voting power across geographical divisions. But it is far more difficult to institutionalize a reliable means of encouraging citizen deliberation on a mass scale.

Deliberation

To explore the argument below we need working definitions of three democratic values: *deliberation, political equality*, and *participation*.

By *deliberation* we mean the process by which individuals sincerely weigh the merits of competing arguments in discussions together. We can talk about the *quality* of a deliberative process in terms of five conditions:

a. *Information*: The extent to which participants are given access to reasonably accurate information that they believe to be relevant to the issue

b. *Substantive balance*: The extent to which arguments offered by one side or from one perspective are answered by considerations offered by those who hold other perspectives

c. *Diversity*: The extent to which the major positions in the public are represented by participants in the discussion

d. *Conscientiousness*: The extent to which participants sincerely weigh the merits of the arguments

e. *Equal consideration*: The extent to which arguments offered by all participants are considered on the merits regardless of which participants offer them

Achieving these five conditions to a high degree distinguishes deliberation from much ordinary conversation. Democratic deliberation is about questions of collective political will—about what should be done. It is about arriving at views that represent collective, informed consent. What combination of benefits and burdens, or of favorable or unfavorable factors applying to an option, would the public be prepared to live with? Just as when individuals offer informed consent to a medical or a legal procedure, we think they should know what they are agreeing to, and we think they should have considered competing reasons for agreeing or not, we can apply generally similar considerations to the outlines of an acceptable *collective* process of achieving something analogous—the consent of "we the people." When an isolated individual offers informed consent to a medical procedure, he or she should also be deliberating, but we often accept such deliberations in isolation from others. It is only an isolated individual, after all, who is offering consent in that case. But, for public policies, we all have to live with the results. Of course some of us may benefit and some of us may be disadvantaged, but that is precisely why we need a shared public discussion of the implications for us all.

When I use a phrase like the consent of "we the people" I do not mean to imply that all these processes are official and binding. They may be informal. They may be unofficial. Note how public polls are often taken as an indication of public support for a policy alternative, or even as the basis for interpreting a "mandate" when they have no official status at all.[3] It is because when the people speak, they speak in variegated ways, in multiple voices, and with multiple interpreters. Even methods of facilitating the public voice that have no official standing can take on considerable legitimacy when care is taken about the appropriate conditions. In our view the key conditions are deliberation and political equality when there is transparency about their realization.

Considering democratic deliberation as a form of collective informed consent, let us turn to each of these five indicators of quality in deliberation. First, consider the need for information. As participants weigh competing options for action, they will find that information is relevant to their assessment of the arguments for and against each possible alternative. In a Deliberative Poll on US foreign policy, a national sample came in thinking that foreign aid was one of the largest items in the US budget. Initially there was a majority for cutting it. Before deliberation, only 18% correctly answered the information question that foreign aid was less than one per cent of the US budget. After deliberation, 64% answered that question correctly and support for foreign aid went from a majority for decreasing it to a majority for increasing it. If the results of a conventional poll or referendum were crucially determined by the public's inaccurate knowledge about the magnitude of the current cost (a situation suggested by the pre-deliberation results and how they changed), then such opinions do not plausibly represent collective informed consent. Rather they seem to represent only a "top of the head" impression as opposed to a considered judgment. By contrast the preference reversal after deliberation does seem to have a recommending force—it is what the people would want if they were better informed and weighed the reasons for and against. It is a representation of what they would approve of, or agree to, on reflection.

A second element of deliberation is substantive balance. It is worth recalling that the root of deliberation is "weighing." Substantive balance gives us confidence that the relevant considerations on competing sides of the argument have been raised. I specify "substantive balance" because it is not merely a matter of balancing the affect or the expressions of support for competing sides. Political broadcasts may consider that they offer "balance" when candidate (or policy advocate) A gets to criticize candidate B's policy positions and B responds with charges about A's personal life. The affect might be balanced for the audience; perhaps the time and attention devoted to each side are balanced. But the criticisms of B's policy positions are left in a pre-deliberative condition. What is the country to think about a position that has been criticized without the response to those criticisms also being aired? Furthermore, if the personal charges are relevant to the political choices, what is the country to think about A's character if the responses to those criticisms are not aired? Hence the balance necessary for deliberation has to be about whether the considerations offered in favor of, or against, a proposal, candidate, or policy are answered in a substantive way by those who advocate a different position.

Broadly, these considerations are likely to fall into three general categories: the *benefits or burdens* of a policy or political choice, the *causal arguments* about whether those benefits or burdens will actually result from one choice or another, and the *values* by which those benefits and burdens might best be evaluated. Considerations falling into these three categories that are raised in favor or against a policy option need to be answered by proponents of competing options. To require substantive balance rather than mere affective balance is to say that if, for example, someone offers reasons for thinking that a policy option will not have the desired effect, and those reasons are not responded to, but the speaker's sex life is discussed instead, balance of the sort required for deliberation has not been achieved. Substantive balance would require instead an airing of the best considerations advocates can offer on either side for thinking that the desired effects will or will not be achieved, the best considerations for thinking that the effects would or would not be desirable, and the best accounts of how those benefits and burdens compare to those that are alleged to follow from other policy options.

In a national British Deliberative Poll about crime, the respondents came in thinking that the solution to crime was to put more people in jail and to build more prisons. Advocacy of this "get tough" position was intense. But during the weekend participants learned that Britain already had the highest rate of imprisonment in Western Europe, that prison was very expensive, and that only a tiny proportion of crimes could be expected to lead to people going to prison. And in this situation, the prisons were already overcrowded and very expensive. These considerations argued for supplementing prison with other strategies such as differential treatment of juveniles and adults and at least some focus on the root causes of crime. Some of what the sample learned could be classified as information. Indeed there were large information gains, as measured by knowledge questions and, as in later Deliberative Polls, the information gains drove the opinion changes.[4] But a great deal of what participants learned was not captured by the information questions so much as by their exposure to competing arguments about the limitations of a position they had held but had probably not examined much. Hence they thought more about the limits of what prison by itself would achieve given its cost and the numbers affected. Put simply, a deliberation without substantive balance would be impaired, because the considerations that weigh for and against the claims at issue would never get considered. If we are interested in conditions of public will formation where the competing arguments are aired, then substantive balance is fully as essential as information.

Diversity of viewpoints is a third condition affecting the quality of deliberation. Deliberation is crippled if only the advocates of one side or one point of view are in the room. Of course, diversity of viewpoints will have some connection to diversity in demographic categories. Diversity in this latter sense is also relevant as it will affect values and interests and those values and interests provide relevant premises for deliberation. Put another way, they can be expected to have an effect on the way policy options are evaluated—particularly if people are thinking about the issues. Our diversity criterion will specify that the range of competing viewpoints on the issue in the population at large should be represented in the discussions. So the diversity of participants criterion attempts to guarantee that a range of viewpoints is represented and the balance criterion guarantees that considerations for and against each of those viewpoints are offered and answered in turn.

There is a long-standing debate about whether ascriptive representation is necessary—whether or not people of one race or class or gender or even geographical location can be represented by those of another.[5] The United States was born in a dispute about representation. The British parliament was supposed to offer those in America "virtual representation." Even though no colonists elected members of Parliament, MPs in London were supposed to take account of their interests. The idea of taxation without explicit representation was thrown overboard along with the tea in the Boston harbor. But even when there is a mechanism of choice, such as elections, which can be employed to give people an actual role in selecting their representatives, there is a debate about whether people of one race or gender can be represented by another. The debate has to do with whether or not the arguments, concerns, and values of one group can be adequately voiced by those outside the given category. This concern is directly relevant to the quality of deliberation since if the arguments, concerns, and values of one group are not included in the argument, then the basis for choice will have been impaired, the range of competing arguments will have been cut short.[6]

Random sampling offers a means of representing the diversity of viewpoints in the population at large. It is not the only method but if done well it should be sufficient.

It is worth noting that we are leaving more precise claims of representativeness to the criterion of political equality. If everyone is equally represented, either by having the entire population participate or through random sampling, then the diversity criterion will automatically be satisfied. We defined it in terms of a diversity of viewpoints comparable to the diversity of viewpoints in society as a whole. There are, however, a few complexities.

First, even if the collection of all those deliberating is comparable in diversity of viewpoints to the population at large, the size of groups that can effectively deliberate together is relatively small. Focus groups tend to be eight or ten. Deliberating groups in Deliberative Polls sometimes range as high as eighteen or so (depending on practical constraints). But once groups get much larger than that, it is hard for individuals to meaningfully participate and engage with each other. Small group democracy begins to turn into audience democracy.[7] Each person has too small a share in the dialogue to be an effective participant.

A simple solution is to randomly assign participants to small groups of sufficiently limited size. This strategy will provide for diversity in most groups. And if there are panel discussions or plenary sessions in addition to the small groups, then the range of viewpoints in the panels can be carefully balanced to ensure diversity as well. The use of small groups and then larger plenary sessions with competing panels is part of the design of both the Deliberative Poll (DP) and Deliberation Day (DD). If implemented well, both the DP and DD would represent viewpoints, as we specified, in their proportion to the overall population.

However, suppose the population as a whole has only a small representation for a viewpoint that is crucial to the discussion. One way in which a viewpoint could be crucial to a discussion is if the question at issue is in fact explicitly policy toward group X, but group X has only a very small percentage of the total population. In that case, random sampling may not provide a critical mass of people in the discussions representing that viewpoint. In a Deliberative Poll in Australia about policies toward Aboriginals, we faced such an issue (working with our Australian partners Issues Deliberation Australia). Aboriginals are only perhaps 1.5% of the population so a random sample that included Aboriginals would not have enough to ensure even one Aboriginal per small group. Furthermore, it is arguable that if one is alone in a small group of fifteen or eighteen, then one might not feel very motivated to participate actively.

We addressed this issue by oversampling Aboriginals and randomly assigning the oversample to a random half of all the small groups. As it turned out, all the groups moved in the same direction (broadly toward policies promoting reconciliation with the Aboriginal population). But the groups that had more Aboriginals in them moved more in that direction. This result suggested the importance of having viewpoints actually voiced by the relevant participants. But it also showed that balanced deliberation was possible even when there was an impairment in the degree of diversity in the small groups.[8] One might have argued for greater oversampling in order to improve the deliberation but note that the oversampling undermines claims to representativeness (or in the terms developed here, political equality).[9] For that reason, the institutional aspirations for the Deliberative Poll would suggest that it is generally preferable to maintain random sampling and deal with the special case where a small population is the explicit subject of the deliberation through the briefing materials and the balance of experts in the plenary sessions. However, there are clearly trade-offs.

The reason for maintaining random sampling is that the key claim of the DP, and indeed, as we shall see, the key claim of deliberative democracy more generally, is the simultaneous realization of deliberation and political equality. Departures from random sampling distort or undermine the claim to political equality even if they might, under these circumstances, contribute to the further realization of deliberation.

A fourth condition is conscientiousness. Deliberation requires that participants sincerely weigh the issues on their merits. They should decide in the end on the basis of the "force of the better argument."[10] One could imagine, for example, that they might instead engage in bargaining about other considerations (perhaps bribes or campaign contributions?) they might receive if they were to depart from their considered judgments or that they might behave strategically. Of course the incentives to do so will vary with the institutional design. It may well be that if a deliberative design requires a consensus "verdict" as in a jury, then a combination of social pressure and bargaining may yield results that depart from the conscientious judgments of the deliberators. However, the DP is set up to simply solicit the individual opinions in what are, in effect, secret ballots. And there are usually not multiple rounds so that there would be no basis for calculating that if I vote for my second best choice in this round that might increase the chances of my first choice in the next. There is just a one-shot confidential ballot about what I really think about the merits.

If participants spend hours trying to decide what they think, and if they believe that there is a reason why what they think will matter, then it seems plausible that the deliberators will offer their sincere views at the end of the process.

Ordinary citizens have less opportunity to bargain (at least under most institutional designs) and less opportunity to behave strategically (at least with any consequence) than do political elites. Ordinary citizens hold an office (citizen) for which they are not running for election. They have no need to spin doctor their positions in order to gain advantage. Of course they are subject to social pressure and since they are often inattentive, they are vulnerable to manipulation, but we can usually assume their responses to well-designed deliberative consultations are genuine.

There is some suggestive evidence that DPs motivate sincere rather than strategic behavior. While this has not yet been studied systematically,[11] consider that when we did a national DP in the 1997 British General Election there was an extraordinary rise in the support for the third party, the Liberal Democrats. Some pundits suggested that when it came to the real vote, the DP supporters would not actually vote Lib Dem as they would be under pressure to vote for one of the two parties that had a better chance of winning. Yet when we went back to respondents right after the election, their self-reports of how they voted corresponded almost perfectly to the final DP results.[12] Their considered judgments seemed to resist pressures for strategic voting, not only in the DP but in the actual election. Similarly, in a Greek project in which we employed the DP for an actual candidate choice, we were able to simulate the final secret ballot choices from the considered judgments in the Deliberative Poll even though there were multiple candidates and plenty of opportunities for strategic behavior. Of course there may be strategic behavior in terms of calculations of electability. Nevertheless sincere preferences seem to play a predominant role in deliberative processes.

A fifth condition is that considerations offered in the deliberations should be given equal consideration regardless of whom they are offered by. More precisely, we want to create a safe public space where *the merits of the reasons* are considered rather than the *prestige or social standing* of the articulators of those considerations. Deliberation with a scientific sample will engage people from very different social backgrounds and perspectives. It is a common criticism of the idea of deliberative democracy that it will advantage the more educated and the more powerful. Those who benefit from social inequalities in the world outside the deliberation would seem likely to benefit from social inequalities during the deliberative process itself. To the extent that happens it would seem plausible to conclude that participants are not weighing the considerations based on the merits. It would not be the force of the better argument, but rather the exalted position of the speaker that would sway the outcome.

Of course if any group, large or small, is deliberating, there will be variations in their perceived competence and expertise on the subject at hand. Why not just defer to those who know more? A rational economy of time and attention, it might be argued, should dictate that I not waste my time thinking about public issues which I cannot do much about, but simply take my cues for my tiny part in the decision from those who specialize in the given topic.

But if I simply defer to experts or prominent people, am I deliberating? Am I thinking for myself if I simply vote for a candidate endorsed by my local newspaper rather than considering the merits myself? It may well be reasonable for us faced with scarce time and resources to do this. But when we do so we are not deliberating, we are just employing cues or shortcuts. Perhaps this is what can realistically be expected of citizens in mass society for many policy problems.

But while this may be a reasonable shortcut for a citizen voting in mass democracy, in say a referendum or election, at least for elections or topics she is not much interested in, it would be more of a limitation if it also predominated in those few institutional designs intended to produce citizen deliberation. And I think it is worth noting that it surely does happen to some degree even in such settings. The degree to which it does, and to which it makes a difference, would be a worthy topic for more empirical work. It is very likely the case that informed citizens use shortcuts or heuristics. First, because the fact that a proposition has been endorsed is itself information that is often scarce and informed voters may be more likely to have that information. Second, because such voters will have more context for considering the merits and limitations of any endorsement. Third, because such voters may also be aware of counter-endorsements, competing expertise that needs to be weighed as well. Even if all this is admitted, the key is that deliberating citizens will weigh the merits of competing arguments for themselves. And to the extent they are doing so, they are deliberating.

Furthermore, in weighing the merits of competing arguments they have to consider complex issues about what policy options are likely to produce what effects. Some conversational partners may have better information about such matters than others. It is part of equal consideration of the merits of arguments to make the best judgments one can about the means–ends relations of key propositions. For example, suppose I am deliberating with persons X and Y and I know that X knows something about the topic. If I decide to support a given policy merely because X does, then I am not deliberating. But if X says that the policy will likely produce a given outcome which I value, then that is relevant for me to consider. And if Y who does not know much about it, dismisses the causal connection offered by X, then I might reasonably weigh the empirical claim offered by X more than the dismissal by Y in calculating whether or not the proposed policy is likely to produce the desired outcome. In that sense I am weighing something X says more. However, I am still independently coming to a judgment about the proposed policy because it produces my desired outcome rather than simply because X wants it. Indeed I might find out that X desires a given policy option because it will produce tax breaks that benefit him or his company and which are not of concern or benefit to me. So the mere fact that X is in favor should not settle whether or not I also support the same policy.

J.S. Mill asked a question at the beginning of *Representative Government*: Why not simply leave governing to a benevolent dictator? Leaving aside the complexities of securing one who is really benevolent and of institutionalizing continuity of wisdom (a problem political philosophy began with in *The Republic*) if we succeeded in securing a benevolent dictator, what kind of people would we be left with? We would be left with people who were not accustomed to thinking for themselves and not accustomed to exercising any of their collective judgments? To the extent that we evaluate arguments based on their source, rather than their content, we are not deliberating but rather using an endorsement or cue to substitute.

These five conditions together define a process of public will formation in which the discussions are informed, they consider the merits of competing considerations for and against the alternatives, they know that the main positions in the society at large have been represented in the discussions, they have considered the issues on the merits and the inequalities participants bring with them to the process have not short-circuited the deliberations. If any of these conditions were absent, there might be grounds for disqualifying the considered judgments that result. Lack of information (or the provision of misinformation) the participants believe to be relevant can lead the deliberations astray. If arguments offered are not answered, then the imbalance can tilt the discussion toward conclusions the participants might not have supported if only they had heard the other side. If they fail to consider the issue on its merits but decide for some other reason, or if inequalities privilege some voices and disqualify others so that they do not get an effective hearing, then the deliberations have been sidetracked.

Political equality

Deliberative democracy is treated here as the combination of political equality and deliberation. The ancient Athenians achieved political equality (within the limited population of citizens) first via random sampling,[13] and second via processes exhibiting political equality (equal counting of votes) among those selected randomly. But random sampling is only one strategy for implementing political equality. The more common way, throughout most of the history of democratic practice, has been to give everyone in the mass public a single vote and then to count the votes equally. There are many complexities depending on the voting system. Most obviously, one might give everyone a single vote and still fail to achieve political equality because the voting districts are of unequal size. Or a theoretical claim to political equality might be vitiated if the voting districts, even if equal in size, are gerrymandered with predictable voting patterns in mind to create permanent minorities effectively disenfranchising some populations.

The root notion of political equality is the equal consideration of political preferences. Everyone's preferences need in some sense to count the same. A key metric is captured by the notion of equal voting power.[14] The basic idea is that if we imagine that each citizen has an equal likelihood of supporting each alternative (candidate, party, or policy that is being considered), then the system ought to give each citizen an equal likelihood of being the decisive voter. Of course, in real life people do not have an equal likelihood of supporting every possible alternative, but this is a way of testing the extent to which the scheme for aggregating preferences gives everyone's preferences equal consideration. Equal voting power is not by itself enough for political equality, but let us focus on it for the moment.

My tiny share of the decision should be equal to anyone else's in terms of the counting of votes. In addition, one might hope that there is some equality in each person's opportunity to determine the views that are given equal consideration. However, in this argument, we will treat those issues of preference formation under the heading of deliberation.[15]

Note that in terms of having an equal chance of being the decisive voter, there is no difference in the root notion of political equality whether (*a*) all voters vote and those votes are counted equally so that I have an equal chance of being the decisive voter or (*b*) there is a lottery among all voters to select a microcosm and the microcosm votes and those votes are then counted equally. In each case, whether the process unfolds in one or two stages, I can have an equal chance of casting the decisive vote. It is just that in the two-stage method, it is equal and small in the first stage while large in the second. And in the one-stage process it is equal and always small. The problem of rational ignorance arises for ordinary voters in the large-scale nation-state because of the latter, because when everyone votes, each has such a small part of the decision. The solution to the problem of rational ignorance for microcosmic experiments in deliberation is that the share is large in the second stage for those selected. Once selected, they have every reason to pay attention.

Unless there are some restrictions, the idea of equally counting votes or preferences, as measured by the idea of equal voting power, is insufficient for a plausible account of political equality. First there is the issue of equality in the opportunities for preference formation. As noted, we will handle that problem under the heading of deliberation. A deliberative process that meets our proposed conditions will give everyone reasonably equal opportunities for preference formation. But there is also the problem that equal voting power is a measure of a kind of merely formal political equality that does not take account of predictable political coalitions. As a result, it does not take account of the fact that equally sized voting districts could be gerrymandered to create permanent minorities. While, in a formal sense, the result would be a kind of political equality, realistically, the permanent minority would have been robbed of its vote.

For our purposes here, we will restrict the idea of equal voting power as a definition of political equality to cases that *also* have politically competitive conditions. If there is not effective political competition, then there is no issue, beyond a sham one, for the public to decide. In the extreme case, consider a one-party state that holds elections. Every voter has the same equal voting power but there is nothing to decide in that the decision has already effectively been made before any election is held. A less extreme case would be a gerrymandered election district where competition is effectively removed and one-party domination is assured. Each voter as a formal matter would have equal voting power but the decision would in effect have been made before any vote. Hence a working notion of political equality would combine equal voting power with a requirement that it be applied to public consultations (whether elections, or referenda, or issues) where there is effective political competition—where, in effect, the consultation is not a foregone conclusion.

It is worth adding that deliberation, were it to occur at the mass level, would make the conventional predictable political coalitions, the ones that make gerrymandering possible, less likely. After deliberation, whites might well vote for a black candidate, or blacks for a white candidate, depending on the substance of their positions. Or long-time Democrats might vote Republican in the case of a given candidate or vice versa. Because we live so far from a world in which large numbers actually deliberated, we can barely glimpse such possibilities. It is voters with non-deliberative preferences who are most easily gerrymandered. But because boundaries can be effectively manipulated in the real world to eliminate political competition, we need the political competition restriction in our definition of political equality.

Participation

The participation at issue for our discussion is mass political participation. It engages the bulk of the population in participation that is political. By *political participation* we mean behavior on the part of members of the mass public directed at influencing, directly or indirectly, the formulation, adoption, or implementation of governmental or policy choices. Voting has become by far the most widely shared form of political participation, but contributing money, time, or effort to political causes, demonstrating, writing letters or emails to governmental officials, signing petitions are all activities that involve large numbers of people. For some purposes, it might be useful to include comparatively passive (but valuable) activities such as watching the news, but we need not extend the concept that far here.[16]

When citizens vote, or write letters or emails to their representatives or gather in demonstrations, sign petitions, or contribute to candidates or causes intended to influence politics or policy, they are engaging in mass political participation. The extent of mass political participation is a matter of how widely such behavior is spread throughout the population (perhaps in percentage terms) and how much activity there is per person. More people participating and the same people doing more are both ways for mass participation to increase. Even so, we will specify that for there to be a high level of mass participation, there must be participation on the part of the bulk of the population.

As we will see, some theorists do not see mass participation as a good to be encouraged. From this perspective, mass participation is a threat. The people have passions or interests, which if aroused, can motivate factions, can motivate mob-like behavior that may do harm to the rights of others. The original design of the US Constitution was intended to filter the public views and through an indirect process, lead to the distillation of public opinion rather than permit any direct impact on politics or policy. From other perspectives, however, mass participation is a cornerstone of democracy. Mass participation signals a form of mass consent. When the people participate and they approve certain results (whether in an election or referendum) there is a mandate for whatever policy outcomes result. The idea is that those who are subject to living with decisions should have an actual share in the decision processes.

Three conflicting options

The three principles—deliberation, political equality, and mass participation—pose a predictable pattern of conflict. Attempts to realize any two will undermine the achievement of the third. The resulting pattern suggests the three outcomes set out in Chart II, which together pose a trilemma, a kind of dilemma with three corners.[17]

The challenge posed by the trilemma is not insuperable, at least in theory. We can imagine ways around it, but at great expense and with departures from the range of reforms usually regarded as feasible. An example is Deliberation Day, which attempts to insert deliberation at the large scale into mass democracy.[18] But barring such a major departure from our usual political practices and constraints[19] or barring some unforeseen new

Chart II. Options in the trilemma

	Political equality	Participation	Deliberation
Option one: Mass democracy	+	+	−
Option two: Mobilized deliberation	−	+	+
Option three: Microcosmic deliberation	+	−	+

innovation or technology, we can reliably expect the trilemma pattern to hold. It has held throughout the long history of democratic experimentation. There has never, in other words, been an institution that reliably delivered political equality, deliberation, and mass participation simultaneously. Conventional elections of representatives, when conducted with political equality, deliver the combination of political equality and mass participation at one stage and then separate deliberation by political elites in another stage. Referenda deliver participation and political equality but routinely fail to offer deliberation at the same time. There have been historical occasions, such as the "constitutional moments" studied by Ackerman, when the whole country is aroused to discuss an issue, but those moments are not reliably delivered by an institution, they occur unpredictably.[20] To the extent the trilemma holds for the design of institutions, democratic reformers face some difficult value choices.

Mass democracy

Let us consider each pair of values in order to see why commitment to any two can be expected to undermine achievement of the third. Suppose, first, that we were to try and realize both participation and political equality. By political equality we mean some institutionalized mechanism for giving equal weight to the views of all citizens in a mass public. The value of political equality can be furthered by expansions in the notion of *who* the citizens are whose views are to be given equal weight or by improvements in the degree to which those views are, in fact, counted *equally*. As we noted earlier, there are indices of voting power that would have us imagine all possible combinations of votes and then compute the "voting power" of an individual by the likelihood that a given person could turn out to be the decisive voter. We determine these probabilities a priori, by the structure of the voting rules or the institutional design and not by, say, what we know of historical voting patterns or the actual preferences of various groups. We can say that if a system for consulting the public would give equal voting power to each citizen then it has fulfilled the formal notion of political equality we are concerned with here. On this view, if there are electoral districts of grossly unequal size (such as between US states in the vote for the Senate) then political equality is, to that extent, undermined. The share of a California voter in the election of a US senator is far less than the share of a Wyoming voter in the election of her senator. Note that this notion of political equality applies equally well to selection by lot or by random sample as it does to mass voting in a referendum or election in which votes are counted equally. The notion of an equal chance to be the decisive voter can be given precision, whether that equal chance comes in a single stage of selection in which everyone votes or in which a sample is selected by lot (or random sampling) and then the group that is selected votes in turn. We can say that your views count equally if the mechanism for assessing each person's views gives you equal voting power.

Much of the history of democratic reform has focused on the extension of political equality to groups that were previously left out because of race, ethnicity, religion, economic status, or gender. These extensions of the franchise are very great accomplishments. They increase the range of persons to whom the equal consideration posited by political equality is applied. At the same time the one person, one vote reforms, for the US House and for most state elections has increased the *degree* of equality applied to those who are included.[21]

These expansions of political equality have often been accompanied by increased opportunities for political participation, thus combining two of our fundamental values.

The primary direction of democratic reform not only in the United States but in most of the major Western democracies has been a simultaneous movement in the direction of both increasing political equality and increasing opportunities for mass participation. In the long sweep of history, the major formal barriers to participation of various groups, considered in terms of race, gender, or economic status, have all tended to fall (at least in comparison to eighteenth- and nineteenth-century benchmarks). From the standpoint of both political equality and participation these improvements have been dramatic and laudable. However, opening up political processes to facilitate mass participation has had the unexpected effect of lessening the realization of our third key value— deliberation.

Mass democracy has increased the weight of raw public opinion on many decisions, and it has even, with initiative, referendum, and recall, moved the effective locus of some decisions to the mass public. In addition the use of public opinion polling to calibrate and anticipate public opinion has intensified the same process. But the result of these well-intentioned efforts to move government and policy closer to actual, raw public opinion has been a lessened impact of deliberation. As we have seen, there are normally strong disincentives for mass public opinion to be very deliberative.

This problem—that there is little rational motivation for citizens to deliberate about public issues in mass democracies—does not depend on citizens being selfish or merely self-interested. Even if citizens have altruistic or ethical reasons for valuing the provision of a public good to everyone, even if they are valuing alternatives, not merely for their effects on their own well-being, but rather for their effects on the whole society, they still can face this problem. As Mancur Olson showed years ago, there is a general problem motivating individual participation in collective action intended to bring about the provision of public goods where the groups involved are large and the individual effect on the provision of the public good is small.[22]

The problem of deliberation for ordinary citizens fits within this general collective action argument. If, for example, there is little rational reason to vote, there is also little rational reason to become informed about one's vote or little rational reason to put a lot of time and effort into weighing competing arguments about how one should vote. A similar case can be made for arriving at considered judgments about public issues one might hope to affect in other ways at the level of the large-scale nation-state. All of this is regrettable from the standpoint of democratic aspirations about the role of informed and engaged citizens in a democracy.

However, as Olson showed, one solution to this problem of effectively motivating individuals to contribute to the provision of public goods in large groups (including mass electorates) when their individual contributions will be very small, is to provide *selective incentives*, that is, to provide incentives that apply to the individuals only if they participate. Obviously, our plan for Deliberation Day takes this into account as there will be significant "selective incentives" for each individual to participate—incentives that the voter will receive only by doing a day's work of citizenship in shared discussion and then following that up with an actual vote in the election.

Our account of mass democracy, thus far, has been that the pursuit of participation and political equality will, because of the debilitations of mass opinion that can be reasonably expected, provide little basis for public deliberation. However, even this picture is too optimistic, as it seriously overstates the degree to which familiar institutions that attempt to realize participatory equality succeed in doing so. Our pursuit of participatory equality has been seriously flawed, even in terms of the two values it has focused on, participation and equality. Our actual practices of political participation suffer from "participatory distortion"—the people who choose to participate are unrepresentative of the entire electorate.[23] In the United States, those who actually participate are generally more white, more prosperous, and more educated by far than those who do not. In that sense, effective political equality has been achieved far less than the breakdown of formal barriers to participation (in terms of voting rights) would suggest. A strong claim of political equality would attempt to minimize participatory distortion, making those who choose to participate as much like the entire electorate as possible. By the entire electorate we mean the electorate of eligible not just registered voters. The United States is the only country in the world to put the entire burden of registration on individual voters so that registration becomes, in itself, a barrier to participation. Only about 72% of eligible voters are registered, and while we get a percentage of registered voters to actually vote comparable to other major democracies[24] many voters do not even get to the starting gate because they do not get registered in the first place. So if one calculates the percentage of voters in terms of what we believe would be the correct denominator, the number of eligible voters, whether or not they have taken the trouble to register, then our realization of political equality has a long way to go, even though many formal barriers to participation have been dismantled.

"Participatory distortion" is the name Verba, Schlozman, and Brady give to differences between those who participate and the total population of those who could participate, for example, those who vote and those eligible to vote. In a landmark study, they note that participatory distortion has significant effects on the voice of the people that is articulated. "Unequal participation", they say, "has consequences for what is communicated to the government. The propensity to take part is not randomly distributed across politically relevant cleavages." As a result "the voices that speak loudly articulate a different set of messages about the state of the public, its needs, and its preferences from those that would be sent by those who are inactive. Were everyone equally active, or were activists drawn at random from across the population, an unbiased set of communications would emerge."[25]

Of course the idea of "activists drawn at random" from across the population has the air of an oxymoron. Activists are precisely those who select themselves because they feel intensely, and hence they differ in their views from those in a random sample. Note of course that with the Deliberative Poll and other forms of microcosmic deliberation, we are recruiting at random, but the people recruited are not especially activists. As representative citizens drawn at random they avoid participatory distortion—which is another way of saying that they realize political equality as well as participation.

Participatory distortion may even have been increased by efforts to further open up the political process and increase the opportunities for public consultation. Low turnout referenda, the proliferation of mass primaries, the use of "town meetings" for self-selected groups to voice their views on policy issues all have the laudable goal of participatory equality. However, the goal is usually realized quite imperfectly because most people do not care enough to take up the offer to participate. The result is often an imperfect realization of participatory equality, one that further undermines deliberation. The very process of opening up politics to more participation has made it easier for intensity to count while other voices are silent. On many issues, while most of the public is inattentive and uninvolved, self-selected activists can express strong and sometimes angry views. The intensity may come from nimby "not in my back yard" interests[26] or from moral/political ideologies that intensely engage a few[27] or from mobilization by interest groups. The resulting participatory distortion gives the general public as well as public officials a misleading sense of the distribution of public opinion and the range of voices that are relevant to the dialogue. It models public discussion on an exchange of messages from the already convinced who intend to persuade, rather than on an exchange of reasons among the open-minded. Of course, if there were a better realization of the political equality component of participatory equality (because those less intensely interested also participated) then this problem would be lessened. However, for many public issues, it is difficult to get the broad and non-intense portions of the mass public sufficiently engaged. And the result is not good for deliberation. If the public dialogue is mostly an exchange of angry voices, it may turn off those without some special stake in the issue.[28] Opening up the process to more participation does not help the public dialogue if those who take up the offer are mostly limited to those who feel intensely. There is a special value in safe public spaces where people can listen to each other without expecting an exchange of expletives. And that is less likely to happen on its own than through conscious institutional design.

However, there is a long-standing line of argument that just because the people who vote (and participate in various other ways) are not like those who do not vote, that does not mean that it actually makes any difference to the way elections turn out. For many elections, the nonvoters and the voters have similar policy preferences and similar political preferences. Hence it is arguable that it would not make any difference to the outcomes of those elections if we somehow got the nonvoters to vote.[29] While the nonvoters are even less well informed than the voters, their policy and political preferences, to the extent that they have them, tend to echo or reflect much the same views as those of voters. On this basis, Wolfinger and Rosenstone argued in a classic discussion that it would not make much difference to the outcomes of elections if nonvoters voted. On this view, "participatory distortion" does not really distort much, because it does not, in the end, change the outcome of elections.

Depending on the election and the issue, there is clearly some merit to this argument. However, it also demonstrates the problem of taking political equality and participation in isolation from deliberation. For if we imagine nonvoters voting—and also discussing the issues—before they vote we get a quite different picture of the counterfactual scenario of the consequences of involving nonvoters in the democratic process. If nonvoters were to deliberate and then vote, we can easily imagine that the impact would be consequential. It is arguable that nonvoters have different interests and viewpoints than voters. The half of the electorate that does not vote is, in general, less well-off economically, less educated, and more likely to be minority. Their inattentive, raw public opinion may not differ from that of voters, but if we could really engage them in the political process and get them to discuss the issues, it seems reasonable to expect their opinions to differ from their "top of the head" impressions. That is generally true for participants in Deliberative Polls. All participants tend to change their policy and political attitudes with deliberation—regardless of education, income, or social stratum.

Of course, for our purposes, the classic Wolfinger–Rosenstone argument, to the extent that it is true, only demonstrates that political equality and participation without deliberation would not make as much difference as some advocates have hoped. On some issues, even if everyone voted, it would not make much difference to the outcome of elections, and on other issues, participatory distortion would, in fact, give a misleading picture of the public voice. It remains, however, for us to explore what could be achieved if we came close to realizing all three fundamental values.

With these limitations of mass democracy noted, the key point is the difficulty of adding our third principle, deliberation. Once the incentives and vulnerabilities of mass public opinion are taken into account, involving everyone on an equal basis is likely to produce only raw, and potentially manipulable, public opinion. If we achieve mass participation and political equality we are likely to end with plebiscitary democracy. An ambitious and expensive innovation like Deliberation Day might break the trilemma, at least for a day, but this would require the political will to make a large change Of course, the limitations of mass democracy only dramatize how such an innovation might be worth the investment.

Mobilized deliberation

Suppose we attempt another pairing—participation combined with deliberation. In recent years, there have been a number of notable efforts to pursue this strategy, which we may call *mobilized deliberation*. These efforts are worthwhile in that they contribute to the civic education and deliberative potential of thousands of citizens. But they are modest in that, thus far, they have affected many thousands, but not millions, in a nation in which the mass public consists of millions of voters. The strategy is the encouragement of the mass public to participate in deliberative forums. The encouragement consists in the provision of infrastructure to make serious deliberation possible. The infrastructure is the development of carefully balanced, nonpartisan briefing materials suitable for citizen deliberation, the training of moderators who can lead deliberative forums, and the creation of networks of local groups who can spread the word and help organize such forums. In the United States, this kind of activity has been carried out most notably by the National Issues Forums supported by the Kettering Foundation, the Study Circles Resource Network[30] supported by the Topsfield Foundation and the Great Decisions dialogue series supported by the Foreign Policy Association. In all these cases, excellent and balanced briefing materials are developed and provided to forums of citizens in many parts of the country, forums in which trained moderators facilitate the discussions among self-selected participants.

Note that these are nonpartisan, self-consciously balanced efforts at informed discussion. Of course, there are many other efforts, some online and some face-to-face, that combine partisan advocacy with discussion. Following Cass Sunstein, we can label these *enclave deliberation*.[31] Enclave deliberation by its very nature will attract partisans or even true believers and hence is even less likely than nonpartisan, balanced discussion, to attract a representative microcosm. It will just attract those who share a point of view. But the experience of balanced nonpartisan discussion is basically parallel—combining deliberation with mass participation is likely to undermine political equality.

Studies of these self-selected deliberative forums confirm much the same pattern as among microcosmic deliberations, such as the Deliberative Polls, or with smaller numbers, the Citizens Juries. Various studies show that the participants demonstrate increased knowledge, increased efficacy, significant opinion change, and increased sophistication in their political views.[32] However, the self-selected character of these forums must inevitably have some effect on the deliberation. Self-selection is likely to limit the diversity of participants and may also help attract people who have some special reason to be interested in a given topic. Unlike Deliberative Polls or Citizens Juries (or Deliberation Day), the participants are not paid significant incentives nor are they generated by any form of scientific sampling. Without such efforts, they can easily accommodate larger numbers, hence serving the value of mass participation.

My assumption here is that it would not be possible to reliably motivate millions to deliberate without either incentives or compulsion. Compulsory deliberation raises conflicts with liberty that would seem to put it off-limits in a liberal democratic society. And incentives significant enough to motivate a large percentage of voters take us in the realm of Deliberation Day. Barring such large expenditures we can assume that if one were to try and spread deliberation to large numbers of ordinary citizens one would get those who were disproportionately interested in the topic and disproportionately informed about it. One might get fairly large degrees of voluntary participation but it would not be representative and in that sense would violate political equality.

Deliberative microcosms

There is one remaining combination among our three values. Suppose we try to achieve both deliberation and political equality. Let us call that *Deliberative Equality*. While such efforts are rare, they illustrate how some of the deficiencies of mass democracy can be overcome—although with other costs. While it has proved possible thus far to achieve deliberation and political equality in combination, such progress has generally come *without* mass participation.

When political equality, achieved through random sampling of a population, is combined with face-to-face deliberative processes we get a picture of *microcosmic deliberation*: a representative mini-public of participants become informed as they weigh competing arguments on their merits. Political equality comes into play if the group is representative of the population and if the views of each person in the microcosm count equally in whatever tabulation or decision process takes place. Deliberative Polling is an effort to realize this kind of microcosmic deliberation. However, it is not the only possible version. There are other variants on the same basic idea. The most prominent are: Citizens Juries, Planning Cells, Deliberative Panels, Consensus Conferences, and Televote. Each has advantages and disadvantages but they all aspire to offer representative deliberations by a microcosm of the public.

The ideal of microcosmic deliberation was suggestively expressed by J.S. Mill in his account of the ideal role of a legislature—to act as what he called a "Congress of Opinions":

> Where every person in the country may count upon finding somebody who speaks his mind as well or better than he could speak it for himself—not to friends and partisans exclusively, but in the face of opponents, to be tested by adverse controversy; where those whose opinion is over-ruled feel satisfied that it is heard, and set aside not by a mere act of will, but for what are thought superior reasons and commend themselves as such to the representatives of the majority of the nation; where every opinion in the country can muster its strength and be cured of any illusion concerning the number or power of its adherents.[33]

The Congress of Opinions has a distribution of opinion that is like that in the country as a whole ("where every opinion in the country can muster its strength and be cured of any illusion concerning the number or power of its adherents"). Each person can find that his perspective is advocated "as well or better than he could speak it for himself" and then it is "tested by adverse controversy," by continuing dialogue in which opinions expressed are answered and, presumably, those are answered in turn in a continuing dialogue. And finally, when conclusions are reached, those "whose opinion is over-ruled feel satisfied that it is heard, and set aside not by a mere act of will, but for what are thought superior reasons." We get a picture of a deliberative body where people are informed by the arguments of others, where there is some measure of substantive balance in the exchange of arguments, where the diversity of views is comparable to that of the society as a whole and where the representatives are participating conscientiously and weighing the arguments on the merits.

The idea of microcosmic deliberation is to take a relatively small, face-to-face group which everyone has an equal chance of being part of, and provide it with good conditions for deliberating on some policy or political issue. Citizens Juries, like Deliberative Polls use public opinion research methods to gather a sample to deliberate. But the Citizens Jury is more akin to a single discussion group in that the size is comparable to that of a modern jury—twelve or perhaps eighteen or twenty-four.[34] A benefit of such a group is that it can continue to meet in a local community for an extended period, sometimes for several days or on successive weekends. The "jurors" hear testimony, call witnesses, ask for evidence, and at some point come up with recommendations to some local or governmental authority. The limitation of the process is that with such small numbers it is not possible to establish the statistical representativeness of the deliberating group. Citizens Juries are too small for there to be a scientific basis for connecting their conclusions to the counterfactual informed opinion of an entire society, to what the country would decide if it were better informed—even though the results of Citizens Juries are often represented in that way. However, the now extensive experience in both the United States and the United Kingdom with Citizens Juries adds to our picture of citizen competence with complex policy issues—once citizens find themselves in a social context that supports deliberation.[35]

Another variant of microcosmic deliberation is the "Planning Cell" developed in Germany by Peter Dienel. The Planning Cells are small group discussions that employ random sampling in many decentralized locations, for example, different towns in a region. The results of those decentralized discussions are aggregated to provide enough numbers to offer statistically significant generalizations. However, selected local random samples do not add up to a random sample of an entire region or population. Nevertheless, if Planning Cells were conducted from a regional random sample, with respondents invited to decentralized assignments in local communities, then the process could offer the same kind of basis as a Deliberative Poll in representing counterfactual but informed opinion. Of course, with different events occurring in different places at different times, one would worry whether the process was sufficiently similar in each location for it to make sense to aggregate the results. Nevertheless, the method can be thought of as providing, or attempting to provide, a decentralized microcosm of the entire population, whose parts are gathered in different locations. In that sense the Planning Cell is a very partial realization of a vision akin to Deliberation Day—many separate communities having local deliberations on the same issue.

An alternative would be to attempt to spread the panels out in time rather than in space. This is essentially the approach to creating Deliberative Panels on a local level that a group called Viewpoint Learning pursues. Small groups are convened in the same location for successive weekends, each for a day of deliberation on the same topic. After seven or eight of these, the numbers may be large enough for statistically significant conclusions to emerge. Provided the world does not change in some dramatic way on the issue in question during the weeks of deliberation, and provided that efforts are made to keep the experiences of the group comparable, this method may offer a practical alternative for some local consultations.[36] However, the main product of these projects is a consensus statement rather than quantitative before-and-after results in confidential questionnaires. The focus is on qualitative rather than quantitative analysis of the sources or explanations of change.

Consensus Conferences are a model that originated in Denmark for public consultation, primarily on ethical issues applying to scientific and technical questions. Respondents are recruited from newspaper ads and then selected on the basis of diversity. The deliberations resemble those of Citizens Juries. However, it is worth pointing out that if one begins with those who select themselves, by responding to a newspaper ad, one is already limiting the universe of participants to those who feel some special interest in putting themselves forward. Citizens who are less involved or who do not already have a view on the issue are much less likely to put themselves forward. Efforts to ensure some demographic representativeness do not make up for the fact that it is only those who put themselves forward who are being selected from in the first place. In addition, the Consensus Conference, like the Citizens Jury, has the problem that it lacks the secret ballot. By prescribing that the group reach a "consensus," as the name implies, and as juries require as well, it exposes the process of decision-making to social pressure toward group conformity. The Deliberative Poll, by contrast, employs what is, in effect, a secret ballot by soliciting opinions in confidential questionnaires at the end of the weekend. Deliberation Day will avoid this problem by not soliciting opinions on the main question, voting intention in the election, on the day at all. Rather, the participants will cast their votes by secret ballot a week later when the election is actually held. In addition, Deliberation Day offers the combination of a significant monetary incentive, a national holiday, and massive publicity. Together these should motivate participation on a large scale.

Two other institutional strategies, Televote and the Choice Questionnaire offer examples of alternatives that add up to microcosmic deliberation but only through the aggregation of many individuals thinking in comparative isolation. In Televote, the respondents are given a survey on the phone and then sent materials on the issue. They are urged to discuss the topic in their homes, with friends and family. Then, at a later time, they are called back to see what their opinions are after further thought and discussion. A merit of Televote is that it employs scientific random sampling rather than self-selection as in Consensus Conferences or the quota sampling typical of Citizens Juries. A difficulty, however, is that the deliberation encouraged by the scheme is modest. Even for those respondents who do actually read the materials and discuss the issue with friends and family, the effect will usually be to discuss the issue with the like-minded. As we have seen, one of the principal deficiencies in citizen deliberation in natural settings is that when we discuss issues, we are most likely to discuss them with people like ourselves, with friends and family, and more generally with people with similar social and political viewpoints. Those are the people near at hand. But they are also the people who are likely to reinforce our views rather than challenge them with conflicting viewpoints. Perhaps for these reasons, the opinion changes recorded in Televote experiments are modest compared with those from Deliberative Polls and other microcosmic deliberations that require discussion with people from alternative viewpoints (through say random assignment of random samples to small group discussions).[37]

The Choice Questionnaire is another approach that employs random sampling but with very limited deliberation. Like Televote it is meant to encourage thinking with more information. But unlike Televote, it attempts to provide further information within the survey instrument itself. And unlike Televote, the time for deliberation is limited to the duration of the survey. It is a variant of the standard sample survey with information provided in the process of asking questions. For these reasons the intervention is even more modest than in Televote. The amount of thought and deliberation stimulated by information in a survey over the telephone is necessarily very limited. A merit, however, is that it is a cost-effective way to investigate the effects of information on scientific random samples and, also, to incorporate control groups in the design who can be subjected to different variations of the same questions, for example those without the information as compared to those with it.[38]

Compared to these versions of microcosmic deliberation, the Deliberative Poll has a number of merits. As opposed to the Citizens Jury and the Consensus Conference, the Deliberative Poll gathers large enough numbers of respondents and relevant kinds of data so that both the representativeness of the sample (attitudinally and demographically) and its opinion changes can be studied statistically. Compared to the Planning Cells and the Deliberative Panels, it has the merit that it combines unity of space and time. It puts the whole country (or the whole region or the whole state or the whole town) in one room where it can think. This allows for a dramatic event that the media can cover and it helps render the small groups comparable. Compared to Televote and the Choice Questionnaire, it offers a more intensive intervention, one that allows people to experience dialogue with a greater diversity of views over a more extensive period and one that also offers the prospect of more substantive balance. With both more time and greater diversity in an interactive process of questioning competing experts and competing politicians there is a great deal of information exchanged and a great variety of viewpoints expressed.

Whatever their merits, none of these models, including the Deliberative Poll, does much for our remaining value—mass participation. The numbers involved are miniscule fractions of the population, sometimes selected by random sampling, sometimes by quota sampling, and sometimes from self-selected groups. But all the people who are not selected do not participate except possibly vicariously through television or the Internet or though press reports. We have some modest evidence that viewing a microcosmic deliberation, such as a Deliberative Poll, on television can have a small effect on people's views about themselves and their political efficacy and sense of civic engagement.[39] But such media effects do little actually to encourage people to deliberate themselves or to become better informed.

By its very nature, microcosmic deliberation is for the few, not the many. To engage our value of mass participation alongside political equality and deliberation, we would need to engage the many. However, as we saw in the discussion of mass democracy, once we engage the many—the millions of voters in a large-scale mass society—we run into problems of rational ignorance and the lack of incentives for those who participate to also become well informed. Once again, we face an apparent forced choice in which we cannot achieve all three values simultaneously.

If we combine participation and equality, we count everyone's views equally and we have an expression of actual mass consent. But it is not generally informed or thoughtful consent. It is the acquiescence of an inattentive and possibly manipulated public. On the other hand, if we combine equality and deliberation, we count a representation of the public's considered judgments, but the connection to the mass of voters is only through their being equally considered via random sampling. There is no token of actual mass participation. In the case of the third option, deliberation and participation, we can reliably expect "participatory distortion" or a lack of equal counting undermining representativeness. It is mostly certain groups who are especially interested who will participate. The rest will be left out. Under most foreseeable practical conditions, one can go round and round this trilemma and never get all three principles satisfied.

Avoiding tyranny of the majority

The three values in our trilemma—deliberation, mass participation, and political equality—apply to the design of the democratic process itself. In sum, they apply to how people's views are constructed (deliberation), how they are collected (mass participation), and how they are counted (political equality). But there is another key value that has had a major role in democratic theory. It is not internal to the design of the democratic process but rather it provides a way of evaluating its effects. We might call it *non-tyranny*, since it is about avoiding what has often been called "tyranny of the majority." The concern is that the people, even if they decide democratically, can do bad things.

If we consider democracy to be a political method of decision, then the concern is that the method may have as its effect some fundamental injustices—injustices that would justify overriding or abandoning the method in at least some cases. Consider this famous challenge by Joseph Schumpeter:

> Let us transport ourselves into a hypothetical country that, in a democratic way, practices the persecution of Christians, the burning of witches, and the slaughtering of Jews. We should certainly not approve of those practices on the ground that they have been decided on according to the rules of democratic procedure.... [T]here are ultimate ideals and interests which the most ardent democrat will put above democracy.[40]

Among many others, Madison, Toqueville, and Mill all discussed how majorities may do bad things, how they may commit "tyranny of the majority." Of course, minorities may also do bad things. Yet tyranny of the majority is especially troubling since it poses a starker conflict between the apparent will of the people and justice. The definition of the objectionable outcomes that might be produced democratically has never received adequate treatment, but it is usually discussed as some kind of fundamental injustice.

Fear of majority tyranny was one of the principal motivations for the original design of the US Constitution. Famously, Madison did not embrace the term "democracy" preferring "republic," by which he meant "a government in which the scheme of representation takes place." By contrast, in the small face-to-face democracy of the ancient city-states, "a pure democracy" without representation (he believed), there was "no cure for the mischiefs of faction. A common passion or interest will, in almost every case, be felt by a majority of the whole... there is nothing to check the inducements to sacrifice the weaker party or an obnoxious individual" (*Federalist* No. 10). The rationale for the Senate was that "an institution may be sometimes necessary as a defense to the people against their own temporary errors and delusions." It was to protect the people, not from their considered judgments, not from the "cool and deliberate sense of the community" but from "the people stimulated by some irregular passion, or some illicit advantage, or misled by the artful misrepresentations of interested men" (*Federalist* No. 63) who might then act as a "faction" adverse to the rights and interests of others, or to the permanent and aggregate interests of the community as a whole. A deliberative institution like the Senate might have saved Socrates, Madison suggests:

> What bitter anguish would not the people of Athens have often escaped if their government had contained so provident a safeguard against the tyranny of their own passions? Popular liberty might then have escaped the indelible reproach of decreeing to the same citizens the hemlock on one day and statues on the next. (*Federalist* No. 63)

The courts were obviously another key bulwark against the passions of the mob, the passions of the public that could be aroused by "designing men." The judiciary could resist the momentary lapses, the immediate passions that lead factions to do things that the people would later regret on reflection and with more information. As Hamilton argued in *Federalist* No. 73:

> The independence of the judges is equally requisite to guard the Constitution and the rights of individuals from the effects of those ill humors which the arts of designing men, or the influence of particular conjunctures, sometimes disseminate among the people themselves, and which, though they speedily give place to better information and more deliberate reflection, have a tendency, in the meantime to occasion dangerous innovations in the government, and serious oppressions of the minor party in the community.

But Hamilton, at least, did not believe the courts would prove a strong bulwark against majority factions. He did not think it likely that judges would have the "fortitude" to "do their duty as guardians of the Constitution, where legislative invasions of it had been instigated by the major voice of the community" (*Federalist* No. 73).

The Framers were clearly haunted by the possibility that factions aroused by passions or interests adverse to the rights or interests of others, could do very bad things. The image they feared seems to be some combination of the Athenian mob and Shays's rebellion. "Tyranny" of the majority is only loosely specified, but they were clearly fearful of substantial and avoidable deprivations committed against life, liberty, or property. While these notions are suggestive, we need a working definition here of those government decisions that would be so unacceptable that there would be overriding normative claims against them even when they were otherwise supported by democratic principles.

For our purposes, we can say that *tyranny* (whether of the majority or minority) is the choice of a policy that imposes severe deprivations of essential interests when an alternative policy could have been chosen that would not have imposed comparable severe deprivations on anyone. By non-tyranny I simply mean the avoidance of "tyranny" in this sense.[41] There are, of course, interesting questions about the definition of "essential interests" and the sense in which policies are alternatives, one to another. I have developed one version of how such issues might be dealt with.[42] Is it an essential interest if people are forced to sacrifice their way of life? Their fundamental convictions? Their health? Are policies alternatives to one another because resource constraints say they cannot both be done? So the people or the policymakers must choose between A and B, even if they are in different policy domains?

The basic idea does not turn on any specific account of these notions. For our purposes here, the root notion will serve: that it is objectionable when people choose to do very bad things to some of their number, when such a choice could have been avoided entirely.[43]

It is worth adding that for a policy choice to violate the non-tyranny condition, it needs to be intended, and those intentions need to be other-regarding (that is, those supporters are motivated in significant part by a desire to have the stated effect upon those who will lose by the policy choice). A further point is that it seems reasonable to include the conscious choice of policy *omission* as well as commission. In other words, if there is a debate that without, say, disaster relief for the next hurricane, group X will suffer, and a coalition blocks the disaster relief, if the consequences are sufficiently dire the decision could count as "tyranny of the majority" or indeed, minority (depending on the size of the coalition needed to block new action) even though the consequences in question were the result of an action not taken (the explicit decision not to offer disaster relief).

To have a fully developed account of non-tyranny (or of tyranny of the majority) one would need a substantive discussion for classifying the unacceptable severe deprivations that are visited upon the losers. For our purposes here we can talk of loss of human rights that are essential for survival or human dignity or harms to essential interests. I have developed one such account elsewhere. However, we do not need the discussion here to depend on any specific account. We just need to specify the idea that non-tyranny is violated when a policy is chosen that imposes severe deprivations when an alternative policy would not have done so. At least that definition can signal enough of the key cases for us to proceed. How to deal with difficult cases where every possible alternative imposes severe deprivations on someone is a more difficult subject for (nonideal) theories of justice.

There have been efforts to develop an account of tyranny of the majority without any substantive discussion of effects. In his classic *A Preface to Democratic Theory*, Robert Dahl offered the balance of intensities as a modern analogue to Madison's discussion. The idea is that if a minority feels really strongly about an issue and they are overruled by an apathetic majority, then the overall weight of opinion (numbers and how strongly people feel) can favor the minority and overruling them could be considered tyranny of the majority. Such calculations are even more likely to protect a group when it is in the majority (if the issue is to protect against minority tyranny).

However, this effort to turn a substantive discussion into one that focuses merely on process seems, in retrospect, to have been doomed. Of course if one begins with the sort of case we invoked from Schumpeter's "mental experiment" and considered a majority that would "burn witches" or "slaughter Jews," it is hard to relate the balance of intensities to the claim of majority tyranny. Yes it is the case that the minority would feel strongly. But if the calculation of intense feeling can be measured (say we had some scheme for considering cardinal interpersonal comparisons), then whether or not we object to the Nazis would hardly turn on how enthusiastic they are. No matter how strongly the minority feels, if the numbers and intensities of the majority are strong enough, it could, in theory, have the weight of opinion on its side. And that would hardly

seem relevant to whether or not the policy consequences were objectionable. The key is that the majority wants to do very bad things to the
minority—impose avoidable severe deprivations—not that the minority
feels more strongly about it than does the majority.

With these explanations, it suffices here simply to say that non-tyranny
is a condition that is violated when a winning coalition imposes avoidable
severe deprivations on a losing one. We can leave open the exact definition of severe deprivations but specify that the more severe they are, and
the more clearly avoidable they are, the more compelling is the case of
majority (or minority) tyranny.

3

Competing Visions

Four democratic theories

Now that we have enlarged our account of fundamental democratic concerns to include four basic principles—political equality, deliberation, mass participation, and non-tyranny—we can consider a range of democratic theories in terms of their positions on these four principles. While there are, in theory, sixteen possible combinations of commitments to these four principles, the ones that have serious normative interest reduce to four. The additional positions are either variations of these four, or they are ruled out by the trilemma, or they make less ambitious claims (such as committing to only one of the principles and rejecting all the others) or they reject all of the principles or in utopian fashion, assert them all at the same time. For more detail see the appendix.

The four democratic theories each make an explicit commitment to *two* of the principles and leave open what they say about the other two. Their position on the other two can be taken as an empirical question or as a question that they are just not concerned about. I indicate their commitment to the principles of central concern by a "+" and their agnosticism about the other principles by a "?".

Chart III. Four democratic theories

	Competitive democracy	Elite deliberation	Participatory democracy	Deliberative democracy
Political equality	+	?	+	+
Participation	?	?	+	?
Deliberation	?	+	?	+
Non-tyranny	+	+	?	?

There is not one democratic theory. Rather there are competing theories. The four positions we focus on here are, to some degree, ideal types, in that some theorists who largely fit require a bit of careful packing to capture their positions within a given category. I would argue that the careful packing serves the interest of making the positions stronger. For example, the prime proponent of competitive democracy was not actually interested in counting votes equally. But competitive democracy is more compelling when votes are counted equally.

The four positions clarify issues in that they represent clear positions for which arguments can be made (and have been made). In addition, we will treat the four positions as variations in commitments about the four principles and how they deal with the merits of the component parts. As a result, we will have an apparatus for discussing a whole range of possible democratic theories. My purpose is not to offer a thumbnail guide to the history of democratic theory. Rather, it is to get a handle on the range of competing visions of what democracy should be.

Competitive democracy

First, consider a minimal position we will call Competitive Democracy. It focuses on competitive elections and on the institutionalization of rights that might protect against tyranny of the majority. It was most famously advocated by Joseph Schumpeter and has been taken up by many theorists since.[1] It lowered expectations about the meaningfulness of any process of public will formation, but focused democratic thought, instead, on the "competitive struggle for the people's vote" with the additional requirement that rights needed respecting. On this view, the key challenge for democracy is to provide peaceful transitions of power and some alternation of political leadership. In addition, parties will usually have incentives to satisfy the preferences of the median voter, and hence the parties will not differ as much as they sometimes appear to. Of course, if the voters were to cluster at ideological positions that are far apart, or if turnout expectations were to give incentives to parties to mobilize their bases rather than appeal to the middle, or if gerrymandered political boundaries were to make elections noncompetitive, then the inference about the median voter would not hold. Ultimately, the substance of the "public will" does not really matter for this position. Whether parties or candidates are close to the median voter is a side issue and a question for empirical research. On this view of democracy, the key is that competitive elections provide a peaceful alternation of governing elites and the system somehow provides clear limitations on what the governing elites can decide (via legal and constitutional constraints). On the competitive view, to expect the "will of the people" to mean much, if anything at all, is a delusion. But if the game settles who is in power without revolution or violence and if rights are protected, these are considerable accomplishments.

Schumpeter himself did not advocate political equality. In fact, notoriously, he was not willing to require that his ideal of political competition mandate the inclusion of blacks in the American south or of nonparty members in the Soviet Union. When political equality is to be instituted via party competition, there are obviously two issues: (*a*) the extent of the franchise and (*b*) the equal counting of the votes of those included. Schumpeter did not offer criteria for either except to avoid the questions.[2]

However, the minimal or competitive democracy position has its most defensible interpretation when it is taken to include claims about the political equality that is realized via political competition. To the extent that major groups are denied the vote, this position can be tarnished with unnecessary criticisms about exclusion. And to the extent that boundaries are manipulated or access by candidates or voters is denied, then the ideal of competitive elections is undermined. Further, to the extent that votes are not counted equally, the competition is open to charges of unfairness. In discussing each position, we will try to construe the strongest version. So while one could have competitive democracy without political equality, it is an unnecessary additional burden for the position and in a modern context, unnecessary.

With this caveat, it is of course obvious that we fail to achieve political equality in the United States in many dimensions. Some of the obvious cases: our eighteenth century structure of an Electoral College for presidential selection and the bicameral design of Congress with senators apportioned regardless of population. Similar degrees of political inequality follow from the legacy of the Progressive reformers for candidate nominations—a sequential presidential primary system with enormously greater influence for some unrepresentative, small states such as Iowa and New Hampshire. Despite these complications, we can grasp the appeal of the ideal of combining political equality with competitive elections, on the one hand, with guarantees that would protect against majority tyranny, on the other. And in some key court cases applied to redistricting, we have of course moved much closer to "one person one vote" in areas such as the design of congressional districts.[3]

Competitive democracy is agnostic or even hostile to the other two principles in our scheme. On this view, there is no particular value in deliberation. Indeed, in some versions of the argument the ideal of deliberation is attacked as a wasteful investment in decision costs. If public will formation is not meaningful, why should we waste our time and energy attempting to foster it? And if the parties are going to basically converge on the median voter, then there is no use spending a lot of time helping people decide which of them should win. The parties, while they might try to appear starkly different are actually so fundamentally similar that who wins will not make much difference.[4]

In both Schumpeter's view and Richard Posner's recent revival of the argument, the idea is to contrast some "classical" theory that aspired to public will formation and a modern competitive view which made no such claims. While there are issues about what exactly the classical theory is that poses the alternative, the basic idea is to build on the contrast between public will formation and a simple decision about who wins the electoral game to achieve and hold office.[5] Posner treats the contrasting deliberative model of democracy as a kind of illusory ideal. He dismisses it "as a pipe dream hardly worth the attention of a serious person." Focusing on citizen deliberation as a way of improving democracy, he says, would be like asking Odysseus to sprout wings as a way of leaving Calypso's island. What makes deliberation unattainable, in his view, is the inability of citizens to deal with complex policy issues.[6] Thus democratic reforms should focus simply on improving the conditions for party competition.

Of course, whether or not ordinary citizens (or voters or residents) are indeed capable of dealing with complex policy issues is an empirical question—one that the Deliberative Polling initiative, along with many other efforts, is devoted to exploring.[7] The prospects for competence in decision-making by the mass public should not be dismissed without evidence. Whether or not ordinary citizens appear competent may well depend on whether they have reason to pay attention, whether they think their voice will matter, how discussions and interactions are conducted, and how any data about their views is collected. And of course any inferences from a deliberative consultation to the broader population will depend crucially on who the participants are, how they were recruited, and what kinds of data are available to evaluate claims about their decision-making capacities.

Proponents of competitive democracy such as Schumpeter and Posner are also worried about another empirical issue: whether mass participation will lead to an aroused public that might do bad things and, hence, commit tyranny of the majority. The idea is that there is a possible (and often assumed) causal connection between mass participation and violations of what we are calling non-tyranny. The most prominent interpretations of the competitive position would actually reject mass participation and deliberation but in order to be inclusive I am representing the position in the chart with just a question mark in order to include the possibility that a position might embrace one or the other.[8]

Proponents of competitive democracy are often fearful of mass participation because they ask, why would large portions of the public participate unless they were aroused by mob psychology, or the passions or interests that might motivate "faction" as Madison hypothesized.[9] The supposition is that unless there are strong emotions involved, the mass public is likely to stay disconnected from politics or policy. From this perspective it may be a sleeping giant that is better kept dormant.

But within the framework of purely instrumental effects for the individual vote or the individual act of participation in large-scale competitive democracies, it is hard to explain even the low levels of participation in a non-aroused public. The paradox of voting or political participation is sometimes referred to as the "monster that ate rational choice theory."[10] The idea is that if one thinks of the benefits of voting (to oneself or alternatively to the public at large) and one takes into account the probability that one's individual vote or opinion will make any difference to the outcome, then the only way that a calculation comparing costs and benefits of participation can be balanced is to include an ethical concern say, satisfaction with the ethic of voting.[11] Many people do in fact vote because they feel they have some kind of a duty to do so. There is a long discussion about whether or not this duty can be plausibly constructed so that even with miniscule individual effects I should feel obligated to go to the polls.[12] For our purposes here, we need only note that if getting people to participate in large numbers often depends crucially on their feeling *obligated* to do so, then we can think of an alternative moral psychology that is motivating them that is less threatening than the mob, less threatening than the angry passions that are taken to motivate factions. In this sense the supposition is undermined that we should expect there to be a causal connection between mass participation and the mob psychology ending in tyranny of the majority.

For competitive democracy, the key is simply to settle the question of who is in charge through a competitive struggle for the people's vote.

By settling that question with ballots not bullets, we get peaceful transitions and can have judicial protections for individual rights (the latter presumably to help protect against tyranny of the majority, although that can be a frail bulwark as Hamilton concluded). Hence the combination of political equality and non-tyranny, with agnosticism about the other two principles, defines a viable position in our chart.

Elite deliberation

A second position, which we are calling Elite Deliberation, has much in common with the competitive model. Like the competitive model, it avoids any commitment to mass participation. In its Madisonian version, emphasizing "indirect filtration" of mass public opinion, the idea was that deliberating representatives could better pronounce on "justice and the common good than could the people themselves if convened for the purpose." The public views needed to be "filtered" or "refined" by representatives if they were to express "the cool and deliberate sense of the community."

A developed version of this position can, of course, be found in Madison. The Founders had little concern for political equality or mass participation but they were focused on deliberation and on avoiding tyranny of the majority.

Madison offers an elegant and compact argument in *Federalist* No. 10. However, it is one that includes a puzzle. After defining factions ("by a faction I understand some number of citizens, whether amounting to a majority or minority of the whole, who are united and actuated by some common impulse of passion, or of interest, adverse to the rights of other citizens, or to the permanent and aggregate interests of the community") he offers two methods for controlling them—removing their causes or controlling their effects. The causes cannot be eliminated without eliminating liberty so the problem is to control the effects.

He then considers two cases, minority and majority factions. In the minority case "relief is supplied by the republican principle, which enables the majority to defeat its sinister views by regular vote." But the solution is not so easy in the case of majority factions. "When a majority is included in a faction, the form of popular government, on the other hand enables it to sacrifice to its ruling passion or interest both the public good and the rights of other citizens." How to control majority factions is the "great object": "To secure the public good and private rights against the danger of such a faction, and at the same time to preserve the spirit and the form of popular government, is then the great object to which our inquiries are directed."

Note that Madison has just identified the "republican principle" with majority rule in claiming that minority factions can be controlled simply by use of the republican principle. But how to "preserve the spirit and form of popular government" and at the same time control majority factions is the "great object."

The extensive discussion of *Federalist* No. 10 has been dominated by the second of two arguments he offers in response to this problem. The second argument is a justly famous one:

> [E]xtend the sphere and you take in a greater variety of parties and interests; you make it less probable that a majority of the whole will have a common motive to invade the rights of other citizens; or if such a common motive exists, it will be more difficult for those who feel it to discover their own strength and to act in unison with each other.

But this argument is about how majority factions are less likely to form in large states, or, if they form, how they are less likely to make themselves felt. It does not deal explicitly with the apparent incompatibility between the "republican principle" itself and the principle that majority factions adverse to the rights of others should not carry the day (how to satisfy what we are calling the non-tyranny condition).

The conceptual problem, in other words, is that if the "republican principle" is an expression of majority rule (and for that reason can control minority factions), why should it not also carry the day with majority factions? Madison's solution was basically that the republican principle is applied to elites who represent deliberative or filtered public opinion. And when they deliberate they will not behave as factions but will, rather, act in the public interest.

When Madison defines a republic as "a government in which the scheme of representation takes place" he says it is this fact that "promises the cure we are seeking." He then explains the function of representatives in the famous phrase: "to refine and enlarge the public views by passing them through the medium of a chosen body of citizens whose wisdom may best discern the true interests of their country and whose patriotism and love of justice will be least likely to sacrifice it to temporary and partial considerations."

As noted, this "refined" view of public opinion will be different from what we would get if we convened the public and asked them their views on the spot. It is not the mirror but the filter. As such it is usually a counterfactual picture of public opinion, held on behalf of the public by its representatives. But there is a sense in which it can also be a majority view—what the public *would* think if it were able to consider the issue in the way that representatives can in a deliberative body. It is not just the views of the representatives, because it is a refinement and enlargement of the "*public* views" not just those of the representatives. It is an application of the "republican principle" but not to the opinions people actually have but to those they would have if they could think about them in the sense Madison advocates.[13]

Madison's "cure" is to apply the republican principle only to representatives refining deliberative public opinion. Madison believes this can best be discovered by the deliberations of a small representative body, such as the Senate, and, hopefully, the ratifying conventions to the Constitution. These were, in effect, gatherings aimed at discovering refined public opinion.

Madison offers the outlines of a political psychology that would also explain why he thinks the deliberative process, the filter, applied in this way also solves the faction problem. The answer lies in the distinction between the "cool and deliberate sense of the community" (*Federalist* No. 63) and the "passions and interests" that would support factions adverse to the rights or interests of others (*Federalist* No. 10). Deliberation filters the public views in a calm and dispassionate way to arrive at collective solutions to public problems supported by reasons that the representatives have weighed in their discussions together in a manageably small deliberative body. Madison and Hamilton both argue consistently from the distinction between the passions and interests that motivate factions and "the reason, alone of the public that ought to regulate and control the government" (*Federalist* No. 69). Madison is positing the rudiments of a political psychology connected with deliberation. The filtering of public views arrives at a dispassionate and shared account of the solutions to public problems. It is not motivated by immediate passions directed against others or interests that seek profit at the expense of others.

Elite deliberation, in this case, the deliberations of representatives on behalf of the people, filtering their views, offers a protection against tyranny of the majority and through indirect filtration, a picture of what the people would want, on reflection. In this sense it will offer a representation that has important similarities to another position we will call deliberative democracy. But we are reserving that position for deliberations by the people themselves, for deliberations that satisfy not only the principle of deliberation but also that of political equality. The elite deliberation position does not offer each voter an equal chance of being decisive on substantive decisions. It only allows elites to represent and decide. The Madisonian version emphasizes deliberation and non-tyranny and we will take those two commitments as its defining features. To be clear, the Madisonian elite deliberation position is deliberation *for* the people. The position we will later identify as deliberative democracy is deliberation *by* the people.

J.S. Mill's Congress of Opinions offers some further refinements to the Elite Deliberation position by suggesting how the deliberating elites are connected to ordinary citizens. In Mill's picture, each citizen can see his arguments made as well or better than he could make them and answered by others from different points of view, as well or better than those from contrasting points of view could make those arguments, and then those arguments can be imagined as answered in turn. At the end of the day, the decisions are made, not as mere acts of will but on the basis of the better arguments. Mill's representatives deliberate just as Madison's do, without regard to faction or party and on the basis of the best arguments about what should be done. Mill's representatives were primarily a debating society, not a decision-making body. And elite deliberation as a theory of how parliaments might actually work has lacked an account of how the elites are supposed to focus on substance while they are also concerned with getting re-elected and hence serve their partisan loyalties.

Of course, the Madison–Mill picture of deliberating representatives seems far removed from most of our political experience since the Founding. It is far removed from a contemporary world of political parties, campaign contributions, television advertising, and candidates who function as issue entrepreneurs in an environment of near-perpetual campaigning. Madison, who lived at least part of his life in an era when letters from Virginia to Massachusetts would slowly travel via England, had no inkling that technology might transform politics as it transformed political communication. Madison thought elections would be less subject to "the vicious arts" in large electorates than in small ones. He was thinking primarily of bribery, and it is of course harder to bribe a large population than to bribe a small one.[14] However, the opportunities for demagoguery and manipulation of the public are clearly available in large electorates, particularly when technology makes communication to vast numbers so easy. Vicious arts, conceived more broadly than just bribery, may actually be easier to practice in large electorates, requiring communication via the media, than in very small ones where vestiges of face-to-face democracy remain.[15]

The relevance of Madison's "cure" for our purposes lies, first, in the suggestion that representatives might properly take account of a counterfactual—what the "public views" *would be* if "refined and enlarged." Second, it lies in the fact that while this refined public opinion may well be counterfactual for the entire mass public, it can be made real for a representative group. By applying the republican principle in "spirit" to the deliberations of a restricted elite it is likely to avoid tyranny of the majority and serve the public interest.

This account of Madison suggests a middle ground in the apparent dilemma often facing representatives.[16] Should they follow the polls or should they vote their own views of what is best for the country (or their state or district)? This crude dichotomy dominates the discussion about how members of Congress and other legislators should approach their task, yet each of these two basic possibilities has difficulties. If members of Congress follow the polls, then they can be dismissed as leaderless weathervanes for the shifting winds of public opinion. Given how ill-informed the public tends to be on most policy issues, the blind would literally be doing the leading. On the other hand, if they follow their views of the substantive merits when their constituents disagree, then they can be criticized for imposing their personal value judgments on an electorate that thinks otherwise.

A slight variant is to think of representatives not as weathervanes, but as weather predictors—as attempting to anticipate what their constituents will think about an issue as it actually evolves. However, from a normative standpoint, this is not a clear improvement. It is quite obvious that on many issues, the public will never be well informed and may even become increasingly misled. What the public would think if it could get some reasonable account of the relevant information is very different from what it is likely to think over time in an environment of attack ads and sound bite campaigning. Representatives admittedly have strong incentives to pay attention to the latter. Yet, there may still be occasions when they can pay attention to the former.

The middle position, between following public opinion as it is, and following one's personal views on the merits, is so obvious that it hardly requires explicit statement. It is easily overlooked and only occasionally articulated. Representatives can take account of what they think their constituents would think about an issue, once they were well informed and got the facts, heard the arguments on either side, and had a reasonable chance to ponder the issues. This view of a representative's role provides grounds for resisting the pressure of polls on issues that the representative knows the public knows little about. On the other hand, this position is not the same as just the representative's own views on the issue in question. The representative may know that his or her values differ from those of constituents on a given question or that constituents would never accept a particular policy, even with a great deal more information and discussion. The representative may also know his or her constituents well enough to have some idea of what they would accept if only they had the information. This deference to the counterfactual deliberating public provides a way of thinking about the representative's role that avoids the difficulty of following the public's uninformed views, on the one hand, and of following the representative's more informed but (perhaps) merely personal views, on the other.

While this view of the representative's role is not often explicit, it does surface in rare moments when Congress or commentators are self-conscious. Consider Samuel Beer's recommendations to the House Judiciary Committee during the preparations for the impeachment trial of President Clinton. Beer's claim was that the Congress is "a creature of the people ... acting in lieu of the people between quadrennial elections. *At their best, the legislators will do what the people, at their best, would do* (emphasis added)."[17] Several members of Congress publicly rationalized their role in the impeachment process by reference to a version of the same basic notion—what the public would think if they were as informed as the members.[18]

Impeachment is, of course, a rare and momentous event. But because of its seriousness and novelty, it brings to the surface a rationale for the role of representatives which is only implicit on other occasions— the aspiration to represent the public's considered judgments. Later, when we turn to the position we are explicitly labeling deliberative democracy, we will discuss the idea that the people, or some portion of them, might themselves give expression to their considered judgments, rather than have the elites do it for them. That position, which shares the value of deliberation with this one, adds the value of political equality. However, before turning to that position, consider the position that emphasizes what both deliberation positions do not—mass participation.

Participatory democracy

As we saw, the early American expression of elite deliberation was challenged when the Founders' scheme for the US Constitution was subjected to a referendum in Rhode Island. While that event was a minor skirmish in the battle over ratification, it is worth noting because it dramatizes competing conceptions of democracy. The referendum provided something that elite deliberations in a convention missed—mass participation which could serve as a proxy for actual consent. Every freeman's liberty was at stake the Anti-Federalists argued. Why should each not get to vote on the issue? Mass participation has long been taken as a means of expressing actual consent. In many countries constitutional changes are subject to referenda, and that is the practice also for constitutional changes in many American states. Even in countries such as the United Kingdom, where referenda are rare, there is precedent for putting especially momentous matters (such as membership in the European Community) to referendum as a way of demonstrating the consent of the governed.

Participatory democracy does not require that all decisions be made directly by the people. In large-scale nation-states this is obviously impractical, although it has had advocates.[19] But the idea is to shift the mix so that direct consultation is frequent and consequential. From the standpoint of participatory democracy, direct consultation is not merely about the choice of policy elites but also about the choice of policies. In contrast to competitive democracy, the people should be consulted about more than which team takes office. It should be consulted about the substance of what is to be done. In contrast to competitive democracy, the expectation is that public will formation is meaningful and worth consulting.

Note that participatory democracy places a positive value on the *combination* of political equality and participation. So to the extent that mass participation is subject to participatory distortion, that is an indication of a democratic deficit. Participation is the means by which the public will is given voice. Hence if some sectors of society, some demographic groups, some widely shared viewpoints, are left out, then that voice is distorted. In the case of our first two theories, there was no concern for representative participation. The competitive and the elite deliberative views were agnostic, and sometimes overtly hostile to mass participation—because of its possible causal connection to "tyranny of the majority." There was no commitment to encouraging participation, equal or not. Within the competitive view it is fair game, and according to some studies probably good tactics to employ negative ads to encourage demobilization and lower turnout, especially of your opponents' supporters.[20] Of course, we have interpreted the competitive view as committed to political equality—at least so far as this is applied to the equal counting of whatever votes are cast. But there is no commitment on this position that participation be widely shared since the spread of participation was feared as a possible expression of dangerous factions.

One could have mass participation without political equality. In fact, we do, to a great extent, given some of our territorial and eighteenth-century legacies in the US system. Consider the many ways in which our votes are not counted equally—the Electoral College, the US Senate, and the primary system. Even if there were a perfect counting of votes *within* electoral boundaries (an ideal we fall far short of[21]) there is an obvious lack of political equality *across* electoral boundaries. There is vastly more influence per vote in some states than others—more voting power because of the overrepresentation of small states in the Electoral College and the US Senate and the over-influence of key early states in the primary process. Yet to the extent that a participatory system violates political equality its normative claims are weakened. Hence, we will focus our attention on the version of the position that seems strongest. We picture participatory democracy as defined by a commitment to both political equality and mass participation. However, it is agnostic on the other two principles.

Why might a proponent support the ideal of participatory democracy? We have already mentioned that actual participation can be considered a proxy for mass consent. It is the people, after all, who must live with the choice of policies. They must live with the benefits and burdens. Why not consult them about the policies they must live with? Of course, this claim of being affected could be taken as a basis for consulting more with those most closely affected.[22] Such a system is likely to be unworkable, precisely because disputes about the degree to which groups are affected would become the battleground determining the approval of policies. But if one thinks, rather, of mass participation as a token of consent to the overall system, to which all are equally subjected as a matter of right, then equal consultation in some sense begins to make sense.

There are additional arguments. Much of the revival of interest in participatory democracy was spurred by the argument that it serves an "educative function." Those who participate learn how to be citizens by doing. They get a greater sense of efficacy and become more informed about public issues. Most importantly, they acquire a sense of "public spirit." As they discuss public problems together they appreciate different points of view and learn to weigh and to value interests broader than their own. As Pateman argues, the distinctive aspect of the participatory view is its posited effect on human development. J.S. Mill reacted to Toqueville's account of a society with a great measure of social equality, in which there were key institutions that gave citizens responsibility—such as the New England town meeting and the jury. In those "schools of public spirit" citizens discussed public problems together and took responsibility for the broader public interest.

As we saw earlier, it is always important to consider the social context and the scale of interaction when thinking about public involvement. Much of the appeal of participatory democracy comes from a picture of small-scale institutions, like the town meeting or the jury. Democracy on the scale of face-to-face democracy allows for a richness of interaction and a solution to collective action problems. It is really a category mistake to classify together New England town meetings and California-style initiatives. While both, technically, offer instances of direct democracy, the difference in scale means that the initiative becomes a variant of audience democracy, in which the primary information sources come from the mass media and in which the individual's role is diluted to inconsequence by the fact that it is accompanied by so many millions of others. The town meeting or the jury, by contrast, allow for active rather than passive involvement and a meaningful share of the decision process for each participant. The educative function is most compelling for the face-to-face variants, whether in the "schools of public spirit" that impressed Mill and Toqueville or in other small-scale contexts such as economic enterprises with substantial worker democracy.[23]

Two caveats are worth noting. First, the four theories of democracy we are considering all need to be theories applicable to the large-scale nation-state. Hence, if the real benefits of participation are only available at the small scale, then the participatory theory is open to objections that do not apply to the others. It is an open question how much efforts to open up local control and decentralization might create spaces for face-to-face democracy within a larger polity.[24] Even supposing the success of such strategies, it is worth asking whether what is being valued with the educative function is participation or deliberation. Note that the influential examples such as the jury or the town meeting involve a combination of responsibility with discussion. Juries and town meetings discuss public problems together and through those discussions each individual learns to consider interests other than his or her own. If the participation does not involve discussion, if it is mute and anonymous, like the modern secret ballot, it is not obvious that the act of participation by itself serves an educative function.

Progressive reformers, in pressing for mass decision-making hoped that voting in the large-scale nation-state would have the same educative function as envisioned in small-scale democracy. To facilitate matters they advocated voter handbooks to be made available to every voter as well as other forms of civic education.[25] Yet their reforms—the mass primary for candidate selection, initiative and referendum for policy issues, recall for those already in office, have provided battlegrounds for low information conflicts in sound bite democracy.[26] There is little dispute about whether or not the public becomes well informed in these contests. The only dispute is about whether or not the public can use shortcuts to approximate the informed preferences that they do not have. Hence, the educative effect of participation at the large scale is normally small.[27]

In the small-scale context, the educative argument for participation is really valuing something like deliberation. The "schools of public spirit" cited by Toqueveille and Mill were discursive institutions—juries and town meetings. And even the modest educative effects of larger-scale participation in referenda are surely linked to the fact that they stimulate a vast public discussion. People talk about the issues in anticipation of having to vote in a referendum. But the actual act of voting in a referendum or primary in a large-scale mass society is not a discursive act. It is a private communication by secret ballot. There is clearly a trade-off. If one wants an educative effect then something like deliberation seems required. But if one wants an effect on the mass of the public then the issue of spreading that effect to scale arises, an issue we grappled with in Deliberation Day. The point here is that to the extent that one is valuing participation, the core of the value should be tied to the nature of the act as it is constituted in the social context in which it takes place. To value participation because of its effects in town meetings does not mean that comparable educative effects will occur in referenda or mass primaries. And if an educative effect is the effect that is desired, then aiming at deliberation directly—or at institutional designs that have a necessary deliberative component—may be more to the point.

On the other hand, to the extent that one is valuing mass political participation as a proxy for actual consent then the educative effects are not intrinsic to the argument. They are a welcome bonus from most perspectives, but the case for participation does not depend on them. Regardless of educative effects and how they may vary with social context, there is a clear and viable position, which we will call participatory democracy, that is committed to the combination of mass participation and political equality and is agnostic on the other two principles in our scheme.

Deliberative democracy

The last of our four democratic theories attempts to combine deliberation by the people themselves with political equality. As we noted earlier, one strategy for achieving political equality would realize it through mass participation—in theory everyone participates and their views are somehow counted equally. While this approach has predominated throughout the history of democratic reform, it has some limitations. First, when participation is voluntary there is usually substantial participatory distortion—the better-off and the more educated tend to participate more. Some voices are just much more likely to be left out. The less well-off are struggling to just survive and are only occasionally mobilized. While this problem might be solved with respect to voting through compulsory voting, compulsion has an obvious cost in liberty. It also means people who have not taken the time or trouble to prepare will be forced to vote. Setting aside the trade-off between participatory distortion versus issues of liberty (in compulsory voting) there is also a second problem with the idea of achieving political equality via mass participation. In the large-scale context, there is little to effectively motivate informed voting or citizen deliberation. One can achieve political equality by equally counting votes or opinions, but the scale of mass democracy leads to the politics of the disengaged audience rather than the empowered participation idealized in the town meeting.[28]

Combining political equality with deliberation requires that the deliberation take place on a human scale, on the scale of face-to-face democracy. This fact was recognized by the Founders when they specified relatively small institutions for their elite deliberations—a constitutional convention or the Senate or even the Electoral College in its original vision. But as noted earlier, these were deliberations *for* the people but not *by* the people. How can the people, much more numerous than their representative bodies, deliberate themselves? As mentioned earlier, one scheme might be to seriously incentivize voluntary mass deliberation in many decentralized forums. Each such forum could be small enough to allow face-to-face deliberation on a human scale. Our proposal for Deliberation Day was an instance of such a strategy. However, such an effort is expensive precisely because it involves coordinating and motivating many millions. If participatory distortion is avoided because the incentives are good enough to motivate participation throughout all strata of the population, then political equality and deliberation might both be served by such a strategy. However, the downside is the cost and massive scale of such a strategy.

There is no reason to think that technology will solve this problem. The self-selection problem, with its attendant participatory distortion applies in the same way to those who choose to opt into the dialogue, whether it is virtual or face-to-face. However, technology would serve to eliminate a separate bias in local face-to-face dialogues in that it can erase geography and create a truly national deliberation for each subgroup. In virtual space I can as easily be in a dialogue with someone on the other side of the country as with someone on the other side of town. Surely this increase in geographical diversity enriches the dialogue. However, when deliberation is inserted into a federal system with state and local governments, it is not clear that this is a distinct advantage since the relevant demos for the decisions in question may well be smaller.

Instead of a massive effort along the lines of Deliberation Day, I want to focus here on a more modest and practical strategy for realizing deliberative democracy—microcosmic deliberation. The microcosm, like a convention or senate, is of modest scale. But unlike elite institutions it is a representative group of ordinary citizens, preferably constituted on the basis of random sampling. Note that there is no upper limit to the size of the population a microcosm can represent. Essentially, one does not need a larger sample to represent a larger population. So with very nearly the same level of precision, a sample of a few hundred can represent San Mateo County, or the state of California or the entire United States or even a much larger political entity such as the entire European Union (whose population now approaches half a billion).

Ideally, the sample should be large enough that its representativeness can be evaluated statistically, but small enough that each participant can speak—particularly if it is organized with alternating small and large group discussions so that each participant is meaningfully engaged in the small groups. If it is too small, its claim to statistical representativeness cannot be established. This problem applies to Citizens Juries and Consensus Conferences (typically in the same size range as modern juries). On the other hand, so long as it is subdivided for small group discussions, there is no clear upper limit on its size, except for practical constraints of cost (incentives for participation, cost of transportation, lodging, etc.).

The idea of microcosmic deliberation goes back to ancient Athens, where a variety of institutions chose participants by lot (from a list of those who had previously agreed). These institutions would typically engage 500 or more for at least a day of deliberation. Juries of 500 had a far greater purview than those in modern legal cases. In addition, there were legislative commissions, or *nomothetai*, that in some cases made the final decisions on legislation. Another institution called the *graphe paronomon* would allow prosecution of a speaker in the Assembly who made an illegal proposal. This device provided an incentive for better deliberation in the Assembly in that speakers knew that an irresponsible proposal could be subject to penalty.

Most importantly, the agenda for the Assembly, and many of the operative decisions of government were made by the *Council of 500*. The Council, unlike the other microcosms, met for an entire year. It was randomly chosen with fifty from each of the ten (artificially created) tribes or demes and each tribe's representation took the lead in meeting almost full time for a bit more than a month. As a result, there was a great deal of small-group interaction. The council differed from the other microcosms both in length of deliberation and in the variety of face-to-face interaction. The other microcosms were usually limited to arguments presented in a single day with the 500 sitting as an audience in an amphitheater.

Microcosmic deliberation realizes political equality via random sampling in the choice of participants as well as an equal counting of their views once assembled. It achieves deliberation through balanced exchanges of reasons and arguments. With the Deliberative Poll and the Citizens Juries as well as the ancient Athenian Council, these exchanges occur in face-to-face discussions. In the Athenian law courts, the exchanges were more limited because the participants were mostly in the role of audience. Later we will also discuss virtual microcosms of the public which gather people together for voice-based discussions but can extend a succession of meetings over several weeks. Voice-based discussions online have some of the interactivity of face-to-face but do not require bringing everyone to the same place.[29]

With good random sampling and an effective motivation to participate the process should avoid participatory distortion. At least in the case of the modern versions, when an extensive questionnaire is administered before people are invited, it is possible to know if the microcosm is in any way unrepresentative—in terms of attitudes as well as demographics (since this information is collected before the invitation is offered). We have little information about the ancient microcosms, but we do know that there was commentary at the time that the courts were mostly populated by the old and the poor who came just to collect the fees.[30] Modern Deliberative Polls usually have relatively few statistically significant differences between participants and nonparticipants. Of course, each case may differ depending on the incentives offered and the nature of the issue, the amount of travel required, etc.[31]

Suppose a microcosm is a good representative sample and that it engages in a substantive and balanced deliberation. What is accomplished? A representation of what the people would think under good conditions—a representation embodying both political equality and deliberation. However, the limitation is that it is a representation. The entire people do not all deliberate, only a representative microcosm. Hence, if we view the results as representing a form of collective informed consent—what the people would accept on reflection if they were informed—it is important to note the use of the word "would." The people in their actual state of raw public opinion may not have thought much about the issue, may not be informed, may never have considered competing views, and may in fact have no opinion at all.

Hence, the main downside of this approach is the gap between the deliberating microcosm and the mass population. But this is, of course, a problem for all representative institutions. And the deliberating microcosm is an alternative or supplementary representative institution, one that is composed of random sampling rather than election. Here again, there are trade-offs. On the one hand, one could argue that the microcosm is not accountable because it is not running for re-election. On the other hand, one might argue that it is able to focus sincerely on the merits precisely because it is not running for re-election. The only office the participants hold is citizen (or in some cases, resident) of the relevant population. They will continue to hold that office regardless of what they decide. They will, of course, have to live with the result, just as will those from the larger population from whom they were drawn. By giving up valuable time for a public purpose, they become engaged in a community service attracted in large part because they think their voice will matter. The result is an effort to arrive at their own conscientious views, not a preprogrammed, spin doctored stance designed to attract votes for re-election.

As we will see, the gap between the deliberators and the mass electorate is often a manageable problem. The issue turns on the exact policy context and on the way the microcosm is connected to decision processes. We will return to these issues in Chapter 4.[32] In the meantime, why should the conclusions of a deliberating microcosm have any normative claim on us? Why should they have any recommending force?

The microcosm experiences good conditions for coming to a considered judgment about the issues. If we think, at the individual level, that it is more relevant to pay attention to a considered judgment than a distorted or ill-considered one, then why not also pay more attention to our *collective* considered judgments? They are also more likely to have a good basis than those we have not thought about, or those for which we have neglected relevant arguments.

Consider John Rawls's characterization of "considered judgments." His focus is on morality, on those conditions where our moral capacities can be displayed "without distortion," but he says the same issues apply to "considered judgments of any kind." Considered judgments are those made "in circumstances where the more common excuses and explanations for making a mistake do not obtain. The person making the judgment is presumed then, to have the ability, the opportunity and the desire to reach a correct decision (or at least not the desire not to)."[33]

Consider our criteria for quality deliberation. They all address the distortions that might lead us astray. Our criteria were *information, substantive balance, diversity* of viewpoints, *conscientiousness*, and *equal consideration* of the arguments offered on their merits. Lack of any one of these could lead us to reasonably question whether we had reached considered judgments. First, we might lack the relevant information. So recalling our earlier discussion of foreign aid, our participants in a national DP on US foreign policy wanted to cut the level of foreign aid, but they erroneously thought it was one of the largest parts of the US budget. When they realized it was less than 1% they wanted to increase it.[34] Second, we might fail to have been engaged by competing sides of the argument. So recalling our discussion of "clean coal," we might have learned that clean coal was cleaner than dirty coal, but we might not have heard how much dirtier it was than national gas or wind power. If we made a choice between coal and these other sources without hearing the competing sides we could easily make what we would later regard as a mistake. Third, we might lack diversity of viewpoints in the positions represented. If Bulgarians deliberate about the Roma, without the Roma position represented in the dialogue, or if Australians deliberate about policy toward the Aboriginals without the Aboriginals represented, then any achievement of substantive balance among the viewpoints represented in the room will fail to do justice to the diversity of viewpoints in the society at large. In that way the criteria of substantive balance and diversity of viewpoints both need to be fulfilled for the participants to be able to weigh competing arguments. Fourth, the participants might not consider the arguments conscientiously on the merits. If they are simply acting strategically, or worse, attempting to disrupt the deliberations for others, then they will obviously fail to offer considered judgments. Hence the relevance of Rawls's observation that participants must have a "desire" to reach a correct decision. Fifth, participants must consider arguments on the merits regardless of who offers them. So if some participants are of lower status that should not mean that their viewpoints are discounted. One could have substantive balance, in that arguments offered are answered, but if the arguments from certain strata are just not listened to, then those arguments would not have had an effective hearing. The possibility of this sort of distortion has been a concern of deliberation critics[35] and it is a fair issue for actual research to assess the degree to which deliberative designs are subject to the problem of effective exclusion of some persons from the dialogue. We believe that the problem varies with the design of the deliberative process and that with the right design, it can be avoided.

Note that the result, if all goes well, is an aggregation of individual considered judgments. But on some accounts there is supposed to be a contrast between deliberative democracy and the aggregation of individual views. Aggregative and deliberative democracy are supposed to be rival and incompatible viewpoints. However, I will argue that this division oversimplifies the possibilities.

Deliberation versus aggregation?

We supposedly face a forced choice between "aggregative" and "deliberative" theories. The aggregative theories are identified with what we have been calling competitive democracy. They count votes and allow for a winner to be declared. They are not concerned with the will of "we the people." Rather their concern is a peaceful process of determining which competing team of elites takes office. Ultimately, on this view, that is all democracy is about. The deliberative theories waste a lot of time and effort on decision costs by having long debates and then seeking some kind of forced consensus. If the ideal of deliberative theory were a Habermasian "ideal speech situation" where we are to imagine that there is no limit to the possible time spent to reach consensus, then the decision costs would be truly unlimited.[36] And in the real world, if the debate is not actually unending (although it may seem so) the necessity of a consensus will require something closer to a false consensus—like a jury verdict reached under great pressure for a decision but which may well be arrived at despite sincere misgivings of many jurors. The consensus that results is subject to distortions of social pressure. Why should we pay heed to a false consensus? Why should we interpret it as a legitimate mandate for action when it may be no more than a product of arm-twisting that covers over real disagreement? Furthermore, even if, on occasion, there is an actual consensus it may be the result of unequal persuasive power, inattention by the others who are persuaded, ignorance of alternatives or of crucial information, or the ability, as Posner argues, of an elite intelligentsia to push their ideological propensities on unsuspecting and less sophisticated members of the mass public. So-called deliberative democracy may simply reflect the intellectual hegemony of the more educated and more advantaged. It does not make a serious moral claim. Variants of this argument are ably put forward by Richard Posner and by Ian Shapiro, both of whom use it to defend competitive democracy.[37]

To assess this argument first, consider the initial move—the often discussed division of democratic theories into two broad categories—aggregative and deliberative. I believe such a division only tells part of the story. Deliberation is a condition of preference *formation*. Aggregation by majority rule or other voting rules is a property of the *decision rule* by which those preferences, however produced, culminate in some kind of conclusion or decision. A point that seems to have gotten lost when this simple division is invoked is that there can be deliberative approaches that use individual preference aggregation—indeed the Deliberative Poll offers an example[38]—and there can be deliberative theories that prescribe consensus,[39] which some, but not all, do.

Similarly there can be aggregative theories that use raw preferences (preferences that have not been subjected to a balanced and informative deliberative process), and aggregative theories that employ deliberation. Hence the aggregative/deliberative distinction really conflates four theoretical possibilities into two. The four possibilities are: deliberation with aggregation (I); deliberation with consensus (II); raw preferences with aggregation (III); and raw preferences with consensus (IV)—Chart IV.

This fourfold table covers over important differences. There are many possible decision rules for aggregating preferences and many possible ways in which consensus might be arrived at. Key concerns might focus on the degree to which a decision rule is majoritarian or if supermajorities are required, the effect of a supermajority requirement on making change

Chart IV. Preference formation and modes of decision

Mode of preference formation	Decision rule	
	Aggregative	Consensual
Deliberative	I	II
Raw	III	IV

difficult—in effect privileging the status quo as an option.[40] Furthermore, the degree to which voting rules satisfy political equality is not addressed by this simple division. One could have aggregation, for example, in a system that had what Mill called "plural voting," in effect extra votes for some people. And alternatively, there are many possible ways in which consensus might be arrived at. Does it come through equal or unequal public participation? How are options proposed and considered? What is the role of any chair in the way alternatives are posed for consensus affirmation? One can think of many variants in the ways in which aggregation and consensus operate.

With these complexities noted, the fourfold table can serve to reveal that the apparent forced choice between aggregation and deliberation is a false dilemma.

The Deliberative Poll and the Choice Questionnaire fit in Category I (assuming for the latter that even modest efforts to provide balanced information can count as contributing to deliberation). There are, in fact, prominent examples of deliberative democracy, such as the positions offered by Cohen and by Gutmann and Thompson that would fit in Category II.[41] Category III comprises mass democracy with nondeliberative preferences, particularly as embodied in mass referenda, primaries, and conventional public opinion polls. Our entire discussion of mass participatory democracy would fit in this category. As for Category IV, it is possible to imagine nondeliberative modes of preference formation producing consensus. At a minimum, deliberation requires balanced argument and access to good information.[42] Hence, approaches that prize consensus without deliberation would fit in Category IV. For example, consensus through collective brainwashing would constitute consensus via nondeliberative preferences, providing an obvious example of Category IV. Or, if brainwashing sounds too extreme, we can simply imagine a form of mass democracy in which elites make decisions and employ massive advertising campaigns to persuade the public to agree with those conclusions. Such a system offers the appearance of meaningful public will formation but it is actually just a charade. Furthermore, a strict advocate of "competitive democracy" who had abandoned all aspirations for deliberation could find no grounds for objecting to such a development.[43]

This way of dividing up the terrain is different from our basic classification of four democratic theories. Competitive democracy will usually fit within III as it is just a matter of aggregating raw preferences to find out which team wins. Mass participatory democracy aspires to Category I but usually will fall into III, since the mass public usually has relatively raw and uninformed preferences. Elite deliberation will sometimes fit under II, when a real consensus is achieved in a committee meeting for example. But it will often fall in I, as when members of the Senate agree to disagree and end up taking a vote. Consensual decision with raw preferences, IV, does not correspond to one of the four normative theories discussed here, but as noted could be realized by a brainwashing consensus.

The key point for our purposes, however, is that it is quite possible to combine deliberation for preference formation with a method of decision that employs aggregation. One can avoid a requirement for consensus and still have deliberation. In my view, there are legitimate arguments against a push for consensus, since it is vulnerable to the criticism that it is likely to yield a false consensus born of social pressure. A comparison of all four possibilities highlights some of the advantages of position I but, in contrast to arguments made by Posner, Shapiro and others,[44] does not constrain us to adopt position III (competitive democracy with raw preferences).

Scale and the forms of democracy

This book has charted the terrain of democratic possibilities from various perspectives. We have classified forms of public consultation (Chart I), hard choices in the trilemma of democratic reform (Chart II), four basic democratic theories committed to different combinations of fundamental values (Chart III) and the relation between preference formation and modes of decision (Chart IV). However, we have not yet faced the issue of how social scale intersects with forms of public opinion.

In Chart V below, we return to the two questions with which we began in classifying forms of public consultation—who and what? Who participates and what form of opinion do they offer? In our other engagement with the "who and what" questions, we considered "the who"

Chart V. Participation and opinion

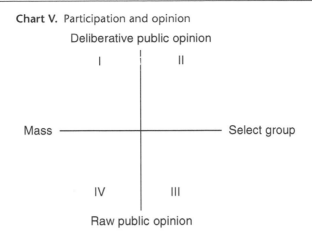

Deliberative public opinion

I   II

Mass ——————————— Select group

IV   III

Raw public opinion

problem in terms of particular methods of selection. In this case, consider a simple classification picturing horizontally the *scale* of participation and picturing vertically the form of opinion (degree to which it has been refined by deliberative processes or whether it is raw opinion in the form we usually find it in mass society).

To fix ideas focus on the two poles of the horizontal or social scale dimension. Suppose at one pole we imagine everyone participating and suppose at the other we imagine only some small-scale group. This small or select group can be chosen in some way to signal a form of representativeness, as with random sampling or with election. Or it can be just a self-selected form of expression. The point is that participation is not widely shared. Hence, at one end we might imagine a successful realization of Deliberation Day in which almost everyone deliberates for a day before almost everyone votes. At the other end of the scale, we can imagine a small representative body, whether an elite deliberative body or a statistical microcosm as with a Deliberative Poll or a Citizens Assembly. In such cases the percentage of the population deliberating will obviously be miniscule, but that, by itself, does not prevent such a group from serving a representative function as deliberators.

Taking these two distinctions together, there are four basic possibilities[45]:

  I Deliberative mass opinion
 II Deliberative opinion of a select group
 III Raw opinion of a select group
 IV Raw mass opinion

The first quadrant, everyone participating in a deliberative form of public opinion, suggests how the considered judgments of the people could be regarded as compelling if they were also widely shared. The idea that deliberative democracy represents a form of collective informed consent is easier to establish when it is also *actual* collective consent—when everyone, or virtually everyone, does actually share the views in question.[46]

As we have seen, opinions that are to some significant degree the product of deliberation require that the persons in question reflect on the merits of competing arguments. Reasons for and against the alternatives need to be voiced and answered. Deliberative opinions should have a number of indicators of quality. Participants have considered competing arguments with substantive balance so that arguments offered are answered and those arguments have been answered in turn. They have achieved a high degree of relevant information. They participate conscientiously, sincerely weighing the merits of competing arguments. The participants represent a diversity of viewpoints. They have listened to the diversity of viewpoints with equal consideration, regardless of who offers the arguments. This kind of opinion is more difficult to find in natural settings. Confronting alternative points of view may be difficult in a partisan environment. It may even be unpleasant and decrease participation. It may well be easier in an organized setting than it is in ordinary life to create a safe space for people to share diverse and competing viewpoints in an atmosphere of mutual respect.

Yet, imagine that somehow everyone had deliberative opinion and Quadrant I of Chart V was fully realized. Surely this is an ideal for deliberative democracy—what the people would all think after appropriate reflection under good conditions. The difficulty is that, as we saw with our trilemma of democratic reform, the very effort to achieve both political equality and mass participation poses impediments to deliberation on such a scale. Deliberation best takes place with small-scale face-to-face democracy—an insight motivating the original Madison strategy of selective filtration in conventions and the Senate as well as Toqueville's later observations about the town meeting and the jury. Of course, as we have seen, the design of these settings influences how successful they are (on various criteria). The scale is clearly a facilitating factor in making the dialogue manageable and in motivating individual participation.

While face-to-face deliberation can be replicated online, technology does not, at least thus far, alter the problem of each individual needing to engage with only a manageable number of others if there is to be deliberative discussion.[47] Of course, whether online or face-to-face, a population can be subdivided, as with our Deliberation Day proposal, envisioning many small groups. But this scenario requires the organization and expense of a massive new kind of institution. Left to our own devices in mass society, Quadrant I is a thought experiment, or a rare historical occurrence, a "constitutional moment."[48]

Quadrant II is realized whenever there is a select group that deliberates for the rest of us. This can be the representative group that Madison has in mind, in *Federalist* No. 10, that "refines and enlarges the public views by passing them through the medium of a chosen body of citizens." It can be the Senate, the Electoral College (in its original aspiration), or a "convention" in the sense meant by the Framers. Using a different method of selection, it can also be the sample in a Deliberative Poll or a Citizens Assembly, a select group that either officially or unofficially can serve a representative function in deliberating for the rest of us.

Quadrant III, raw opinion of a select group, is filled out by the participants in poll-directed mass democracy. Ordinary public opinion polls permit select groups of citizens, chosen by random samples, to have their raw, unfiltered preferences inserted into the policy process and the public dialogue. To the extent that conventional polls influence politics and policy, we have a realization of Quadrant III—the raw opinions of a select group (chosen by random sampling). Or poll-driven elected representatives offer an instance of policy elites guided by raw public opinion.

Quadrant IV, raw opinion of the entire mass public, is the realization of mass democracy. The long-term trajectory of American democracy, and indeed of most democracies around the world, has been to consult the mass public more and more directly. This process has brought power to the people—with referenda and other plebiscites, with primaries in candidate selection, with the elimination of more indirect modes of election of some office-holders, and with expansion of the number of office-holders who are directly elected, etc. The end result has been that innumerable decisions that were once made in Quadrant II, through a select or elite group deliberating, are now subject to the incentives for rational ignorance and "top of the head" engagement typical of the mass public. Increasingly, we have brought power to the people under conditions where the people have little reason to think about the power we would have them exercise.

Of these four possibilities, Quadrant I has special merit. It is strategically located in the array of democratic possibilities. There are reasons to move North in the diagram, to realize deliberation and there are reasons to move West in the diagram to realize mass consent. But our tendency has not been to move North and West, but rather, to move either Northeast or Southwest—more deliberation by the few or less deliberation by the many. When the Founders developed the Electoral College, the Senate, or the convention, they envisioned decision-making in the Northeast direction, believing it was the only way of realizing deliberation. When democratic reformers, from the Populists and Progressives to the post-McGovern–Fraser reformers of the modern American primary system, instituted more democratic consultation, they moved our institutions in the Southwestern direction believing it was the only way to realize mass consent. As waves of reform and counterreform occur, there is an oscillation between degrees of Northeast and Southwest movement in the diagram. Empowering super delegates who are not selected in the primaries with a voice, perhaps a pivotal one, in national party conventions, is a move in the Northeastern direction, insulating decision from the influence of mass democracy in the primaries.

Lacking any reliable way to achieve Quadrant I, we can think about what forms of Quadrant II can be offered as a *representation* of what would be the opinions in Quadrant I. Here there are two particularly influential and plausible candidates. The select group can be elected in some way (directly or indirectly) or it can be chosen by scientific random sampling. The former is what we have been calling Elite Deliberation. It is the original idea behind the convention and the Senate. The latter is the microcosmic deliberation we have been focusing on with Deliberative Polling and the Athenian Council. Elite deliberation was defended as a way to "refine and enlarge" the public views, whether in Madison's account of successive filtration or in Mill's Congress of Opinions, with its explicit representation of public views as the material for deliberation. But note that the normative case has to include the additional move—this is what the people would think under good conditions.

The main practical alternative is to give primacy to some version of Quadrant IV, mass opinion in its nondeliberative or raw form. Indeed this is the primacy of mass politics, often poll-driven, sanctioned by both the theories we called Competitive Democracy and Participatory Democracy. Note that this approach embodies the actual will of the people whether or not the people have thought about the issue, and whether or not they have been manipulated in their views. Given competitive incentives to mislead and misinform the public, the result may well be very different from what the people would think under good conditions. Yet this position avoids the charge of elitism that could be directed at deliberative democracy, that it presumes to place the public's potential considered judgments above its actual views.[49]

In this forced choice I have ignored Quadrant III, elite raw opinion. To give this verisimilitude, think of poll-driven elites. Why would elites not act on deliberative opinion but rather defer to the public's raw opinion? Because they find doing so yields electoral advantage. We will include in this category even those cases where the elites have managed to manipulate or reshape opinion for electoral advantage as those resulting opinions are also nondeliberative.[50] Quadrant III is really derivative of Quadrant IV, through its deference to raw mass opinion.

Another way of thinking about it is that social science opens up the possibility of Quadrant III representing IV just as Quadrant II can represent I. In other words, if random sampling is the form of selection, then Deliberative Polling or other deliberative microcosms (in Quadrant II) purport to represent what people would choose if everyone deliberated (Quadrant I), just as conventional polling (a way of filling out Quadrant III) purports to represent what everyone is actually choosing (Quadrant IV). Once one sees that II, at its best, is a representation of I, and that III at its best is a representation of IV, then the effective choice is between the bottom half (III or IV) and the top half (I or II). If that is the case, then the normative forced choice is ultimately between thinking and not-thinking, between deliberative and nondeliberative preferences.

But this move ignores the representational aspect of the right side of Chart V. The left-hand possibilities are the ones that are actually the views of the mass public. Since Quadrant I is by stipulation here not normally available, then we have to realize that II is a second-best possibility compared to I. Is it appropriate to pay special attention to Quadrant II compared to IV, nondeliberative mass opinion? After all, Quadrant IV is what the people are actually thinking, even if they are not paying much attention.

Our effective choice is between Quadrants II and IV. Quadrant III is just a stalking-horse for IV. And Quadrant I is under normal circumstances unattainable. We face a dilemma between small-scale, but representative, deliberation and large-scale nondeliberation. Unlike the false choice in the last section (aggregative versus deliberative), this choice is recurrent and poses a real problem of institutional design.

If we are to embrace the possibility of deliberative microcosms, we must do so with great care to establish the representational connection between the select group (whether elected elites or randomly sampled citizens) and the claim that this is what the public would think. In the case of elected elites the claim is based on a responsibility entrusted to representatives to deliberate in the public interest. But we saw that this original aspiration of the Founders has gotten enmeshed in party and electoral calculations. Representatives aspire to fill out Quadrant II but they are often driven by electoral incentives to fill out Quadrant III. Even Madison himself went off to cofound a political party.[51] As we saw, the idea that elected representatives are supposed to stand for what their constituents would think if only they knew what the representative did, surfaces occasionally and may express a sense of responsibility for how to deal with both the merits of the issue and the shape of public opinion about it. Yet it is also an idealistic notion that has to be constrained by electoral incentives if the representatives are to stay in office.

Our other focus for how to fill out Quadrant II, microcosmic deliberation, is a very old practice, but one that has only recently revived. If it is to acquire credibility, it needs buttressing with systematic investigation. Social science can be employed to give credibility to the claim that a particular strategy of institutional design has been realized to give expression to deliberative democracy—to the combination of political equality and deliberation. The aspiration is to undertake a research agenda that credibly explores the conditions under which deliberation might be realized by ordinary citizens who constitute a credible microcosm. The tighter this connection, the more transparent it is; the more evidence there is that it has been achieved without distortion, the more force there is to the claim that we can accept a realization of what the people would think (Quadrant II), rather than what they actually do think when they are not thinking very much (Quadrant IV). Now we will turn to an overview of some initial efforts in this direction.

4

Making Deliberative Democracy Practical

Bringing the public sphere to life: Four questions

The problem of democratic design we posed at the outset was whether it is possible to combine inclusion and thoughtfulness. Stated in terms of political principles: whether it is possible to combine political equality and deliberation. Consider four central questions. First, if and when this combination is achieved, *how inclusive* is it? In what way can it represent all the relevant voices or perspectives in the population? Second, if and when this combination is achieved, *how thoughtful* is it? We need to look at specific indicators of deliberative quality to evaluate the process and ensure that the results really are driven by consideration of the merits of competing arguments and not distorted by some pattern of domination or group psychology. Third, if and when this combination is achieved, what effects does it have? What effects does it have on participants or on the broader public dialogue? Most importantly, can it be situated in the policy process or the public dialogue in such a way that it has some effect on policy? Fourth, under what social and political *conditions* can any of this be accomplished? Even though we have only limited experience with the revival of deliberative democracy among ordinary citizens in the modern era (a revival of a process that once was influential going as far back as ancient Athens), can our modern experience thus far show us anything about the kinds of conditions under which it can be applied? With a limited number of cases, can we say anything about whether this aspiration can succeed when challenged by difficult conditions? Put another way, under what conditions are we likely to get encouraging (or discouraging) answers to the first three of our questions just posed? The idea is to *pilot* deliberative democracy, to see what institutional designs withstand objection, and to explore points of entry where this ancient political life form, suitably updated, can find a modern role.

Projects on different topics conducted with varying kinds of sponsorships in different parts of the world give us a basis for some preliminary conclusions. Chart VI provides a timeline of efforts beginning with the first Deliberative Poll in Britain in 1994 until the time of this writing, in 2008.[1]

The first Deliberative Polls were built around television broadcasts, by Channel Four in Britain or PBS in the United States. Media projects, particularly by PBS have continued at both the national and local levels. But soon other contexts surfaced. In Texas, a series of Deliberative Polls sponsored by the regulated electric utility companies, in conjunction with the Texas Public Utility Commission, led to a series of decisions about investments in wind power and conservation.[2] While there was a media component of these projects (all had local broadcasts), the prime impetus came from the process of consulting the public in order to feed into a policy process. The same might be said of other projects, such as the Deliberative Poll in Rome for the Regione Lazio that contributed to dealing with the state's budgetary issues and the Deliberative Polling projects in Thailand about the health care system. In Greece, as we saw earlier, a project was sponsored by a political party and in both Denmark and Australia projects were led by a broad national coalition of stakeholders before national referenda (and with national broadcast of the process and results). The variety of issues, sponsorships, and contexts does not lend itself to easy generalization. But the four questions we have posed define the key challenges.

How inclusive?

Consider each of our four questions. First, inclusion. We have focused on random sampling as the instrument of inclusion in the process.[3] Random sampling has the additional advantage that it is not limited by social scale. It does not make any appreciable statistical difference whether the same size sample is representing a town, a city, a small nation, or the entire European Union. The precision of the estimates with which that sample can represent a population will be essentially the same. Hence the representative microcosm selected by random sampling has great practical advantages if one is interested in adapting deliberative democracy to the large scale. The main disadvantage compared to a form of inclusion in

Chart VI. Deliberative Polls, 1994–2008

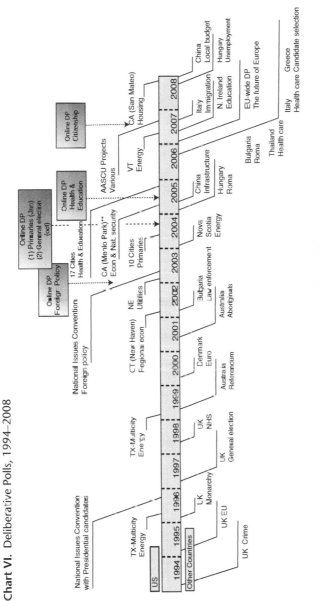

* Altogether eight Deliberative Polls were conducted in Texas on energy choices between 1996 and 1999. The cities are (in chronological order): Corpus Christi, Abilene, Shreveport (LA), El Paso, Houston, Beaumont, Amarillo, and Dallas.
** The Deliberative Poll at Menlo Park, CA, was held with a sample of local high school students.

which everyone does actually deliberate is that the connection between the microcosm and everyone else is representational. Citizens in the broader population who have not deliberated may have different actual views (or no views at all), just as they may have different actual views from their elected representatives.

The gap between deliberative public opinion in the microcosm and raw public opinion in the broader population poses a problem of justification. On what basis might the deliberative opinions have a recommending force for policymakers and the broader public? Such a case depends on the credibility of the inference that these considered judgments are the ones the public would support under good conditions for considering the problem. Hence, the need for a social science research program assessing the merits and limitations of various institutional designs that might realize deliberative democracy. Social science must form the basis for defending the inference that a given design is producing its conclusions through the normatively appropriate deliberative processes (questions of internal validity) and that it is in principle generalizable to the larger population (questions of external validity). The generalizability is an inference about what the public would think under comparably good conditions—admitting that the public will rarely face comparably good conditions in a world of campaigns and interest groups more interested in manipulation and impression management than in informing public opinion. Nevertheless, if we can create these conditions for the microcosm and show that they are generalizable in terms of what the public would think under comparably good conditions, then we have defended the rationale for employing microcosmic deliberation.

As we have seen, the alternative strategy of attempting to implement inclusion through the actual participation of everyone recreates the conditions of plebiscitary democracy and the incentives for rational ignorance, disconnection, and the politics of impression management of a (usually) inattentive public. Perhaps some thoroughgoing investment in the infrastructure of deliberation in many decentralized small groups would overcome this problem, as in our scenario for Deliberation Day, but we are focusing here on the more limited alternative of microcosmic deliberation. Note that there is a rough sense in which microcosmic deliberation offers a representation of what public opinion would be like if everyone deliberated, and hence what would be the results, ideally, if something like Deliberation Day were fully implemented.[4]

Another alternative to random sampling and microcosmic deliberation is to hold public forums that are theoretically open to participation by anyone. But this alternative is not really inclusive and leads to domination by organized interests who are inevitably the ones who actually show up, and at best, issue publics (those especially interested in the topic).[5] Such distorted participation must inevitably distort deliberation as well, because of a lack of representativeness. Hence we are drawn back to the strategy of microcosmic deliberation.

How thoughtful?

The essential idea is for a representative sample to engage in high-quality deliberation. The driving question for institutional design is: What would the people think under good conditions for thinking about it? Hence the whole effort rests on the credibility of a transparent account of "good conditions" for thinking about the issue.

The test is not realism. In natural settings, as we have seen, ordinary citizens tend not to be effectively motivated to experience good conditions for thinking about public issues. In fact, many efforts and a great deal of money are usually spent, routinely, to make sure they are not— to distract and even manipulate public opinion with the anticipated effects on election outcomes, on opinions about policy, and on consumer choices. Without artificially sealing off the microcosm or altering it beyond recognition, is there a way in which ordinary citizens can bring their existing values and heartfelt concerns to a deliberative process that manages to refine public opinion—by answering the public's questions and engaging it in active discussion? The difficult part is to effectively convene the public and at the same time facilitate it without predetermined outcomes.

In evaluating the thoughtfulness of microcosmic discussions, we should keep in mind the criteria mentioned earlier for quality in deliberation. These criteria focused on information, substantive balance, conscientious (rather than strategic) participation, diversity of viewpoints represented, and whether ideas were considered equally on their merits regardless of the status of those offering them in the discussion. These are ambitious normative criteria and while there is clear evidence about some of them, the record is spotty on others. Hence our account is an effort to lay out a research program only some parts of which have been fulfilled as yet in these early days of the empirical study of deliberative democracy among ordinary citizens.

Avoiding distortions: The problem of domination

Critics of deliberation worry that the apparent commitment to equal consideration of everyone's views on their merits will in fact mask domination of the process by the most privileged. The problem is that any microcosmic deliberation taking place in a modern developed society will be one in which there are significant social and economic inequalities in the conduct of ordinary life in the broader society. It seems difficult or impossible to "bracket" these inequalities—for participants to behave "as if" they do not exist.[6] Indeed the problem goes deeper. The possibility of doing so is the challenge of the "autonomy of the political," namely, whether or not equality can hold sway in politics in a world in which inequality rules in economic and social relations. The viability and legitimacy of the liberal-democratic project may turn on the answer.

How might the apparent equality of deliberative processes mask domination by the more privileged? Iris Marion Young distinguishes "external" and "internal" forms of exclusion. The external forms are the most obvious. Not letting someone be part of the participating group, either because their participation is barred or because they are not effectively recruited, has been the focus of electoral/political reform for decades. And even in survey work, efforts to get at nonresponse, to reach the more difficult to reach, those with difficult schedules, those without phones, Internet access, or even fixed addresses can rightly[7] justify significant expenditures of time and effort.

But Young's point is that there are more subtle forms of exclusion that turn on manners of speaking and listening. Some people, even if formally included, may not have their voices, if they speak at all, taken seriously. They may give off cues that indicate they are not well informed or not worth listening to. Those who are accustomed to every advantage in the conduct of their everyday lives may be more assertive in pressing their views on others and less open to listening to those without similar advantages.[8] They may also be more accustomed to orderly forms of reason-giving argument that weigh with other participants. Or so the argument goes.

The empirical question for our research program is whether or not those advantaged in actual life use the opportunity for shared deliberation to dominate the process. If all or most of the opinion changes move sharply in the direction of the more advantaged viewpoints, then that might be an indication that the advantaged are dominating. The issue is complex in that the advantaged may be more informed, at least on some issues, and if the idea of deliberation is that participants move in the direction of their more informed opinions, then they may move in that direction because of information effects, not because of distortions by a factor extraneous to the merits of the issues, that is, the social positions of some of the participants.

Those coming to this debate from a feminist perspective will be concerned about men dominating. Those focused on socioeconomic inequalities will be concerned about domination by the rich and the more educated. The metrics for evaluating this claim could turn on the movement of policy attitudes toward or away from the supposedly dominating group as well as on the distribution of speaking time among the participants.

Avoiding distortions: Polarization and groupthink

Regardless of socioeconomic and gender inequalities there are long-standing concerns that the process of group discussion itself may bring distortions. Cass Sunstein, building on earlier work on the so-called risky shift has claimed there is an inevitable "law of group polarization." If there is a dimension for which there is a midpoint, and the mean of a small group starts out on one side of that midpoint, he hypothesizes that it will move farther out from the midpoint in the same direction. If it starts out to the right it will move further right. If it starts out to the left it will move further left. The argument is not dependent on liberal and conservative accounts of left and right just on there being a dimension with a midpoint. The effect is meant to apply generally to any issue dimension that is the topic of discussion.

The idea is that this distortion will occur because of two main dynamics. First, if the group starts out on one side of the midpoint, then there is likely to be an imbalance in the argument pool on that side of the issue. More arguments will be offered to motivate further movement in that direction. The second dynamic is a social comparison effect. People will compare their own positions to that of the others in the small group and feel social pressure to conform to the direction of the new consensus.

The argument is a challenge to the legitimacy of deliberative democracy because if there is a reliable pattern of group psychology that predicts the movement of opinion then it is hard to hold that the movement is based on the merits. Regardless of the merits in a particular case, the group will supposedly move in a stated direction. The issue is an empirical one and may well vary with the precise institutional design of a deliberative process. Sunstein, however, holds that it will apply generally to group discussion processes.[9]

A related distortion was made famous by Irving Janis with his book *Victims of Groupthink*.[10] Here the argument is that social pressure for conformity will lead to an inadequate consideration of the arguments on their merits under various conditions. The result will be consensus prematurely arrived at. Sometimes, of course, the polarization argument can lead to decreased variance around a new, more extreme opinion. But the groupthink argument posits a push to consensus regardless of whether or not it is more extreme.

Both the polarization and groupthink argument can be studied empirically. Whether or not there is a pattern of group discussions leading the mean opinion away from the midpoint or whether or not there is a pattern of decreased variance in opinion after deliberation can be studied when data are collected at the individual level before and after deliberation. We return to these issues below.

To what effect?

Deliberative democracy has been conceived here as a certain kind of talk among political equals. But what effects does it have? Is it just talk?

We should distinguish effects on the participants from effects on the wider world. It is worth listing some potential effects, beginning with the former and moving to the latter. Here are some obvious candidates:

a. Changes in policy attitudes. The ultimate questions in a deliberative public consultation focus on "what is to be done?" Hence policy attitudes supporting (or opposing) one policy alternative or another are central. Are these the same or different as those from conventional, usually "top of the head" polls?[11]

b. Changes in voting intention. Some deliberative consultations take place in the context of an election or referendum. The question "what is to be done?" comes down to the personal level of one's vote.

c. Changes in civic capacities. Here I refer to changes in attributes at the individual level that may contribute to public problem-solving. I will include information, efficacy, public spiritedness, and political participation. First, consider information. One of our indicators of quality in deliberation is that the participants become more informed. Rather than self-reports about whether or not people think they are well informed we ask questions that, unlike those about the empirical premises above, have uncontested correct answers.

Consider efficacy. Will discussion of public problems together under conditions of good information and, potentially, conditions of empowerment increase the sense of political efficacy of those who take part? Will it affect their internal efficacy, their sense that they can have an impact on the political or policy process as a result of their own efforts? Or will it affect their sense of external efficacy, their sense that government will be responsive to their concerns? These issues can be explored by before and after questions and, where possible, questions to control groups as well.

As for public spiritedness, there is a long-standing hypothesis speculated about by Alexis de Tocqueville in his writings about America and by John Stuart Mill, who was partly responding to those writings, that when citizens discuss public problems together they come to place greater value upon the interests of the broader community. There are two versions of the hypothesis—the community whose interests they value is enlarged and the degree to which they value that community's interests is increased. As shorthand, we can refer to either one as an increase in "public spiritedness."

As for political participation, once citizens are actively engaged in the discussion of politics or policy, particularly if it is in a context where they feel their voice matters, they may wish to continue engagement. And some of the other factors potentially affected by deliberation, efficacy, and information, may also contribute to their further participation.

d. Changes in collective consistency. The literature on public choice, from the Marquis de Condorcet in the eighteenth century through William H. Riker, Kenneth Arrow, and modern practitioners confronts the problem that democracy can lead to cycles. In pairwise comparisons majorities can move from A to B to C and back to A again. When this is the case, agenda manipulations can arbitrarily determine the outcome. Any claims to a reasoned public will formation seem undermined. However, when preferences conform to an underlying dimension, say left–right as an example, then they are said to be "single peaked" and cycles are not possible.[12] There has been considerable speculation that when participants deliberate together, the percentage of the participants who come to share the same single-peaked dimensions increases, making cycles less likely or virtually impossible. The idea is that while people may not agree which alternatives are best, they do come, through discussion, to a meta-agreement on what the issues really are and what shared dimension underlies their differences. If this should be the case, then that would show that deliberation helps democracy achieve a collective consistency or coherence that a democracy of "top of the head" opinions can possibly lack. We say "collective consistency" because single-peakedness, while inferable from the preferences of individuals, is a collective property, one that refers to the preference structure of a given group or population that will be doing the voting.

e. Changes in the public dialogue. Many exercises in deliberative democracy receive substantial media attention. When coverage is keyed to the public's deliberative processes, is it different from say the horse race coverage of campaigns or the coverage of policy through a partisan filter on cable news or talk radio? What does it contribute that may be distinctive?

f. Changes in public policy. As we have emphasized, a key to the success of microcosmic deliberation is that the participants believe their voices matter in some way. They overcome inattention and disconnection by a situation that by its very structure undermines any calculations of rational ignorance. They each have one voice in a small group of fifteen (as well as one questionnaire in a gathering of a few hundred at most). What they say and think matters to their self-presentation in a small face-to-face group. In addition, it may seem consequential because it will get media coverage. But finally, they may hope or believe it may have an influence on policy. To what extent is this latter aspiration realistic? Do deliberative microcosms sometimes have an effect on policy? If so, what can we learn so far from the cases where they have?

Under what conditions?

What must people share in order to be able to deliberate together? Must they share fundamental principles? Must they share nationality? Must they share language? Must they share a certain measure of mutual trust and respect? Must deliberative democracy be embedded in already existing democratic systems with full-scale apparatuses of party competition, individual rights, and liberties? Or can credible exercises in deliberative democracy take place so as to push these frontiers? Can they occur when principles are not shared but may in fact be part of the dialogue? Can they occur across the borders of nationality? Can they take root without much trust—and perhaps contribute to the development of trust and mutual respect? Lastly, can they occur in the absence of developed systems of democracy? When they do so are they contributing to the legitimacy of authoritarianism or are they contributing to democratization? Obviously, answers to these questions depend on many more elements of context. But we need to explore issues of how deliberative democracy may exist or even flourish under varying conditions and how those conditions might begin to affect answers to our other questions about the quality of a deliberative process (how inclusive, how thoughtful, to what effect?). Even with limited cases that may fit some of these categories the questions are too central not to be included in our research agenda.

5

Making Deliberation Consequential

A case from China

Our four questions pose a daunting challenge for both research and practical experimentation. Who is included? How thoughtful is the process? What effects does it have and under what conditions?

To focus discussion, consider these questions applied in an unlikely place, local decision-making in a town in China. At first glance such a project would seem unlikely. China has not yet made a successful transition to democracy. There are obvious legacies of authoritarianism. Deliberative democracy is often treated as a possible attribute of only the most advanced forms of democracy,[1] not as one appropriate in systems lacking even the apparatus of Schumpeterian competitive democracy. Further, the level of economic development is very uneven. Poverty and inequality combine with massive internal migration from the countryside into urban settings. A process of transformation like England's industrial revolution which took more than half a century is happening at quick time on a massive scale. In the midst of such tumultuous changes, one might also question whether there is enough public trust to permit deliberative democracy. And with no apparatus of accountability through party competition, and with individual rights only partly implemented, it is less than obvious where the entry points for deliberative public consultation might be.

With the collaboration of Professor Baogang He, a leading expert on local democracy in China, we assisted the government of Zeguo township, Wenling City (about 300 km south of Shanghai), in using Deliberative Polling to make key decisions about what infrastructure to build. The local leadership had identified thirty possible infrastructure projects but had budget for only about ten in the coming year. Hence they faced the problem of making a choice among qualitatively different kinds of expenditure—for local roads, highways, a new town square, sewage treatment plants, various kinds of parks, a comprehensive environmental plan.[2]

Town officials had a long-standing interest in public consultation about such issues. There was a local tradition of "Kentan," of convening "heart to heart discussion meetings" to ask the public its preferences. However, these meetings, much like "town meetings" in the West, had some clear limitations. First, with self-selected participation, those who were most seriously interested or impacted by the issues were obviously overrepresented at the meetings. Second, participation among those who showed up was dominated by the leading citizens of the town, the more prosperous, educated, and self-confident. Third, while the discussions provided an airing of issues there was no clear product, no clear method of decision. The meetings provided some transparency and sharing of concerns but were not focused in such a way as to really provide an input into the policy process.

The local policymakers were attracted to the Deliberative Poll because it offered a possible response to these concerns. First, it could permit consultation with a representative sample, rather than self-selected voices. Second, it might offer a method for getting greater equality of participation, not dominated by the local notables. Third, it provided clear statistical results before and after deliberation. In principle these could provide a clear road map to policy.

A local advisory committee developed briefing materials with arguments for and against each of the thirty proposed projects. Experts were selected who could answer questions in plenary about the projects. Each of the projects had advocates among the experts. A questionnaire was developed with the standard repertoire of questions—policy attitudes about the thirty projects, information questions, values, empirical premises, and for the final questionnaire, event evaluation questions. Local teachers were trained to moderate the small groups, without giving any hint of their own views. A site was selected, the local high school, with a weekend date for the deliberations. All costs for the project were borne by the town, which intended to use the results in making its decisions.

Consider now our four basic questions. First, who was included? A simple random sample of 275 residents was drawn from the household register list. Of these residents, 269 completed the initial survey and 235 showed up on the day, participated in an entire day of deliberation, and completed the final questionnaire. While there was an overrepresentation of males in the initial sample[3] the participant sample was almost the same as the sample as a whole and there were no significant differences between participants and nonparticipants. In both attitudes and demographics, the 235 were a good microcosm of the community of about 120,000 registered voters.

Second, what can we say about the thoughtfulness of the process? There were some clear and coherent changes of opinion. Generally, the participants greatly increased their support for sewage treatment plants and for one main avenue that would connect different parts of the town. Most of the other roads went down in support. A fancy town square went down but a people's park for recreation and a comprehensive environmental plan went up. Twelve of the thirty projects showed statistically significant net change.

In addition, the participants became more informed. Even with a relatively truncated index of information questions (only four questions) there was a statistically significant average gain of eleven points.

A further point is that the pattern of information driving opinion change held to form.[4] In a pattern typical of other Deliberative Polls, it was the participants who gained information who changed their policy attitudes. Hence, the results have a claim to legitimacy in that they represent what a good microcosm of the people would think about the issue after becoming informed about it.

There are two other key factors we have focused on. A sample might be representative and its members might acquire information, but one could imagine that the process of discussion itself brings distortions, either from the notables dominating or from group polarization. Neither of these distortions surfaced in this China effort. The process avoided both the key distortions that critics have offered as possibly undermining deliberation, domination by the more privileged, and polarization.

In the case of domination by the more privileged, if one looks at the time 1 opinions of the more privileged groups, the deliberators moved away from the time 1 positions of the educated on half of the issues, away from the time 1 positions of the men on three-fifths of the issues, and away from the time 1 positions of the economically more advantaged on four-fifths of the issues.[5] In order to plausibly dominate the process, the more advantaged would have to move the opinions of others in their direction. Instead, the movement was generally in the opposite direction, away from the views of those who were more advantaged.

As for polarization, the issue is whether or not the process was distorted by the alleged inevitable law that groups become more extreme after discussion. This "law of group polarization" holds that if a group starts out on one side of the midpoint, it will move further away from the midpoint in the same direction. If it starts out on the other side, it will move further away in that direction. In this Chinese case we found that groups moved away from the midpoint only about half the time and they moved toward the midpoint about half the time. Hence there was no tendency at all for the process to be distorted by a pattern of group polarization. Small group discussion did not drive the groups toward more extreme positions.

Another aspiration of deliberative democracy has been the idea that when people deliberate together they become somewhat more public-spirited. They become somewhat more sensitive to the broader interests of the community. In this case we classified the projects in terms of whether the interests served were narrow or broad: whether, for example, a road would benefit only a single village or whether it was likely to benefit the whole town. After deliberation the priorities among the thirty projects shifted significantly toward the projects benefiting the entire town.[6]

Our fourth question is whether the project had any consequences. In fact, local officials carried through on their commitment to implement the public will as expressed in the results. While they expressed surprise at the public's priorities, the top twelve projects selected by the people were constructed, including all three sewage treatment plants, the people's park for recreation, and the one main road that would link different parts of the town.[7]

The project was featured in Beijing at a conference about reforming the public hearing system.[8] Local Party Chairman Zhaohua Jiang, who was a key decision-maker in conducting the DP, was asked about the process and in particular why he went to the trouble to convene a scientific sample rather than just ask the Local People's Congress. He replied that the Local People's Congress was something of a rubber stamp and that he would not really learn what the people were thinking by consulting it. Then an expert on Public Hearings in Beijing pointed out that decisions in China must conform to three criteria, they must be "scientific, democratic and legal." How could Deliberative Polling satisfy those criteria? The reply was that it was obviously scientific in its method. It was democratic since it was the voice of the people. But how was it legal? Mr Jiang replied that he submitted the results to the People's Congress and it ratified them.

These projects provided a method of consulting the public that had two potential benefits. First, it seemed to increase legitimacy. Mr Jiang commented: "I gave up power and found that I got more." A *New York Times* article highlighted the contrast between Zeguo, where the public was consulted about policy and the local leadership appeared to have legitimacy, and a town nearby where it had not done so and there were riots.[9] A second potential benefit is that by the fourth project it seemed to more effectively connect an elite representative institution, the Local People's Congress, with a mechanism of public will formation. Even though this arrangement lacked party competition, it did now permit thoughtful and representative public input.

What conditions made this possible? First, local government in China has a great deal of autonomy. There is wide room for experimentation at the village, town, and even city levels of decision. Second, while there are also massive variations in local political culture, the tradition of "Kentan" laid the groundwork for more scientific public consultation. The project was sometimes described locally as "scientific heart to heart discussion meetings." Third, the project did not pose a threat to the one-party system. It dealt with sewage and other infrastructure matters, not politics or elections. Despite this limitation, it clearly added to legitimacy while speaking to the demands of the public to somehow have a say. With rapid economic development residents are acquiring consumer power. It is only natural for them, over time, to desire some influence over public decisions.

Would the spread of Deliberative Polling at the local level in China simply prop up local government without contributing to democratization? With a limited number of cases, there is no way of saying definitively. However, it is worth noting how the process, far from yielding a predetermined conclusion surprised local officials with its results. In addition, they found it advantageous to implement the results and to repeat and expand the purview of the process in subsequent years. By increasing public responsiveness to the point where it affected decision-making about the entire budget of the town, it brought transparency to the town's entire budget, and it created, probably for the first time, scientifically representative participatory budgeting by the mass public.[10]

Zeguo's application of local Deliberative Polling provides distinctive and optimistic answers to our four questions. The process was demonstrably representative. It was information-driven and avoided distortions from inequality and polarization. It showed increased public spiritedness. Its results were actually implemented so it clearly had an effect. And lastly, it took place under surprising conditions, in a regime that has not even yet made a transition to party competition.

Of course, the argument for making deliberative democracy practical cannot rely on a single successful case. Nevertheless, it shows what can be accomplished under challenging conditions. Now we should look more generally at our four questions.

Representativeness

The claim of microcosmic deliberation is that every member of the population has, in effect, an equal random chance of being selected and once selected, an opportunity for his or her views to be considered equally with others, before, during, and after deliberation. The first difficulty with many attempts to realize this idea is that often no data are collected to compare the attitudes of the deliberators with those who do not deliberate. Often representativeness is considered in terms of just a few simple demographic categories. But how can a microcosm purport to represent the public's considered judgments at the end of the process if we have no way of knowing whether it was representative in its views to begin with?

Of course, demographics are relevant. However, the issue is not whether there are so many blacks or Hispanics, so many women or men of whatever age in a sample, but *which* members of these demographic categories participate with what viewpoints. If a forum is open to a heavy dose of self-selection, because only a small percentage of the sample actually agrees to participate, then it is especially important that the data should be collected to permit comparison of those drawn in the sample who attend with those drawn in the sample who do not. Of course, this comparison presumes that the initial survey is reasonably representative. The best strategy for ensuring that outcome is to conduct it with a good response rate and a high number of callbacks (since those who are easy to reach may be different from those who are more difficult to reach).

Many deliberative consultations do not employ random sampling and on the perspective offered by some theorists, that is not a problem. For example, in two books, Gutmann and Thompson use the Oregon health care consultations in the early 1990s as an illustration of deliberative democracy made practical.[11] But the community meetings, organized by Oregon Health Decisions were entirely self-selected and heavily dominated by health professionals. While Gutmann and Thompson talk of "well constructed deliberative forums" they do not offer specifications for what makes a forum "well constructed."[12] Rather, they profess to be entirely agnostic about the key question of who participates and how they might be recruited. At the same time, they insist that to count as deliberation, a process must be "binding."[13] To specify binding authority for deliberative processes—however constituted—is to provide an incentive for capture and for mobilization. At the least, it hands over some degree of binding authority to forums whose outcomes may be determined as much by who attends (and by who does not attend) as by what happens once the dialogue begins.

The attraction of random sampling is that it can provide a basis for establishing a microcosm of the entire community. But everything depends on how it is done. An example of the sort of project that *appears* to employ random sampling but actually fails to provide any credible basis for its evaluation is the attempt by a group called America Speaks to substitute "random sampling" for its normal recruitment process of sheer self-selection (combined with a demographic screen selecting only some of the people who volunteer themselves). In the case of its project on health care in Maine, it sent out 75,000 postcards to randomly chosen residents in order to recruit a forum of a few hundred. Recipients were asked to indicate interest in attending a deliberative forum about health care by sending in a response card with their demographic characteristics. Only 2,700 returned the cards and after some demographic screens were applied to these, 300 particpants came on the day. Setting aside the fact that this "sample" was supplemented by others who were recruited by stakeholder groups to make up for low numbers of young people and minorities, this design gives no confidence in any claims to representativeness. There are no data comparing the attitudes of the 2,700 who volunteered themselves with the 75,000 and no data comparing the 300 with the 2,700 or the 75,000. It is important to note that unlike Deliberative Polls, the participants in *America Speaks* are not compensated for their time and effort. They just have to be sufficiently motivated about the issue to want to spend a whole day discussing it. Since most people are not motivated to spend much time and effort pondering policy, it seems obvious that the 300 or so who volunteered themselves from an initial list of 75,000 would not offer a credible microcosm of the views of the entire public.[14]

The lesson here is that the mere invocation of "random sampling" is not enough to ensure representativeness. Everything depends on how it is done, what data are collected at what point, and what incentives or other motivations are employed to try to encourage—and enable—those initially drawn in the sample to show up. When the response rate is miniscule and there are no incentives, an initial effort at random sampling can easily transform into virtually pure self-selection.

A more credible effort, but one still marred by the lack of any data for evaluating attitudinal representativeness on the issues to be discussed, occurred with the now famous Citizens Assembly in British Columbia. The Government of British Columbia sponsored a citizen group to deliberate over the course of eleven months about electoral reform. The distinctive aspect of their charge was that their proposal would go directly on the ballot for a referendum by the electorate on the proposed reform. Change in the constitution required a 60% supermajority. As it happened, the proposal got a majority but fell short of the 60% requirement. We will later return to this innovative effort to combine microcosmic deliberation with referendum democracy. But for the moment it is worth pausing over the issue of how the microcosm was constructed.

A stratified random sample of 23,034 were invited via letters, and 1,715 responded saying they were interested. After some demographic criteria were applied, 1,441 of these were invited to come to "selection meetings," 964 did so, and 158 of these were selected randomly. The issue is that we do not have any way of evaluating how the 1,715 who selected themselves compared to the initial pool of 23,034.[15] How much more interested or knowledgeable about politics and public affairs, how much more skewed to one political viewpoint or another, were they? Similarly we do not know anything about how the representativeness of the microcosm was affected by the other stages of selection. It is a demanding task to volunteer to give up nearly a year of one's life. How did those who put themselves forward for this opportunity compare to those who did not, or, in other words, how do they compare to the rest of the population for whom they are supposed to be a random microcosm?

Based partly on input from our Deliberative Polling research presented to Gordon Gibson, a retired Canadian politician who did the initial planning, the other elements of the basic design of Deliberative Polling were implemented in the Citizens Assembly—moderated small group discussions with the "random sample"; questions posed to competing experts in plenary sessions; secret ballots for determining collective will free of social pressure for a shared decision. And the participants were extraordinarily impressive, indeed inspiring, in their willingness to continue for nearly an entire year. Yet the lack of data at the beginning leaves forever open the question of what (or whom) they represented.[16]

The Deliberative Poll, while far less ambitious in duration, offers a design that attempts to address issues of representativeness for the microcosm that is supposed to deliberate. Consider how the samples are recruited. Unlike *America Speaks* and self-selected open meetings, incentives are paid to encourage representativeness and participation from those drawn initially in the sample and to make it possible for those less interested or less fortunate to participate. Unlike the Citizens Assembly, attitudinal and other data are collected before there is any invitation so that there is a basis for evaluation of the attitudinal and demographic representativeness.

To fix ideas consider the practice of Deliberative Polls to pay incentives. The first Deliberative Poll, about the issue of crime in Britain, offered a financial incentive of a modest fifty British pounds in addition to rail or bus transportation, hotels, and meals. The National Issues Convention paid each participant $300 as a gesture of appreciation, plus free air fare, hotels, and meals. In addition, these events, like most Deliberative Polls, were televised. Some of the participants were undoubtedly attracted by the idea of participating in a national public dialogue. But others were attracted by the incentive or by the idea of a free trip to an interesting place. Special efforts had to be made to facilitate participation for those with special problems. We called employers to try and get permission for participants to take time off from work. One woman had a small farm and there was no one to milk her cow. So we made arrangements for someone to come out and milk her cow while she was gone. Other cases involved payment for child care or help with a sick relative. In some Texas projects, Spanish-speaking participants were provided with headphones for simultaneous interpretation. In the European-wide project, simultaneous interpretation had to be provided in twenty-one languages.[17] In almost all cases, incentives are paid, there is media attention (usually through dedicated media partners as well as the press who can cover all proceedings), and special efforts are made to overcome specific difficulties (child care or care for a sick relative, special assistance for the disabled, etc.). The idea is to make it attractive and possible for anyone drawn in the initial sample to participate.

If the participant group is too small, it will be impossible to evaluate claims to representativeness. The touchstone of deliberative democracy is that it combines political equality and deliberation—it offers at least a representation, if not a realization, of what everyone would think if they were thinking about the issues under good conditions. If a Citizens Jury or a Consensus Conference has twelve or eighteen people, it is too small for the claims to representativeness to be evaluated. Given that usually no initial attitudinal data are collected, the process is beyond evaluation. It is arguable that such small groups should not be considered mini publics or microcosmic deliberation at all. On the other hand, they do embody suggestive results and, like focus groups, reveal qualitative data that could be useful, if they were then subjected to more systematic investigation. A Citizens Jury about health care reform at the time of the Clinton health care proposal showed more support for a Canadian single-payer approach. But with such a small sample, there was no credible way to generalize the results and the project's conclusions could only remain suggestive. Who knew whether or not other small group discussions of health care policy with different participants and different policy attitudes to start, would come out the same way? By contrast, we can more confidently generalize from a design where the total number of participants is large enough to be evaluated statistically, and where there are comparisons between participants and nonparticipants about their views on first contact, before they start changing in anticipation of the event. In these respects there is a difference in kind rather than just in degree between a Citizens Jury of twelve or eighteen and a Deliberative Poll of 150 or 300. It is surprising how few deliberative efforts satisfy these simple prescriptions.

Deliberative Polls, like some of the other mechanisms (Citizens Juries, Consensus Conferences), pay incentives to the participants. It is worth asking whether this practice, aimed at facilitating representativeness, introduces "demand characteristics"—-whether it might be argued that the participants change their views just to please the organizers since they might be grateful for being paid. This notion is sometimes combined with a concern for "Hawthorne effects" in the process of deliberation. The Hawthorne effect showed that when workers in a Westinghouse factory were observed, they became more efficient workers and in that sense unrepresentative of other workers who were not observed. But in the case of deliberative forums like the Deliberative Poll, the aim is to see what participants would think if they thought their voice mattered and if they could experience good conditions for determining what they thought. Our participants become better citizens just as the workers subject to the Hawthorne effect become better workers.

The point of our experimental treatment is to investigate what would happen to the opinions of ordinary citizens if they experienced favorable conditions for considering the issues. Those favorable conditions include an atmosphere of mutual respect where dialogue is possible, balanced briefing materials, an opportunity to pose questions to competing experts and/or policymakers, moderated small group discussion—and the effective motivation to participate in all these aspects of the experiment. It can readily be admitted that those most favorable conditions do not apply most of the time to most citizens. Most citizens believe their views will not make a difference and in any case, they are subjected to continuous efforts intended to distract, manipulate, and often demobilize them.

As for demand characteristics, it is first worth noting that even if participants wished to please the organizers by changing their views, they would not know in what direction to do so. There would have to be an obvious implicit agenda or hidden curriculum of change. Given the work that advisory groups typically do to prepare balanced briefing materials and panels of experts and politicians or policymakers, the transparency and balance of the process should serve to insulate against this difficulty. Second, in Deliberative Polls at least, we emphasize in discussions with the participants that we do not care whether they change or not. We only care that they tell us what they think at the time that they fill out the questionnaire. It does not matter whether it is the same as or different than at any other time that they filled it out.

It is also worth noting that many Deliberative Polls come out differently than organizers would have expected *ex ante*. For example, the local government sponsors of the first Chinese Deliberative Poll firmly expected that the public would increase its support for "image projects" highlighting the towns' development. Instead, the people greatly preferred environmental projects, sewage treatment plants, environmental planning, and also a "people's park" for recreation. In the European-wide project, at least some of the sponsors expected that support for enlargement of the European Union would increase. However, the materials and agenda were scrupulously balanced. And the result was that support for enlargement actually decreased dramatically, especially among the participants from new member states. And in the Vermont project on energy choices, some people expected that support for wind power would go down once the participants realized the limitations of wind power and heard about some of the aesthetic objections to windmills. Instead, support for wind power remained strong amidst a greatly lessened concern for the visual impact of wind farms on the Vermont scenery.

Of course, sometimes the expectations of organizers or stakeholders, if they have them, are in fact realized. But the dramatic cases where they are not offer a caution to anyone who wishes to claim that the participants somehow discover an implicit agenda of how things are supposed to change and then they are so extraordinarily obliging that they follow it. What actually happens, we believe, is that the participants are genuinely empowered to deal in a balanced way with substantive issues and would be unlikely to take instruction from anyone. Instead, they are interested in implementing something that is very much akin to what Habermas famously called the "forceless force of the better argument."

We have assumed throughout that it is the mass public that is being represented. We need to define a population and then draw a random sample from that population. Of course, in practice, there are no perfect random samples. There are many sources of nonresponse. The spread of cell phones as opposed to landlines has complicated telephone polling. The costs of face-to-face recruitment are usually much higher, except in some countries. And the attempt to use Internet polling is complicated first by the digital divide and second by the lack of appropriate sampling frames for random sampling. These are problems facing all public opinion research, not just efforts like Deliberative Polling that attempt to begin with conventional polling and then layer deliberation and subsequent polls on top of that (see section "Virtual Democracy" in Chapter 6). Deliberative Polling attempts to build on the base of established scientific public opinion research. And if there are limitations in the base, it will share them.

In any given case, a decision must be made about what population is being sampled. It is usually all residents or all citizens or all voters of a given area. It could be registered voters or eligible voters. For issues like electricity regulation or affordable housing, it makes sense to get all residents whether they are citizens or not. They all need electricity or housing. Even when an application of deliberative democracy is inclusive of all residents, there are always choices about other groups relevant to the dialogue that may not be adequately represented in the population. In a local DP about affordable housing in San Mateo, we clearly faced the problem that many of the constituencies could not afford to live in the county. That was part of the problem posed by the deliberation. Nurses or teachers were not paid sufficiently to be able to live in the area. However, in organizing the event we stuck with random sampling of the residents of the county and worked to ensure that the interests of these groups were represented in the plenary sessions on the panels.

Some approaches to deliberation are interested not in discussions representative of the general population but rather in those that are restricted to activist groups engaged in what Cass Sunstein has called "enclave deliberation." It is undoubtedly valuable for groups that wish to change society (the civil rights movement, the environmental movement, the women's movement) to deliberate among themselves. Contributions to deliberative *advocacy* by various subgroups enrich the broader discourse in the society at large. But they are not themselves manifestations of deliberative democracy in the sense defined here. Deliberative democracy as defined here has the punch line that it combines representativeness of the population (via political equality) with deliberation. It is a representation of what the public would think. Deliberation among activist groups could in principle be studied or provide consultation if the population of advocates were well defined. So the members of an advocacy group could be sampled randomly and those sampled could deliberate. But the results would represent only that restricted population. Most such studies of activist deliberation do not bother with random sampling but study the modes of communication among those who gather themselves together.[18] Such studies can be valuable in revealing the deliberative or nondeliberative character of activist groups in their internal workings. However, they do not offer an application of deliberative democracy for the society at large. Even for questions of deliberative democracy of an organized group, random sampling might be useful if one is interested in what rank-and-file members think.

Returning now to random sampling of the general population, what can be accomplished in terms of actually getting ordinary people to travel and spend a weekend deliberating? After all, with a standard survey we are only asking for opinion responses for a short time in the convenience of one's home, either by phone or face-to-face interview. Taking a few days to travel would seem an entirely different matter. Each project needs to be evaluated comparing participants and nonparticipants. Consider for example the very first Deliberative Poll, in Britain in 1994 on the issue of criminal justice policy. It set a high standard demonstrating what is possible. There were 102 questions, both demographic and attitudinal, in the initial questionnaire, and only fourteen showed statistically significant differences between participants and nonparticipants. Furthermore, most of the differences, even when statistically significant, were substantively small. While the participants were slightly more knowledgeable than the nonparticipants (between 7% and 11% more likely to know the right answers on a battery of knowledge questions), we could truly say that we had gathered all of Britain to one room.[19]

The first American Deliberative Poll, the National Issues Convention broadcast on PBS from Austin, Texas, in 1996, also gathered a highly representative national sample to one place. While it showed more statistically significant differences between participants and nonparticipants (42 out of 114 items), most of the differences were substantively small.[20] Generalizing across projects in many countries around the world, it is fair to say that it has been consistently possible to gather good random samples to a single place to deliberate face-to-face. Not all the samples are perfect. Often they are somewhat more educated or more interested in politics and policy than the general public. But when these problems occur, the differences, while statistically significant, are often substantively small. Most importantly, there is usually a great deal of attitudinal representativeness. In that sense the projects offer a microcosm of the population's arguments and concerns, a microcosm reminiscent of Mill's Congress of Opinions where all the arguments shared in the society were represented in their approximate degree in the microcosm and where the participants were motivated to consider those arguments on their merits.

Assessing the poll with a human face: Thoughtfulness

Some critics of deliberation believe that the public is either incompetent to deliberate or so withdrawn and disengaged from politics and policy that it would be impossible to motivate it to do so. Posner relies on the incompetence argument in his defense of competitive democracy over deliberative democracy. A competitive struggle for the people's vote— by whatever means—is all that we can expect of democracy since any claims about a public will are supposedly illusory. Advocates of "stealth democracy" add a motivational element. We all have better things to do than to waste time and effort on public problems.[21] It is unreasonable to expect the public to become informed or engaged.

Some of these concerns offer variants of the "rational ignorance" argument that we invoked as a possible explanation for what is a widely accepted fact—the mass public in most countries most of the time is, in fact, not well informed or much engaged in public issues. But that is different from a claim that it is incompetent.

The picture that emerges from Deliberative Polling and indeed from other deliberative consultations is that the public is indeed capable of dealing with complex issues, once it believes its voice matters, once it believes that there is reason to spend time and effort in public discussion, listening to alternative points of view. When we say "complex matters," it is worth distinguishing questions of collective political will from purely expert or technical questions. The public should be consulted about its priorities in answer to the question "what should be done?" Its priorities are more meaningful when they have been tested against competing arguments about the pros and cons, the benefits and burdens, of a given policy compared to its alternatives. One complexity of course is that there will be competing, contested accounts of what those benefits and burdens might be. For this reason, the format of the DP permits interrogation of panels of competing experts to explain why they believe one account or another. Making use of expert input, in a balanced way, is one of the more difficult design challenges for public consultation. By embedding experiments in the Deliberative Poll, we have found that most of the change in policy attitudes comes in the balanced on-site deliberations rather than in the (probably unbalanced) anticipatory learning before the deliberations begin.[22] This result is also compatible with the self-reports of the participants who consistently rate the small group discussions the most valuable part of the experience in their post-event questionnaires.

Our impression from observation is that once participants learn that the experts disagree they feel freer to reexamine the issue for themselves. But it is important to note that we are *not* asking them for an expert judgment. It is rather a question of collective political will or public judgment. And this is an area that experts cannot reasonably substitute for the public, or its surrogates.

Consider the series of Deliberative Polls that we helped the Thai Ministry of Health conduct in 2008 about whether or not kidney treatment should be extended to everyone, and if so, how to pay for it. Alternatively, the question was that if it were not extended, on what criteria might it be rationed? In either case, the extraordinarily dedicated health professionals who had brought what was originally called the "30 baht" universal health care system to Thailand, felt that the extension of kidney treatment, and, in particular, questions of to whom it would be given, were not primarily questions for expert judgment. This decision turned on the value trade-offs the people were willing to make. It was a matter of the people's values not those of the technocrats. Technocrats could inform the public about whether or not the investment was cost-effective, in that other forms of lifesaving might go farther. And they could inform the public that other health plans, available to civil servants and politicians, already covered the treatment so that there was an equity argument for extending coverage. And they could inform the public of the likely effects of increasing sin taxes such as those on alcohol and tobacco, as a way of paying for an extension of this treatment. But in the end, the people would have to weigh how a decision about whether or not to extend the treatment fit their values and priorities, duly considered.

Even if medical professionals might not want to provide the values and goals to determine a policy, one might imagine philosophers would. Applied philosophy is a lively area of scholarly debate. But that does not mean that a group of political philosophers or ethicists should easily be able to substitute its values for those of the people, or its judgments about what is on reflection desirable for the people's judgment.

If the people are to decide, or at least have an input to these questions, what are some indicators that they are actually deliberating about them, rather than just offering "top of the head" responses, conforming to social pressures or deferring to experts?

The first indicator that something is happening is that opinions change. More than two-thirds of all the attitude items in Deliberative Polls result in statistically significant net change.[23] In that sense the recommendations of opinion after deliberation are different from those offered before. It is worth noting that there is a sense in which even the opinions that do not change are valuable as a democratic input, since those opinions will have been tested against alternative arguments in the deliberative process. To know that the public thinks X after it has considered a range of counterarguments is different from knowing that it thinks X when it has not really thought about the issue or is not well informed.

The second indicator that something is going on is that the participants always become significantly more informed. We always include information items and these routinely show statistically significant gains, as in the first Deliberative Poll in Britain,[24] the National Issues Convention in the United States, and almost all others. Sometimes the changes are large. Consider the Deliberative Poll in Northern Ireland on education policy. Even though the sample was drawn from parents only (because that is what the government authorities regarded as directly and legally relevant to education policy), there were massive gains in knowledge. On average, the sample answered only 22% of the information questions about Northern Ireland's education system correctly before deliberation but answered 50% correctly after deliberation. For example, the percentage knowing that schools receive more funding for older pupils increased from 21% to 79%, and the percentage knowing that the new entitlement curriculum requires that "every school provide all 14-year-olds with a choice of at least 24 subjects" increased from 21% to 74%.[25]

In addition to learning information, the participants learn about competing perspectives and the views of people very different from themselves in face-to-face discussion. In New Haven, we launched the first in a series of controlled experiments embedded within Deliberative Polls, in which we isolated the effect of face-to-face deliberation from the other elements of the broad Deliberative Polling treatment.[26] The broad treatment includes all the anticipatory learning before people come; it includes the

121

small group and plenary sessions on-site, even the informal interactions between participants in the coffee breaks and meals. To begin to separate what happens on-site, we conducted a project at Yale with the fifteen towns of the New Haven metropolitan region about two issues—the possibility of regional tax sharing and the future of the airport. The participants were assigned to sixteen small groups with half deliberating about the tax sharing first and half about the airport. When the first issue was complete, they all took a second questionnaire (the first was administered at home on first contact), and then those who first discussed taxes discussed the airport and vice versa. In that sense, each portion of the "split half" served as a control group for the other. On the issue that showed most of the change, the regional tax sharing, most of the change came from the on-site deliberations. Both issues showed significant changes overall, but the changes in the low salience issue (the regional tax sharing) were much larger.[27]

Consider the four defects in raw public opinion with which we started our discussion: rational ignorance, phantom opinions, selectivity of sources, and vulnerability to manipulation. Microcosmic deliberation in Deliberative Polling offers a basis for responding to all four problems.

First, the participants are effectively motivated to become more informed. Each has one voice in say 300 and, in the small groups, one voice in fifteen or so persons engaged in face-to-face discussion.[28] Information questions asked before and after, show substantial changes. The information gains noted above occur because the participants believe their voice matters so they are effectively motivated to become informed. The process is also designed to make it easy for them to have access to good information and competing arguments in a safe public space.

The changed incentives for becoming more informed were crystallized for me by a woman who approached me during the first Deliberative Poll, on crime in Britain in 1994. She said she was a spouse accompanying her husband and she wished to thank me. In thirty years of marriage, her husband had never read a newspaper. But since getting invited to this event he had started to read "every newspaper every day" and he was "going to be much more interesting to live with in retirement." We had given him a reason to become informed. Once experienced, such an event can change the habits of a lifetime. When we went back to the sample from that event some eleven months later, we found they were just as informed as at the end of the weekend. Presumably, they continued to read newspapers and pay attention to the media, once activated by the intense discussions of a deliberative weekend.

The second problem with which we began was that sometimes the opinions reported in conventional polls do not exist. They are non-attitudes or phantom opinions because respondents almost never wish to say that they do not know. This phenomenon was originally discovered by Philip Converse of the University of Michigan. There was a National Election Studies panel that was asked the same questions from 1956 to 1960. The questions included some low salience items such as the government's role in providing electric power. He noticed that some of the respondents offered answers that seemed to vary almost randomly over the course of the panel. They cared so little about the issue that presumably they could not even remember what they had said the previous year in order to try and be consistent. Converse concluded that there were not real opinions being reported but that a significant portion of the people were answering randomly.

In the Deliberative Poll, ordinary citizens are effectively motivated to consider competing arguments, get their questions answered and come to considered judgment. Even if they do not have an opinion when first contacted, many will form conclusions by the end of the process. In 1996, we began conducting Deliberative Polls with electric utility companies in Texas who faced a new requirement that they consult the public as part of "Integrated Resource Planning" for how they were going to provide electric power in their service territories. Were they going to use coal, natural gas, renewable energy (wind or solar power), or demand-side management (conservation policies reducing the need for more power)? The companies faced the problem that if they used polls, they knew that the public did not have the information, or even opinions about the issue worth consulting. While they were not specifically aware of Converse's earlier discovery of non-attitudes on their issue, they had the basic idea. Alternatively, if they were to consult focus groups or small discussion groups, they knew that they could never demonstrate to regulators that such small groups were representative. And if they were to hold town meetings, open to everyone, they would get forums dominated by lobbyists and organized interests. They would not actually get the mass public.

They concluded that Deliberative Polling offered a more viable solution. With several conditions we agreed to help them. Those conditions specified that an advisory committee of stakeholders representing all the major constituencies have supervision of the briefing materials, the questionnaire, and the agenda for the weekend. This advisory committee included consumer groups, environmental groups, advocates of alternative energy as well as more conventional energy sources, and representatives of the large customers. In addition, we wanted the event to be public and transparent, including television coverage of the weekend process to the rest of the service territory and participation in the process from the Public Utility Commissioners who would answer questions from the sample.[29]

In eight such Deliberative Polls in various parts of Texas and nearby Louisiana, the public went for shrewd combinations of natural gas, renewable energy, and conservation. Averaging over eight projects, the percentage willing to pay more on its monthly utility bill to support renewable energy went from 52% 84%. The percentage willing to pay more for conservation went from 43% 73%. The resulting Integrated Resource Plans all included substantial investments in renewable energy—transforming Texas into the second leading state in wind power and by 2007 the leading state, surpassing California.[30] Undoubtedly, many of the opinions expressed at the end replaced non-attitudes or phantom opinions. But the point is that the opinions expressed in the end were the considered judgments of representative microcosms—what the public would think under good conditions and after great efforts at balance and transparency had been undertaken to guarantee those good conditions.

The third defect in public opinion that the Deliberative Poll attempts to address is that even when citizens discuss public issues, they discuss them overwhelmingly with the like-minded. Ordinary social conditions do little to facilitate people taking seriously arguments from opposing points of view. Our experience in the Danish national Deliberative Poll on the Euro[31] shows the difference between face-to-face discussion in people's home environments and then in the Deliberative Poll. The country was about evenly divided on adopting the Euro. Our questionnaire had information questions, half of which were the sort of item that someone supporting the "yes" side would likely invoke and half being the sort of information that someone supporting the "no" side would invoke. Between the time respondents were first interviewed and the start of deliberations on the weekend, an additional questionnaire was administered on arrival. This showed that in preparation for the event, the "yes" supporters tended to learn the "yes" information but not the "no" information. The "no" supporters tended to learn the "no" supporting information but not the "yes" information. But in the final questionnaire, administered at the end of the weekend, the gap closed. The "yes" people had learned the "no" information and the "no" people had learned the "yes" information. Randomly assigned to small groups for face-to-face discussion, people learned from those discussions what they had not learned in their home environments——the information supporting the other side. The Deliberative Poll created a safe public space where people could actually talk about the issues on a reasoned basis, despite their fundamental disagreements on an issue sharply dividing the country.

Sometimes the weight of the other side of the argument is emotive as well as cognitive. In the 1996 National Issues Convention broadcast on PBS with presidential candidates and a national random sample, one of the issues was welfare reform and the current state of the American family. An 84-year-old white male Conservative happened to be in the same small group as an African-American woman who was, herself, on welfare. At the beginning of the discussions, the Conservative said to her, "you don't have a family," explaining that a family meant having both mother and father in the same household with children. This comment tested the social skills of the moderator to keep the discussion going. By the end of the weekend the Conservative was overhead asking her, "what are the three most important words in the English language? They are 'I was wrong.'" I have always interpreted that comment to mean that he came to understand her situation from her point of view. A hallmark of moral discussion is learning to view a problem from the point of view of those who are affected——a kind of ideal role taking. In this case, by sharing a discussion group with her for a whole weekend, he came to appreciate the world from her point of view as well as his own. Normally those two would never have had the opportunity for a serious discussion about the family, and women on welfare would have remained sound bites on television. If we are to understand competing arguments we need to talk to diverse others and to understand their concerns and values from their own points of view. Discussions in a safe public space with random samples, randomly assigned, can accomplish that.

The fourth defect that the Deliberative Poll attempts to respond to is vulnerability to manipulation. Raw public opinion is vulnerable to manipulation because it is volatile, based on low information levels, susceptible to misinformation, strategically incomplete information, and priming. In the setting of a deliberative microcosm, a scientific sample of ordinary citizens should become thoughtfully empowered rather than manipulated. It should arrive at considered judgments which are usually less volatile than "top of the head" opinion. After all, participants have spent a great deal of time and effort discussing and pondering the issues in question. They have already weighed the competing considerations and come to some conclusions. Such considered judgments have considerable staying power, even when people return to their normal environments.[32]

When people have low information levels they have little basis for judgment other than shortcuts or heuristics. If they know nothing about policy they will evaluate candidates based on their personality traits or likeability. We have found that when citizens deliberate they take account of issues in addition to candidate traits.[33] When they have more information they have more of a context for evaluating both candidates and policy proposals. Also, with the deliberative process they should be less vulnerable to misinformation. The DP is designed to sort out misimpressions and incorrect information that may serve as the basis for discussion. The briefing materials, agreed to after extensive consultation by stakeholders representing different points of view, are certified as balanced and accurate. Questions the participants are unsure about are brought to the plenary sessions where they are answered by competing experts. The whole process is designed to replace impressions of misinformation with a better account of what is known and what is contested by experts from different points of view.

The design also works for strategically incomplete information. If advocates of one side offer a point of view that has a clear counter, then advocates of the other side, if they are represented on the panel, should be able to respond. In our Texas Energy projects, the coal advocate could not oversell the benefits of clean coal compared to natural gas and renewables because he shared the panel with the advocates of those other approaches. They had an equal opportunity to fill out the discussion with counters from their point of view. A similar point can be made about priming. The competing stakeholders will at least have a chance to articulate different frames for the whole discussion. Priming economizes on scarce attention. But in an environment in which people have more time to consider competing arguments and points of view, it is harder to push the unique claim of only one construction of the issue.

Earlier we specified five indicators of *quality* in deliberation:

a. *Information*: The extent to which participants are given access to reasonably accurate information that they believe to be relevant to the issue

b. *Substantive balance*: The extent to which arguments offered by one side or from one perspective are answered by considerations offered by those who hold other perspectives

c. *Diversity*: The extent to which the major positions in the public are represented by participants in the discussion

d. *Conscientiousness*: The extent to which participants sincerely weigh the merits of the arguments

e. *Equal consideration*: The extent to which arguments offered by all participants are considered on the merits regardless of which participants offer them

As we have already seen, information questions establish considerable learning in the deliberative process. We do not rely on self-reports but rather on questions with demonstrably correct answers and with enough options so that participants will not do well by simply guessing (hence no true/false questions).

The Danish experience cited above offers an indication of substantive balance, inferable from questionnaire responses before and after deliberation. Partisans of each side on the referendum learned information supporting the other side during the small group discussions. Another way to approach this question would be to look at the deliberative process itself. Alice Siu has opened up the black box of deliberation by studying transcriptions of recordings and then coding the arguments offered in the small groups. Based on five American Deliberative Polls which had complete recordings of the small groups, she coded statements in the small groups (*a*) for whether the participants offered reasons or simply took positions (whether they offered justified or unjustified statements) and (*b*) for which side of the issue they were on. The latter classification would allow study of the degree of balance or imbalance in the argument pool expressed in a given small group.

Two conclusions emerge shedding light on deliberative quality. First, justified statements move opinion more than unjustified ones. In other words, statements offering reasons have more of an effect on opinion change than do statements that simply express support for a position. Second, imbalance in the argument pool has an effect on opinion mostly among the uninformed. Imbalance has little effect on those who become more informed. Hence we get a picture, among those who become most engaged in the deliberations, of participants who weigh balanced arguments and become more informed.[34]

An informed consideration of balanced arguments speaks to our first two indicators of quality in deliberation. The third criterion is diversity in the extent to which the major positions in the public are represented by participants in the discussion. By design, the DP recruits participants only after they complete an extensive questionnaire. Hence, the data are always available to evaluate the degree to which the policy attitudes and values of the participants differ from those of the population at large. As noted earlier, we usually turn up few statistically significant differences between participants and nonparticipants. Hence, for projects that are well executed, there is a clear basis for claiming that the viewpoints in the microcosm represent the same diversity of viewpoints on the issue in the society at large.

Our fourth criterion for quality in deliberation is that participants sincerely weigh the merits of the arguments. Since the poll with a human face offers opportunities for gathering qualitative as well as quantitative data, we have extensive observational experience with deliberations on multiple topics. It is hard to observe the small groups in a Deliberative Poll without believing that the participants are weighing the pros and cons sincerely. They are not coming in with settled preferences and preparing to behave strategically to get their way. Instead, there is ample evidence that they come with open minds and the amount of preference change provides evidence that they are open to competing arguments. Random samples of the public do not behave like activists with firm opinions. They have spent much less time cogitating about the issues than would activists and so the picture of strategic rather than sincere behavior intended to implement predetermined opinions is less applicable in a context in which everyone is arriving at a considered judgment in a safe public space in an atmosphere of mutual respect.[35]

The fifth criterion, that participants weigh the arguments on the merits regardless of who is offering them, is a variant of the problem that the less advantaged may have their views devalued and the more advantaged may have their views dominate the deliberations, not because of the merits of their arguments but because of their social positions. We will turn to that issue in the next section when we discuss deliberative distortions such as domination and polarization.

Domination?

The ideal of deliberation requires that the participants come to substantive conclusions on the merits, after weighing competing arguments in a context of good information. There are two common critiques of how this ideal will backfire when implemented, first that it will lead to domination by the more advantaged and second that it will lead to polarization.

Both imply some predictable pattern of group processing that would hold regardless of the merits of the issues. In that sense both would undermine the normative claim of deliberation. How can we think that people are deciding on the merits if some predictable pattern of group psychology determines the results?

The domination argument attacks deliberation for failing to achieve an equal consideration of arguments on their merits, regardless of who makes the arguments. The difficulty is that the proposed atmosphere of equality or equal consideration in the deliberative process occurs in societies whose social structures have great inequalities—in income, in education, in the relative standing of racial, gender, or ethnic groups. Those inequalities in the broader society can be expected to distort the supposedly equal context for deliberation in an artificially designed forum. The inequalities of life contaminate the supposed equalities of the deliberative process.

These distortions are alleged to occur in a number of ways. First, the privileged will take the opportunity to talk more and push their points of view. Second, they will be advantaged in the capacity to make their arguments, in the self-confidence to do so and in the deference that others will likely give them because of their superior social positions, not because of the merits of what they are saying. A further implication is that their success in pushing their own views is likely to serve their interests. In deliberations about politics and policy there are always interests at stake. And those positioned to win the argument can be expected to use a supposedly balanced and neutral process to serve their own private interests.

Because of these concerns, expressed by Iris Marion Young, Lynne Sanders, and Nancy Fraser, among others, it is important for empirical research programs to assess the degree to which these distortions occur and what designs might produce them or tend to avoid them. Most of the empirical literature supporting distortions from inequality, like the literature supporting distortions from polarization, comes from jury studies. But it is important to note the difference between a jury and the DP. A jury arrives at an agreed verdict. The necessity for such agreement creates social pressure for a consensus. By contrast a DP solicits opinion in confidential questionnaires and tries to avoid any pressure for consensus so that the opinions can be studied at the individual level. A jury does not have moderated discussion. The jury foreman is a leader but not a moderator. The foreman is in fact one of the members of the jury and has no responsibility to encourage relatively equal participation. As for substance, jurors are usually not permitted to get their questions addressed by competing experts or policymakers. By contrast, the only interactions in a DP with experts and policymakers are in answer to questions first formulated by the deliberators. In addition, the presentations before juries in a court are driven by an adversary process. Rules of evidence constrain the discussion and the composition and size of juries do not support any claims to statistical representativeness. Furthermore, juries deliberate together only after all the evidence and arguments are presented. By contrast, the DP participants deliberate from the start, and throughout the process, in order to determine the agenda of questions which the experts and policymakers have to answer. So in juries the elites come first and then the citizens deliberate. In the DP the citizen deliberations come first and then the dialogues with the elites follow in response to the public's questions. In any case, differing design elements may well lead to different conclusions about the likelihood of a distorted decision process.

In some of the Deliberative Polls, all the small group discussions were recorded, permitting study of the distribution of words used and the kinds of reasons offered. In her study of five American Deliberative Polls, Alice Siu looked at these two questions. About the distribution of talk, she concluded "that no particular gender, race, or demographic dominates deliberations." In one of the DPs, on health care and education in the United States, by far the most talking (measured in number of words used) was done by nonwhite, less educated females, with nonwhite higher educated females close behind. The least number of words were actually expressed by the white higher educated males. In a separate DP on the 2004 primary campaign the pattern was largely reversed. All of the DPs used representative samples of the US adult population.[36]

Even if talk is evenly distributed, it is possible that influence is not. If we look at issue indices for each topic of discussion and analyze the movement at the small group level, the five DPs had 354 small group issue combinations (the number of issue indices in each DP times the number of groups in each DP). Siu found no significant pattern of movement in the direction of the initial positions of the whites, the males, the high income participants, or the more educated. In each case, movements in the direction of the more advantaged groups occurred only about half the time. In other words, about half the time a group ended up moving toward the initial position of the more advantaged (the more educated, the whites, the rich, or the male) but about half the time it moved away. And when the magnitudes of the movement are examined, rather than the numbers of movements in each direction, the amounts are small considered as a percentage of the total range of possible movement.[37]

While further empirical work, including additional experimental manipulations, will be necessary to sort out exactly why, it is already clear that there is no substantial pattern of inequalities distorting the deliberative process in the way that deliberation critics suppose. First, it is consistently the case that change in the DP cannot be predicted from any of the standard socioeconomic factors, including education, race, gender, and income. The degree of change is not correlated with any of these factors. However, in theory one might still imagine the advantaged dominating by turning the discussions to their advantage, but just doing that so effectively that somehow everyone changes in the same way, to the same degree. Such a supposition would be hard to take seriously. However, as we have seen, analyses of the direction of movement toward or away from the initial positions of the privileged also rebut the worry that they dominate.

Movement to extremes?

The polarization argument put forward vigorously by Cass Sunstein, represents a different kind of distortion. Sunstein argues that there is a predictable pattern: group discussions lead to extremes. If there is an issue for which there is a midpoint, his "law of group polarization" asserts that, if the mean position of the group begins on one side of the midpoint, it will move farther out from the middle in the same direction. If the mean position begins on the other side of the midpoint, it will move farther out from the middle in that direction.[38]

However, we looked at the degree of polarization in fifteen Deliberative Polls with 1,848 group/issue combinations (the number of issue indices in a given DP times the number of small groups in that DP for all fifteen DPs). The proportion of small groups moving away from the midpoint turns out to be 50%. In other words, the other 50% of the time, the movement was toward the midpoint and so there was no tendency at all toward polarization in Sunstein's sense. These DPs took place in various countries, including the United States (six cases), Britain (five cases), Bulgaria, China, Greece, and Australia. All employed scientific random samples and face-to-face discussion.[39]

We did find some modest evidence, not of polarization but of homogenization. There was a slight tendency of groups to converge in the sense that the variance in the groups decreased for 56% of the group/issue combinations. On the other hand, that meant that 44% of the time opinions in the group diverged more after deliberation. While statistically significant, the actual amount of movement in the direction of homogeneity was modest.[40] In addition, one might note that the substance of the "groupthink" argument is that groups will converge without having really considered alternatives. That social conformity will replace thought is the key to the groupthink critique. But the DP process has many indicators that the changes are not thoughtless, but rather the result of an informed weighing of competing arguments.

Why are these small group distortions mostly avoided in the DP? First, recall the two hypothesized mechanisms for polarization—imbalance in the argument poll and a social comparison effect among the deliberators. With mock jury experiments of the sort that Sunstein and his collaborators conducted and studied, it is easy to see how these two mechanisms might come into play. A jury lacks elements of balance in its actual deliberations, either in talking time (no moderators) or in the agenda of discussion. In addition, juries have to reach a shared verdict so there is obvious social pressure that might facilitate social comparison effects.

In the DP by contrast, there are elements of balance in the argument pool right from the beginning. The briefing materials are carefully vetted by an advisory committee of stakeholders, who ensure that there are competing arguments and good information as the basis for discussion. The small groups have trained moderators who try to ensure that everyone talks and no one dominates the discussions. The small groups are diverse as they come from random samples randomly assigned. The plenary sessions in which the questions from the small groups are answered are balanced by competing experts and policymakers who each get to offer rival answers to the same questions. If the moderator of the plenary sessions keeps the discussions on point then there should be considerable balance in the argument pool feeding back into the small group deliberations. Lastly, the DP does not require nor does it aim for consensus. The final considered judgments of the participants are solicited in confidential questionnaires. Moderators are trained to discourage collective position taking or even a showing of hands or counting of votes in the small groups. The only question for which a small group ever seeks agreement is on the questions prepared for the plenary sessions. But people can radically disagree on an issue and still agree that a question is worth asking. From different perspectives they may be expecting quite different answers. In any case, the use of confidential questionnaires lessens the social comparison effect. There is less pressure to conform to a majority position because the moderator attempts to ensure everyone's freedom to continue participating without having to reveal where they finally come out on the issue.

A similar point can be made about the mechanisms for groupthink which principally focus on group pressures for conformity and lack of diversity of viewpoints expressed. A small cadre of decision-makers talking to each other about foreign policy might suffer from groupthink because they have only a truncated argument pool and pressure to come to consensus. But with random and representative samples of the public and a balanced agenda of interaction with competing experts, there is a wide argument pool. And with confidential questionnaires at the end there should be little or no pressure for consensus. So the picture of groupthink, where largely unreasoned agreement is facilitated by pressures for social conformity, should mostly be avoided with the DP.

To what effect?

Earlier we outlined a series of possible effects that DPs could have, either on the participants or on the broader world via the public dialogue or actual decisions. We have a variegated list of projects in different countries on different issues and with different sorts of sponsorship. And there are gaps in the sorts of data that have been collected in past projects if we wished to speak to every item in this catalogue of possible effects. The projects were conducted with local partners with varying agendas about what was to be accomplished. Nevertheless, various projects suggest insights relevant to these categories:

a. Changes in policy attitudes
b. Changes in voting intention
c. Changes in information
d. Building "better citizens"
e. Changes in collective consistency
f. Changes in the public dialogue
g. Changes in public policy

Let us examine each of these in turn.

Changes in policy attitudes

The punch line of a Deliberative Poll is a change in policy attitudes, a change in answers to the question: what is to be done? We studied fifty-eight indices of policy attitudes in nine national Deliberative Polls conducted between 1995 and 2004. Four of these DPs were American, four were British, and one was Australian. Topics varied from US foreign policy (2003) and the US general election (2004) to Britain's future in Europe (1995) and the British General Election (1997.) All samples were national with sample sizes ranging from 238 to 347. Seven of the DPs were face-to-face and two were conducted online.

The first point to note is that there is a lot of change in policy attitudes. Of the fifty-eight indices 72% show statistically significant net change comparing the answers on first contact with the answers at the conclusion of deliberations. The magnitudes of the changes are also large.[41]

A second point is that there is clearly an effect of salience. The more salient the issue to begin with, the less likely is the net change. If respondents have already processed an issue, even with fairly imperfect and unbalanced deliberation in their daily lives, they are less likely to change their views. They may, in other words, have already arrived at fairly firm views. If we proxy salience by the time one knowledge scores, then there is a strong negative relationship.[42]

While there is a great deal of net attitude change, deliberation has a value even when there is no change. If the public thinks X should be done, but has not thought about the issue much, has not tested its views in comparison to alternative policies and the reasons for them, then there is an issue about how seriously, from the standpoint of normative legitimacy, one should take those views. There is a kind of *deliberative discount*. It does not disqualify the opinions. After all, these are the views people actually have. But those views should be viewed within the category of "top of the head" opinion, of impressions of sound bites and headlines that are only incompletely rationalized. They reflect very little thought and little consideration of opposing possibilities. On the other hand, if those views survive a serious deliberation unchanged, then the deliberative discount should be lifted. Those views have been tested in a context of opposing arguments with good information. Hence, regardless of change, the conclusions at the end of a well-constituted DP represent the public's considered judgments. It is those judgments, change or no change, that should have a recommending force to policymakers and representatives and those concerned with the public dialogue. While some of those views may correspond with the views in conventional polls, one can never be sure, unless they have been tested by adverse arguments, unless they have been tested by serious deliberation about policy alternatives.

Changes in voting intention

As noted earlier, it is widely established that voters have low levels of information. Some argue however that they have more than enough information to make the simple voting decisions they are called on to make in modern democracies. As Sam Popkin puts it famously, "low information rationality" can approximate "high information rationality" through the use of heuristics. Or as Arthur Lupia terms it, "short cuts" can approximate "encyclopedic knowledge."[43] Voters need not become massively informed because they can draw inferences from bits of knowledge they collect as a by-product of ordinary life. One may not know the details of a referendum proposition but if one can know which parties, notables, or interest groups are for or against it, that may be more than enough to come to a conclusion without having to reason your way through the ballot proposition and its consequences yourself. Of course, knowledge of the key heuristics (a party, an endorser, or interest group's position) is itself knowledge and may or may not be widely distributed. It may take time and research to figure out which heuristics might be relevant and to make sure that this strategy does not give conflicting reasons about how to vote. But if the unambiguous heuristics are readily available, then such information may be enough to approximate a more informed vote.

In 1999, Australia had a constitutional referendum on whether it should become a republic, replacing the Governor-General appointed by the Queen with a president to be elected by two-thirds of the Parliament. The proposal had come from an earlier "constitutional convention" which deliberated about how an altered constitution might replace the Governor-General. While the convention had included some ordinary citizens, it was primarily an elite deliberation.

In the public debate about the referendum there were actually three options that each had significant support—the status quo, the referendum proposal (for an indirectly elected president), and a directly elected president. The last of these options was widely discussed, mentioned in opinion polls, but was not on the ballot. The split between republicans who wanted direct election and those who were willing to support the indirect model would prove crucial. The direct electionists had to decide whether they preferred the status quo to the indirectly elected president.

The Deliberative Poll before the referendum took place under the leadership of our Australian collaborator, Dr. Pam Ryan of Issues Deliberation Australia. An advisory group very similar to that for the official "yes" and "no" committees for the referendum approved the briefing materials for balance and accuracy. The briefing materials provided a basis for a systematic questionnaire, given both before and after the event as well as to a posttest-only control group administered by the Australian Election Study.

On a weekend two weeks before the referendum, a highly representative national sample of 347 Australian voters was brought to the Old Parliament House in Canberra. The sample deliberated for three days in small groups and with questions to large panels of competing experts and politicians with substantial national television on the Australian Broadcasting Corporation and on Australia's version of *60 Minutes*.

By the end of the weekend, the deliberators moved sharply in support of the "yes" position, from 57% on first contact (a position that was similar to national polls at time of recruitment) to 73%. Other questions give insight into the dynamic of change. On the three-way choice, Direct Election went from being the most popular first choice to having that support from only a fifth (from 51.5% rating it number one in a three-way choice to only 20.5% doing so). The status quo went from being the second most popular first choice to being the least (from 27.5% rating it number one in a three-way choice to only 15.7% doing so). And the referendum proposal went from having the least support as a first choice to having the most (from 21% rating it number one in a three-way choice to 64% doing so).

The Australian DP also showed large information gains. On five information questions the average percentage offering correct answers went from 39% to 78%. For example, the percentage knowing that the Queen appoints the Governor-General on advice of the Prime Minister went from 39% to 85%. In addition, the information gains drove the opinion changes. It was those who became more informed who also changed their views.

Both the elite deliberators at the constitutional convention and the citizen deliberators in the DP realized the merit of an indirect election after considering how direct election would affect the power of the proposed president. The indirect election model was not initially appealing to the public who thought, quite naturally, that if they were going to have a president then they should elect that person directly. But this thought did not take into account considerations about how an elected president would relate to the Prime Minister. And if the public wanted to keep the rest of the system intact, then on further thought they moved in the same way as the elite convention had.

From the standpoint of our democratic theories, a fundamental question has energized the debate between Elite Deliberation, Competitive Democracy (and its skeptical claims), and the aspiration for Deliberative Democracy on the part of ordinary citizens: it is whether ordinary citizens, like elites, are competent to deliberate. The Australian Republic story offers an example of convergence between the conclusions of a convention (the Madisonian model of elite deliberation) and a DP. It was only the mass exercise in plebiscitary democracy, the actual referendum vote, that came out differently. With compulsory voting and low information levels, a mass advertising campaign keyed to the theme "say no to the politicians' republic" brought out the rift between the direct electionist republicans and the supporters of the indirect model.

The nationally televised Deliberative Poll in the 1997 British General Election offers another case in which deliberation, even under intensely fought campaign conditions, produced dramatic changes in voting intention. The project was sponsored by the television network Channel Four and was conducted by the National Centre for Social Research which conducts the British General Election study.[44] Because a general election focuses on many issues and even in an entire weekend of deliberation every issue cannot be discussed, Channel Four made the agenda the economic issues. Such issues are usually central to British General Elections and this one was no exception.

In addition to carefully balanced briefing materials on the economy, each of the three major parties was invited to select a recognized expert who would present its viewpoint in answer to questions from the small groups. A fourth, prominent independent expert, Andrew Dilnott, had the role of responding to the other three experts.[45] On the Sunday the weekend deliberations climaxed with questions from the small groups directed at three candidates for Chancellor: Kenneth Clark (Conservative), Gordon Brown (Labour), and Malcolm Bruce (Liberal Democrat). The project and its results were broadcast in a two-hour special on the Sunday evening, April 28, 2007.

The changes in voting intention were striking. The Liberal Democrats increased their support from 13% to 33% making them a close second to Labour. Labour came in first, as it did in the actual election, but decreased its share from 52% to 44% during the deliberations. The governing

Conservatives, who lost the actual election, decreased their share from 29% to 21%.

As in other DPs the participants became more informed about the issues, both when measured by multiple choice questions and when measured by questions asking respondents to place the parties on issue scales. On factual knowledge the percentage answering correctly went from 47% to 61% and on the party placements the correct answers went up from 41% to 48%.

The respondents were asked to place themselves on the same issue scales as they placed the parties, affording a possible window onto vote choice. There were four issue scales—on income redistribution, taxes and spending, minimum wage, and on full unity with the EU. Participants moved closest to the Liberal Democrats on the issues overall at the same time that their votes for the Lib Dems increased dramatically. They also moved closer to Labour, but less so. In sum, the participants became demonstrably more informed and dramatically changed their voting choices in ways that coherently related to their more informed policy views of the parties.[46]

Another national DP, in 1999 in Denmark before the referendum on the Euro, also shows significant opinion change. A national sample of 364 was gathered in Odense at the University of Southern Denmark in dialogue with competing policy experts and both the Prime Minister and Leader of the Opposition for a three-day nationally televised deliberation.[47] Support for the "yes" position on Denmark joining the Euro moved from 45% to 56% after deliberation, while support for the "no" position moved from 37% to 43%. Of the sample, 20% changed their minds at least once between the three surveys (on first contact, at the beginning of the weekend, and at the end). Counting a fourth survey three months later, the percentage was 25%.[48] There were independent pre- and post-control groups, buttressing the claim to attitudinal representativeness of the deliberating group and the fact that the changes in opinion were due to the deliberations.

As in other DPs there was also substantial learning on knowledge questions and on the positions of the parties. These increases held up in comparison to the gains in the mass public as shown by the control groups. In other words the public gained knowledge in the referendum campaign but the participants gained more. And a survey three months later showed that the learning held up significantly after the event.

As we noted earlier, one aspect of the knowledge gain was that selective learning diminished with deliberation. On five of the seven knowledge questions there was a significant difference on first interview between whether it was known by "yes" supporters or "no" supporters. These were questions about knowledge that would tend to support a "yes" argument or a "no" argument. For example, a "yes" supporting knowledge claim was about whether Denmark could continue to decide its own rates of taxation if it joined the Euro (the answer was yes). A "no" supporting argument was about whether Denmark could continue to set its own interest rates if it joined the Euro (the answer was no). On all five of the questions with a significant gap, the difference narrowed considerably during deliberation. "Yes" supporters had learned the "no" supporting information while "no" supporters had learned the "yes" supporting information.[49] The overall result was that vote choice, under conditions of balanced information after deliberation differed from the initial vote choice when people had given the process less thought and were less informed. These differences held up in comparison to the control groups. While voters do become somewhat more informed in a referendum campaign, they can become even more informed with deliberation and that experience can affect their vote choice. These results are striking as the Danes are known to be the best informed population in Europe about European issues in part because they have had seven national referenda about Denmark's role in the EU. One way to inform the public is to have referenda on the same general topic over and over. Even in Denmark the deliberative treatment clearly made a difference not just to information and policy attitudes but also to vote choice.

We do have only a few cases that focus on vote choice, and so we cannot infer that deliberation will always alter voting intention. But we do have enough cases to show that dramatic changes are certainly possible. Hence, advocates of the heuristics argument, who might wish to say that deliberation is a waste of decision costs, should hesitate to reliably predict that low information rationality will approximate high information rationality. In the cases just cited, high information rationality led to different voting outcomes.

Changes in civic capacities

Under this heading we can consider those attributes that help citizens solve collective problems—information, efficacy, public spiritedness, and political participation. We have already reviewed large changes in the information levels of participants, changes that are routine in every DP. Measuring true information gain is a complex issue since if the questions asked are too easy, there are ceiling effects (everyone will get them right at time 1) and if they are too hard, no changes will be registered. With questionnaire space tight, the questions asked will always be a miniscule fraction of the information relevant to the deliberations.[50]

In the first DP, in Britain in 1994 on the issue of crime, the overall gain in information, counting all the knowledge questions, legal and political, was a statistically significant 9.8%. The legal questions, perhaps the domain most specifically relevant to the deliberations, showed a gain of 20%. And some questions, such as which country had the highest rate of imprisonment in Western Europe, showed a thirty point gain (from 50% to 80%). The fact that Britain had the highest rate of imprisonment already was arguably relevant when combined with the high cost of imprisonment and discussions during the deliberations about the small percentage of crimes that already lead to imprisonment. This combination of facts led to reflections about whether putting more people in prison would be cost-effective, compared to other strategies for dealing with crime such as getting at root causes, separating out juveniles from adults, etc.

Sometimes the information questions can identify a single strategic fact, one that may be crucial in shifting opinion one way or the other. As already noted, this seems to have been the case with foreign aid spending in the 2003 national DP in the United States on foreign policy. The public had the impression that foreign aid was one of the largest elements of the US budget. When they realized just how tiny it was (less than 1%) they wanted to increase rather than decrease it.

Sometimes general political information is relevant to the possibility of a meaningful and informed choice. If one does not know that the Democrats are more liberal and the Republicans more conservative on most policy dimensions, then it is hard to make sense of much of the public debate or to hold the parties accountable. Deliberative Polls that pose general policy scales show significant increases in the ability of respondents to place the parties and themselves on the same scale. Strikingly, in the US National Issues Convention, a DP which did not discuss liberal and conservative terms explicitly, the respondents improved in their party placements by a significant 8% apparently as part of their activation to become more informed.[51] As already noted, the British General Election study provides similar movement and offers insight into the movement toward the Liberal Democrats. In any case, Deliberative Polls routinely show substantial information gains and it is generally those who gain information who drive the attitude change.[52]

When people discuss issues together in microcosmic deliberation, the institutional design is intended to effectively motivate them to engage with the issues at least in part because they think their voice will matter in this situation. Hence it is not surprising that the process regularly produces increases in the sense of internal political efficacy, in the sense that they can have an impact on the political or policy process as a result of their own efforts. So DPs routinely show increases in internal efficacy indices composed of questions asking whether or not "I have political opinions worth listening to," whether or not "people like me have no say in government" and whether or not "politics is too complicated for people like me to understand." In some cases, there have been control groups who do not deliberate and the results hold up in comparison to them.[53]

We also have data suggesting similar results for external efficacy, for the sense that government will be responsive to the concerns people have. There have been significant changes in the extent to which people agree that "public officials care what people like me think" or disagree that "national political leaders are out of touch." When the questions have been asked, the picture is consistent with increased efficacy after deliberation, both internal and external. Participants become more confident that they can have an effect and increase their sense that government will be responsive.

While participants have a greater sense that their preferences will have impact and will be listened to, what will those preferences be? We have noted that the preference changes are driven by information. Another hypothesis about the nature of post-deliberation preferences is that they will be more "public spirited." When people share their reasons in a dialogue about public problems, everyone is sensitized to broader public concerns. They come to understand the interests and values at stake from the perspective of other members of the community. J.S. Mill, reacting to Tocqueville's account of America, was impressed by the "schools of public spirit," the American institutions where ordinary citizens discussed public problems together in a context where they had some responsibility for solving them. Notable examples were the New England town meeting and the jury. Mill generalized to parish offices in England and the law courts (with random samples of citizens) in ancient Athens.

Mill argued that when the private citizen participates in public functions

[h]e is called upon, while so engaged, to weigh interests not his own; to be guided in case of conflicting claims, by another rule than his private partialities; to apply, at every turn, principles and maxims which have for their reason of existence the general good.... He is made to feel himself one of the public and whatever is in their interest to be his interest.[54]

Mill called for more "schools of public spirit" and experimentation with their design. In a sense the DP, like other microcosmic deliberations is potentially a "school of public spirit." But whether or not it functions that way is an empirical question.[55] We have already seen in China that when local citizens were gathered to deliberate about infrastructure choices, they increased their support for projects, among the thirty possible ones, that would serve a broader community, as opposed to projects that would benefit only a single village. In addition, in the eight Texas projects on energy choices, the percentage willing to pay more on their monthly utility bills in order to provide wind power to the whole community rose by about thirty points, averaged over the eight projects. And the percentage willing to pay more on their monthly bills in order to provide conservation efforts for the community (demand-side management) also rose about thirty points. The notion that one would pay more on a monthly bill in order to subsidize the cost of windmills or in order to subsidize conservation efforts seems an indication, in at least a small way, that one is willing to contribute to the broader public interest.

A similar result can be inferred from the project in New Haven about local issues facing the fifteen towns in the metropolitan region. In Connecticut, the town is the unit of government and at the beginning there was a strong presumption that the towns would not share revenue among each other. But after deliberation there was considerable movement toward revenue sharing to promote new development that might benefit the region as a whole. The experimental design of this project allowed us to attribute the movement to the process of discussing the issues together rather than to learning at home in anticipation of the event or any of the other elements of the process.[56]

Information, efficacy, and a concern for the broader public good might all be considered factors that could plausibly contribute to political participation. Participation in a Deliberative Poll is in itself a form of participation. But does it awaken civic interests so that citizens, once engaged, continue to participate? They cannot continue to participate in DPs, even though we have found that, once engaged, participants have requested the chance to do so and have even organized reunions. But they can engage in more conventional forms of political participation. And we do have indications that once activated they are more likely to participate.

In the National Issues Convention, a national DP held in Austin, Texas, in dialogue with presidential candidates, the respondents were asked about their participation on first contact (T1), at the end of the weekend (T2), and then ten months later (T3). Ten months later, there were significant increases in how often respondents talked about politics (by self-report), whether they had worked in an election campaign, whether they had ever contacted a government official, whether they had contributed money to a political party, and whether they voted.[57]

In another project, the 1997 British General Election DP, 82% said on first contact that they would vote, 87% said they would vote at the end of the weekend, and 96% reported that they had voted when they were telephoned after the election.[58]

In sum, the experience of deliberation seems to create "better citizens," if one means by better citizens those who have developed civic capacities for dealing with public problems—information, efficacy, public spiritedness, and participation. As we saw earlier, on some democratic theories, such as Elite Deliberation and Competitive Democracy, there is no need for engaged and informed citizens. Indeed on those views, too much active engagement by citizens might even be dangerous and apathy might be taken as an indication of satisfaction with the status quo.[59] But from the perspective of democratic theories that might ask for citizens to contribute to a collective process of public will formation, the experience of deliberation had salutary effects on their behavior. For both Participatory Democracy and Deliberative Democracy, deliberation is itself a school for better citizens. This result has implications for the spread of deliberation even beyond the confines of scientific samples. Other deliberative efforts, such as the National Issues Forums contribute to civic education. And introducing deliberation into the schools would have lasting benefits as a method for reaching a broader public.[60]

Changes in collective consistency

Since the time of the Marquis de Condorcet writing in the eighteenth century, it has been well known that democratic choices can lead to cycles violating transitivity. In pairwise comparisons democratic choices can move from alternative A to B and from B to C and then from C back to A. This possibility poses several challenges to the meaningfulness of democratic choice. First, it means that individually rational preferences may lead to collectively irrational results. Second, it means that collective decisions may be unstable, in that majorities can successively undo each other. Third, it means that the results of democratic decision may depend on the arbitrariness of agenda manipulation. In a situation with cycles, any of several alternatives may have majority support and so the agenda of decisions and their path dependence can easily be used to determine the result.

Of course, from the perspective of some of our theories of democracy this is not a problem. Competitive Democracy makes part of its case on the basis of skepticism about the public will. All that matters is that there be a competitive struggle for the people's vote and that some result be accepted to determine which team holds office. Of course, if there are only two teams or two parties, then the instability never reveals itself in any case (since cycles obviously require three or more alternatives).

While there is some controversy about the extent to which cycles do occur empirically[61] it is demonstrable that there is a condition that rules out cycles, what Duncan Black called "single peakedness." Preferences are structured so that there is an underlying dimension and (*a*) each individual has a most preferred alternative on that dimension and (*b*) each can place his or her other choices on the dimension according to their distance from that most preferred alternative. One common version of such a dimension is a liberal/conservative left–right continuum. But it need not have any particular substantive content. What counts is that there is a shared dimension that orders the alternatives. If everyone shares such a dimension then cycles are impossible.

Of course, in real life with large numbers of people it may be unrealistic to expect everyone to share the same underlying dimension. We have explored this question by looking at the connection between a dimension being shared by a given *proportion* of the voters and the likelihood of cycles. We call this proximity to single-peakedness.[62] This step has allowed us to investigate a hypothesis that deliberation will increase the proximity to single peakedness, and this increase will in turn provide greater protection against cycles occurring. Note that an increased proximity to single-peakedness is not an increase in people agreeing about the substance of what is to be done. It says nothing about whether or not there is a consensus. Rather, it is an increase in the degree to which people agree about the shape of the issue they are deciding, the dimension on which the choices could be ordered. For example, should they move more left or more right? They can disagree sharply about which direction they should go, but it might still be the case that each person's views can be accurately described as an ordering on that shared dimension.[63]

A number of DPs employed ranking questions permitting us to investigate the possibility of cycles. We looked at six DPs from Texas with ranking questions about energy choices. Participants were asked to rank: (1) getting new energy from coal, (2) from wind or solar, (3) from natural gas, or (4) investing in conservation (to lower the need). They were also asked to rank the goals of energy policy: (1) minimizing cost, (2) maintaining environmental quality, (3) avoiding dependence on any one resource, (4) using renewable resources, and (5) maximizing flexibility to increase or reduce production quickly.

In the Australian Republic Referendum, participants were asked to rank three options for the Australian head of state: (1) maintaining the Queen as head of state represented by the Governor-General, (2) a directly elected president, and (3) the referendum proposal for an indirectly elected president. These were the three options under public discussion even though the referendum only posed the choice between (1) and (2). As we saw earlier, the drop in support for (2) after people deliberated sheds light on the rise in support for (3).

In the British Deliberative Poll on the monarchy, participants were asked about three possible reforms: (1) a continued monarchy with a more ordinary royal family, (2) a republic with a head of state with the same duties as the Queen, and (3) a republic with a head of state with the combined duties of Queen and Prime Minister.

In the New Haven, Connecticut, DP on regional economic issues facing the fifteen towns in the metropolitan area, there were ranking questions in two different issue areas: regional tax sharing and the future of the airport. On tax sharing respondents were asked to rank: (1) complete local control, (2) voluntary agreements with other towns, (3) state-provided incentives to share, and (4) state requirements to share. On the second issue, the future of the airport, respondents were asked to rank: (1) maintaining commercial passenger service to nearby cities; (2) expanding commercial passenger service, providing more flights to more places; and (3) ending commercial passenger service.

These topics provide thirteen cases of ranking questions posed to random samples before and after deliberation. The topics vary in substance and in salience and come from different parts of the world. With these various cases we tested the hypothesis that deliberation would increase proximity to single-peakedness subject to two constraints: first, the rate of increase would diminish to the extent that people had already deliberated, and second, that it would increase the most among those who became the most well informed. We did not have the data to examine the first constraint directly, but proxied it with the degree of salience, reasoning that if an issue were highly salient, then the public had already come to some judgment, at least compared with issues of low salience.

This hypothesis was resoundingly confirmed by our cases. Deliberation consistently increased proximity to single-peakedness, but it did so more in the less salient cases (the electric utility energy choices and regional tax sharing cases, for example, with the lowest salience, the electricity goals with moderate salience) and it did so more among those who became well informed in every DP. Deliberation creates a shared understanding of what is at stake in policy trade-offs. Deliberators need not agree on the solution, only on what they are disagreeing—or agreeing—about.[64] The result has implications for our confidence in the collective meaningfulness of the public will. With high proximity to single-peakedness we can be confident that individually rational preferences will not produce collectively irrational results. We can be confident that arbitrary agenda manipulations will not determine the winners of a democratic consultation. Whatever arbitrariness might apply to "top of the head" preferences, we have greater assurance in the collective rationality of deliberative preferences.

Changes in the public dialogue

The key to any deliberative microcosm is that it effectively motivate the participants to engage with each other and with the issues. Ordinarily, most people do not have the time or inclination to become involved in politics or public policy partly because they do not believe their voice matters. Why spend a lot of time arriving at an informed opinion if you do not think your views will be of any consequence?

One reason people might think their voice matters is if policymakers make clear that they are interested. When policymakers engage directly with the microcosm, the views expressed may actually have an effect on policy, a possibility we turn to in the next section. Another way for the microcosm's deliberations to seem important or consequential to the participants is if they receive significant media coverage. For most ordinary citizens, being on television is a big deal. Just being part of a televised event or one reported in the press, even if one does not appear individually in the media, can seem important. If the media amplify the voices in a dialogue or the conclusions from it, that can increase the motivation for people to take part and to take it seriously.

Most DPs apart from those in China and Thailand have received substantial television coverage. Often there are broadcast partners. Some of these media partners have included PBS (the *By the People* initiative of MacNeil/Lehrer Productions), Channel Four in Britain, the BBC, Danish Broadcasting, Bulgarian National Television, NHK (Japan), the Australian Broadcasting Corporation, the Canadian Broadcasting Corporation, Arte (a French/German television network), as well as newspapers such as *The Independent* (London) and *The Australian*.

These media partnerships serve to amplify, but they also serve a convening function. They provide a further basis for key politicians and policymakers to participate. The media becomes a factor that helps connect a microcosm of the people with key public officials in substantive dialogue. To name just a few who have participated in Deliberative Polls: Tony Blair, Al Gore, Gordon Brown, Kenneth Clark, Phil Gramm, Richard Lugar, Lamar Alexander, Sergei Stanishev (Prime Minister of Bulgaria), Tommaso Padoa Schioppa (Minister of Finance, Italy), George Papandreou (Leader of PASOK, one of Greece's two major parties), Danish Prime Minister Poul Nyrup Rasmussen and the Danish leader of the opposition (and later Prime Minister) Anders Fogh Rasmussen and, at the local level, all the commissioners in the Texas Public Utility Commission, plus mayors of various cities, members of Congress, members of Parliament and party leaders in various countries.

Involvement of the media has made the dialogue seem consequential and it has also helped attract policymakers whose participation adds to the event's importance. These points show how the media can facilitate the DP. There are also ways that the DP may affect the media or affect the public dialogue conducted via the media. Public deliberation is likely to differ from elite political discourse for some key reasons. First, the public dialogue in a DP is not strategically calculated for its effects. It is not pretested by spin doctors. It is not a tool of advocacy groups. Rather, it offers the representative and informed views of the public, sincerely expressed. Unlike campaigners, these members of the public are not running for re-election, but only interested in solving collective problems. Second, the public dialogue in a DP is likely to focus more on how substantive topics for deliberation affect the lives of ordinary people and how they can be dealt with constructively. Ordinary citizens are less concerned with strategic questions affecting the future of one partisan interest or another.

When this "poll with a human face" is broadcast and covered in the press it gives voice not only to the representative views of the public, but to its considered judgments. By doing so, it can affect the agenda and perhaps prime issues that are also of greatest concern, on reflection, to the microcosm. Because the gathering is representative, those concerns should resonate with the broader population. Whether or not the actual coverage of the DP has an effect, the path of argumentation in the DP lays out a route for responsible advocacy that speaks to where the broader public would go if it focused on the issue and became more informed. By responsible advocacy, I mean advocacy based on good information in a context where arguments offered on one side are answered by another. By testing the issues with balanced arguments and good information, one can see the concerns that survive challenge by competing viewpoints.

Sometimes a DP can crystallize a coming change in the public dialogue. In January 1996, almost exactly a month before the New Hampshire primary, the DP entitled the National Issues Convention gathered a national sample of Americans to Austin, Texas, for a weekend of deliberations about the issues in the presidential primary process. There was a considerable amount of press (about 600 newspaper articles) and nine hours of coverage (with some repeat broadcast) on PBS with about 9.8 million unduplicated viewers for the whole weekend. What the press saw was a dialogue distinctly different from the campaign up to that point. As Michael Tackett of *The Chicago Tribune* described the small group discussions in one group he followed:

> For nine hours over two days, the farmer, the waitress, the CTA secretary, the software engineer and others formed an American kitchen table to talk, of all things, about the issues of the day.... They disagreed about a lot of things. But they seemed to concur that perhaps the most profound problem facing the country is one that most politicians don't seem to talk much about: a growing sense of economic anxiety.[65]

Tackett noted the "disconnect" between these concerns and the broader primary campaign up to that point: "the tenor of the Republican presidential debate so far bore little resemblance to the immediate concerns of Group 9."

Almost exactly a month later, Senator Bob Dole was upset by Pat Buchanan in the New Hampshire primary and commented: "I didn't realize that jobs and trade and what makes America work would become a big issue."[66] It did indeed become a central issue that primary season.

Jay Rosen, an inventor of "public journalism," held a seminar on-site with twenty-four journalists who had just covered the National Issues Convention. The journalists reflected together on how covering a microcosm's deliberations allowed them to see public opinion taking shape. They were forced to drop the conventional frames through which they had previously covered politics (the horserace, ideological labels like liberal and conservative, strategic accounts of who might be advantaged or disadvantaged, etc.). Instead, they could report on the dialogue in what must have seemed to experienced reporters like a giant focus group actually representing America. But unlike an ordinary focus group, it was large enough, eighteen groups at the same time, to statistically represent the whole country. Unlike an ordinary focus group, it was recruited through random sampling. And unlike an ordinary focus group, it allowed the participants to become much better informed over three days rather than just an hour or so.[67]

A similar public reframing of the issues occurred in the Danish national DP before the referendum on the Euro. An issue emerged in repeated questions from the small groups to the experts and politicians: Would joining the Euro have any effect on the welfare state and in particular on the pension system? The participants noticed provisions in the proposed Nice Accords that made it clear that there was a possibility of regularizing pension levels between Northern and Southern Europe, between countries such as Denmark with extensive welfare states and countries such as Portugal with much more limited pension systems. Before the DP this was not a noticeable issue in the Euro debate but it naturally arose from the concerns of ordinary citizens who pay high tax rates and enjoy the benefits of an extensive welfare state. As this issue was picked up by the "no" side it came to dominate the debate. "Claims that the state pension would be hit produced a panic-stricken response from the Prime Minister, Poul Nyrup Rasmussen, who announced a "pensions guarantee," pledging that the benefit would remain untouched. But according to press reports, the response "left many experts unconvinced. He then promised assurances from the other 14 EU leaders that the Danish pension would not be touched, but that had to be withdrawn."[68]

The microcosm, when gathered, can have an effect on the ensuing public dialogue. Its deliberations can bring to the surface issues which then resonate with the broader public. In addition, the coverage itself can have an effect. While our data on this are spotty, our NORC partners in the National Issues Convention conducted an experiment with viewers in Chicago, some of whom were randomly prompted to watch the broadcast. There was a surprisingly strong effect on the viewers, in terms of whether or not they disagreed with the statement "people like me have no say in government." However, there was also a strong effect, for those who were prompted to watch both the small group deliberations and the candidate sessions, with people agreeing that "political leaders are out of touch." Many of the candidates treated the DP as a campaign stop and offered standard rhetoric. The disjunction between the heartfelt concerns of the public and the candidate responses was clearly noticeable. In a way this is the same disjuncture that the civic journalists struggled with in covering both the candidates and the citizen dialogue: campaign rhetoric and the public's concerns after deliberation may not match up well.

In the Australian DP on the republic, there was a dramatic result (increased support for the "yes" side) which got extensive television coverage and was front-page news in many of the national papers. We do not have systematic data to demonstrate media effects but the "surge" for "yes" in the closing days of the campaign following the surge for "yes" in the event suggests an impact.[69] Clearly, the effects of media coverage on the broader population are an element for further study when resources permit.

Changes in policy

How can deliberation by a microcosm of the public in a DP actually change policy or politics? We have already mentioned cases where that has occurred: decisions about energy choices in Texas, about infrastructure in Zeguo Township, China, and about the choice of candidate for a party in Greece. Before reflecting on these examples and others like them, let us begin with another.

In 2006 the Regione Lazio, the state in Italy for which Rome is the capital, held Italy's first Deliberative Poll.[70] The state faced budgetary difficulties, especially from a deficit caused by health care costs incurred by the previous government. A principal issue was the cost of maintaining the large number of hospital beds in Rome. With a large number of teaching hospitals, Rome has far more hospital beds than any other part of Italy. While policymakers had long hoped to cut the number of beds and use some of the health care money more efficiently, particularly by investing in poly-ambulatory clinics that could bring health care closer to the people, they were reluctant to cut the number of hospital beds. The fact that Rome had so many more than any other part of Italy was a point of pride and very popular.

On December 3, 2006, a random sample of 119 voters in the Regione was gathered to a state government building in Rome for a day's deliberations. The deliberators were attitudinally representative but slightly older and more educated than the nonparticipants.[71] The most notable result was that the percentage believing the Regione should "convert some of its beds into other resources that make the structures more efficient" went from 45% before deliberation to 62% afterward. Support for converting some of the hospital beds specifically into "poly-ambulatory facilities where you can go for some checks that now you can receive only through hospitalization" changed only slightly, but was very high both before and after—87% before and 85% after deliberation.

After the DP, the state government moved to implement a plan to reorganize the hospital network, lower the number of hospital beds and redistribute resources to poly-ambulatory clinics. Luigi Nieri, the state treasurer, commented on the DP:

> It was an exciting experience that has shown how great is the people's desire to participate and to express their opinion.... It's exactly what we want: encouraging direct participation to democratic life and promoting new transparency practices.[72]

The Rome DP received extensive press coverage in Italy and its perceived legitimacy certainly helped to influence policy. But there is also a sense in which the results gave officials "cover to do the right thing." The informed and representative conclusions of the sample could be invoked as a way out of the budgetary impasse.

The Rome DP encapsulated in a day's deliberations a connection to policymaking that played out over two years in eight projects in Texas. The transparent and representative deliberations of a sample as it became more informed acquired enough legitimacy to be invocable by policymakers. The involvement of stakeholders from different perspectives in the briefing document and in the question-and-answer sessions combined with media coverage of both the process and its results to create a platform for amplifying the influence of the public's considered judgments. Once the microcosm was seen as a legitimate representation of the views of ordinary citizens and once its process was seen as transparent and balanced, the conclusions acquired a recommending force. The results were well received throughout the policy community and were even treated favorably in press releases by the utility companies and the Environmental Defense Fund on the same day.

One difference between the Italian and Texas projects was that the Rome project was sponsored by the state government in conjunction with civil society. In the case of the Texas projects, the deliberations were sponsored by the utilities themselves, with supervision by stakeholder committees and the participation of the Public Utility Commission (PUC). But the basic dynamic was the same—perceived legitimacy and transparency for deliberations by a representative microcosm.

Before the Texas Deliberative Polls, the state of Texas had the lowest usage of wind power on a percentage basis of any state in the United States.[73] Based on the successive DPs, the Integrated Resource Plans which took account of their results, and then the Renewable Energy Standard (RES) that was supported by the DP results, Texas surpassed California as the leading state in wind power in the United States in 2007. The eight projects took place across Texas (as well as across the border in Louisiana).[74] Averaged over the eight projects, the basic choices postdeliberation for sources of energy among residential customers (assuming costs were the same) were:

49% prefer renewables (solar, wind, biomass)
31% prefer reduce need (energy efficiency)
14% prefer fossil (gas, coal)
5% prefer buy and transport from others[75]

Clearly these results supported new investments in renewables and in conservation.

And as we saw earlier, large majorities after deliberation were willing to pay more on their monthly bills when necessary in order to subsidize the first two choices, renewables and energy efficiency. These conclusions represent increases after deliberation of more than thirty points in the percentage willing to pay more. The results were implemented in the Integrated Resource Plans filed with the Commission and then used as the basis for lobbying the legislature for the RES.

The head of the Texas Renewable Energy Industries Association wrote about the eight DPs:

These polls had astounding positive effect. They showed overwhelming customer support for the addition of renewable energy sources. Not only did folks from all regions of the state of Texas say they wanted clean, renewable power on the system, they indicated their willingness to pay more for it (mostly from $1 to $5 a month). There was also a preference for the cost to be shared by all users. This was a significant underpinning for the decisions yet to come. It resulted in the development of 188 megawatts of wind-generation projects.[76]

With the continued operation of the Renewable Energy Standard, the first 188 megawatts was only the beginning. By August 2007, the total was 4,525 MW. Pat Wood, then the George Bush appointed chair of the Texas PUC, took the results of the DPs and had them implemented both in the Integrated Resource Plans and then in the RES. As he commented on the series of eight DPs, all of which he attended, answering questions from the sample: "By the end of the cycle, I had totally changed my mind on renewable energy." Before the DPs he had viewed it as a "boutique industry" that used "public money for pet projects." By the end, reflecting on what he had heard from the public about its priorities after deliberation, he viewed it "as an infant industry that had to be nurtured."[77]

The Texas energy projects set an example for public consultation that led to policy impacts in other jurisdictions that did not have Integrated Resource Planning or any actual requirement that utilities consult the public. For example, in August 2003, the Nebraska Public Power District held a DP with local public television broadcast, to decide on its energy priorities, comparing wind power, methane generation (from animal manure), natural gas, and coal. By the end of the deliberations, 96% supported a large increase in wind power (200 MW) and 81% an investment in methane.[78] Following the DP, the utility's board approved the state's largest wind farm with plans for additional renewable energy investments.[79]

Nova Scotia Power, the province's electric utility company, held a DP in November 2004 to get informed public input from the entire province about its energy choices. As with all the other DPs about energy choices, a media partner produced a broadcast about it so that those who did not participate could be informed about the process and its results. In this case, the media partner was the CBC (the Canadian Broadcasting Corp.). As in other DPs, a highly representative sample of the province was gathered to a single place (Halifax, Nova Scotia) and the participants became far more informed as demonstrated by their answers to information questions.[80] Participants were asked about factors to consider in the generation and delivery of electric power, such as providing enough electricity, contributing to the global effort to control greenhouse gases, controlling emissions locally, and economic factors such as stable cost and securing the lowest price. The importance of the economic factors was strong predeliberation, but after the event it dropped by half. The environmental considerations such as contributing to the control of emissions and to the global effort to deal with climate change went to the top. After the DP the company proceeded with major new investments in renewable energy[81] and also decided not to retrofit a major coal plant.

In November 2007, the State of Vermont sponsored a Deliberative Poll to help its Department of Public Service chart the state's energy future on issues like reliance on energy efficiency (reducing the need), investment in wind, nuclear and hydro, as well as natural gas, oil, or coal.

There was strong support at the end of the day for hydro, wind, solar, wood, and nuclear in that order. There was much less support for oil or coal. Respondents expressed overwhelming support (86%) for the state continuing to buy electricity from Hydro Quebec and from Vermont-based independent Power Producers (97%) but only a slender plurality at the end of the day for continuing to buy from the Vermont Yankee nuclear plant.[82] Much of the initial opposition to wind on aesthetic grounds clearly abated in the face of broader environmental concerns.

The support for Hydro Quebec increased by twenty points after deliberation, and support for the independent Power Producers in Vermont by eight points. There were other significant increases in support for energy efficiency measures and for hydro and wood as fuel sources. Support for coal and oil decreased after deliberation. Within a few months after the project concluded, these results were explicitly incorporated into the Vermont Comprehensive Energy Plan. As of this writing, the plan is out for public comment but it offers a good reflection of the public's views expressed in the DP.[83]

In the various projects on energy choices in eight different utility districts in Texas (and nearby Louisiana), in Nebraska, in Nova Scotia, and in Vermont, the same basic dynamic unfolded as in Rome. A scientific sample was convened, its deliberations were transparently balanced in a dialogue involving public officials, its conclusions showed dramatic changes in comparison to the initial "top of the head" opinions, the participants became demonstrably more informed about the issues, and media coverage amplified the public voice. Relevant officials found the results compelling and reasonable. In Texas, as in Rome, policymakers independently offered the same comment—it gave them "cover to do the right thing."

The dynamic of consulting representative and informed opinion and having it implemented was not much different even in China. While the local projects were not widely covered in the broadcast or print media, they were widely discussed on the Internet. Most importantly, they were big events locally—public and transparent forms of consultation building on the local tradition of "Kentan" (heart to heart discussion meetings). In the Chinese case local innovation provided a novel answer to the question of how citizen deliberations can be connected with elite deliberations. By the time the fourth Deliberative Poll in Zeguo occurred in February 2008, the Local People's Congress had become less a rubber stamp and more an effective decision-making body. In this project the entire budget of the town was opened up to scrutiny by the deliberating sample of 175 recruited, again through random sampling. But this time, sixty deputies from the Local People's Congress observed the entire process. The Local People's Congress (LPC) met a week later and considered both the quantitative results of the DP and their own observations of the process, and then adjusted the budget in light of both[84] After deliberations, participants became more supportive of infrastructure (e.g., rural road construction) and environmental projects (e.g., environment protection and construction), and less supportive of budgeting for national defense affairs. When these results were presented to the Local People's Congress, the LPC revised the township's budget and reallocated monies to increase the budget for infrastructure and environmental projects. The budget for environmental projects increased almost 9%. In addition, the LPC increased the budget for social security. While participants' support for social security increased, the increase was not statistically significant. Presumably the representatives in the LPC were reacting not only to the quantitative results, but also to their observations of the discussions as well as their own political calculations.

The most recent Chinese case highlights the issue of how deliberations by the people might be connected, institutionally to deliberations by actual decision-makers. In the case of the Texas utility projects, the actual decisions were made by regulated utilities but in light of plans that had to be approved by the Texas Public Utility Commission (an appointed government body). In the Nebraska and Nova Scotia cases, the decisions were made by the companies themselves. In the case of the Rome DP, the decision was made by the elected government of the Regione Lazio, while in the case of Vermont the DP played a role in the state's comprehensive energy planning process by the Department of Public Service. In China, however, we see the first glimmerings of another model, one that fuses the two theories of deliberative politics we have been discussing—Deliberative Democracy by the people themselves and Elite Deliberation by an elected body.

Our own American journey of institutional design began with a focus on indirect filtration, on representatives "refining and enlarging the public views" in a relatively small body like a convention or the Senate. But for the Elite Deliberation theory there was always the question of how those discussions might connect with the people, since, except for extraordinary times of constitutional change, the people were mostly not deliberating themselves. In Madison's terms, how do the representatives get the public views they are supposed to refine? In this novel local case in China, we have the example of elite deliberators, for the first time, observing microcosmic deliberation and taking the results onboard in the official decision process. We believe this model can be replicated and may set an example for public consultation in many settings around the world.

All of the cases just mentioned fall short of one last possible step, giving over the formal power of public decision to a microcosm of the people. The people's deliberations were advisory, but advisory in circumstances that endowed them with recommending force. As we noted earlier, some other efforts at microcosmic deliberation, the Citizens Assemblies in British Columbia and Ontario, exercised the formal authority to put a proposition on the ballot for public vote. While in both cases the efforts fell short of the required supermajority, the people in microcosm did have the official power to put the issue on the ballot without further filtering by other government entities. On a smaller scale, the same basic idea was realized in our Greek project for candidate selection. The people in microcosm were given the official authority to make a decision about what was on the ballot (in this case the determination of who was the party's candidate). The final decision, as in the Citizens Assemblies, was made in a public vote. But the Greek project offered two additional novelties. First, it offered a distinctive solution to the problem of candidate selection—a middle ground between mass primaries which realize plebiscitary democracy without much deliberation and elite decisions which realize deliberation without mass participation. Second, it marked the return of formal authority for a step in public decision-making for a randomly selected microcosm to Athens—but after a gap of two thousand four hundred years. These various cases show that formal authority is not necessary to have an input. Indeed, the advisory cases—in Texas, China, and Rome—had more actual impact on final decisions than either the Citizens Assemblies or the Greek project. But both forms of connection to decision—advisory (in varying degrees and contexts) and formal authority—are worth experimenting with to make the thoughtful and representative voice of the public consequential.

Suppose deliberative microcosms were to become institutionalized? How might this occur and would there be a danger that, once institutionalized, the process could be victimized by its own success? Isn't there a problem that the more important the decisions, the more likely the process becomes vulnerable to capture and/or corruption?

First the rationale for the kind of research program described here is to explore the viability of applying deliberative microcosms to the policy process. The idea is to assess the designs that best stand up to critical scrutiny so as to capture the promise of deliberation and avoid potential objections to it. But all these applications have been episodic. They have been based on particular opportunities providing entry points for the process. One ideal model for institutionalization is suggested by the Danish Board of Technology, an office set up by the Danish Parliament to offer the continuing capacity to sponsor deliberative consultations—in this case on the model of the consensus conference.[85] While the consensus conference has limitations as a model for decision, because of sampling and the quest for consensus, the Danish innovation is suggestive for the problem of successful institutionalization. Once this capacity for consultation is established as an independent consultative office of the government, insulated from direct political interference, it can be made available for difficult issues and used by commissions and various government entities that might need citizen input. In this way it offers a readily available alternative to the public hearings and public comment processes that so often engage only lobbyists and special interests. Such an alternative could mobilize a representative and informed public voice as a routine part of the public doing its due diligence on policy proposals.

Second, there are some protections against corruption and capture. The Texas projects on energy choices were part of a regulatory process, Integrated Resource Planning, that affected hundreds of millions of dollars of investment. Yet there was every incentive to create a balanced and transparent advisory group process to supervise the briefing materials and the agenda for the discussion. Any groups left out would have a strong basis for objection when the results of the DP were later submitted to the Public Utility Commission. The briefing materials were transparent, made available on the web or to the press and observers, and the dialogues themselves were open to the media and were the subject of local PBS broadcasts.

Transparency is one protection. Another protection comes from the design. In the Greek DP, a disgruntled candidate who did not make the shortlist tried to interfere with the process by hiring a call center to tell participants that the event was cancelled. But the call center had no way of locating the random sample and found it completely ineffective to try calling the entire population. Thousands of people were called but very few members of the actual sample could be reached. It is also worth noting that in the Citizens Assembly in British Columbia, the deliberations went for a year, with the membership visible to the public. Even though the stakes were large the transparency and visibility of the process protected it against any attempts to interfere with the deliberations. A deliberative microcosm, unlike a modern jury, has a relatively large number of participants. Attempts to bribe or threaten the participants would have to apply to such a large number to be effective that such efforts could not hope to succeed without discovery and would likely backfire.

We do not yet know the limits of this revival of an ancient Athenian notion. Obviously there are practical questions to be faced as the process finds further applications. But it is well worth bringing a modern (and continually improving) version of this process to life because it offers a solution to the problem with which we began—how to devise a form of inclusion that represents everyone under conditions where the people can really think about the issues they are consulted about.

6

Deliberating Under Difficult Conditions

Pushing the boundaries of public consultation

The efforts in deliberative democracy we have discussed so far have taken place mostly within the favorable conditions of "normal politics" in established liberal democracies.[1] But it is worth considering a wider range of conditions to apply the concept. There are two basic components to deliberative democracy that have to be realized: inclusion and thoughtfulness. How can we include everyone, or at least a microcosm of everyone, and how can we establish conditions for their collective thoughtfulness, for a credible deliberative process?

We have already discussed one obvious case that pushes boundaries, deliberating outside established democracies. As we saw, the local Chinese projects do well on our proposed criteria. In terms of recruitment, the legacies of authoritarianism may even have made recruitment of those drawn in the sample easier. In terms of deliberative quality, they also did well on the aspects we could measure—the changes driven by information gain, the balanced materials, discussions that are not distorted by either inequality or polarization, participants who become more public-spirited. In addition, the results have actually been implemented. It does not appear to be the case that an apparatus of established party competition is necessary for applications of deliberative democracy when those applications depend on a deliberative microcosm. However, one of the essential conditions for those projects, the unusual degree of autonomy allowed local government in China, is not necessarily characteristic of other nondemocratic systems.

Consider some other cases where it is arguable that it should be harder to apply deliberative democracy. I have in mind:

    a. Divided societies

    b. Virtual space

    c. Multinational and multistate deliberations

Why are these areas a challenge for deliberative democracy? Our fundamental concerns are inclusion and thoughtfulness. Sufficiently great divisions, such as national or ethnic differences, may make recruitment of a sample difficult. They may also lead to what Iris Young called internal rather than external forms of exclusion: some people may be in the room but without having their views taken seriously. If that happens, of course, the quality of the deliberative process is undermined. Recall our criteria for quality in a deliberative process.

    a. *Information*: The extent to which participants are given access to reasonably accurate information that they believe to be relevant to the issue

    b. *Substantive balance*: The extent to which arguments offered by one side or from one perspective are answered by considerations offered by those who hold other perspectives

    c. *Diversity*: The extent to which the major positions in the public are represented by participants in the discussion

    d. *Conscientiousness*: The extent to which participants sincerely weigh the merits of the arguments

    e. *Equal consideration*: The extent to which arguments offered by all participants are considered on the merits regardless of which participants offer them

The first three of these are addressed by the institutional design of the DP. The advisory group sanctions the information for balance and accuracy, the substantive balance is realized in the small group discussions with trained moderators and with the balance of the expert panels. The diversity of the participants should be guaranteed by random sampling. Any of these aspirations could, of course, be defeated by the intensity of conflict among ethnic groups or nationalities in a divided society or by national differences in a multinational deliberation. Such divisions might, for example, defeat the recruitment of participants or sabotage the advisory committee. But if the design is adequately realized, fulfilling these first three criteria is within reach. It is another story, however, for the last two criteria. They depend on *dispositions* of the participants in how they engage in the dialogue.

While dispositions can be incentivized, they cannot be legislated by fiat or specified by an institutional design. And the dispositions people bring with them into the discussions are part of the background conditions for any project. For the process to work, participants must be *conscientious*, sincerely weighing the arguments on their merits. Hence, severe divisions of ethnicity or nationality might blind them to the merits of some arguments or even prevent them from considering anything but their own group's advantage or the opposing group's disadvantage. A legacy of conflict or deep differences of identity may leave them inured to any appeals about a shared public good—precisely because their minds and hearts are closed to any shared future with the opposing community.

For the process to work, participants must also be willing to grant *equal consideration* to the arguments offered by all participants regardless of who they are. Obviously, a legacy of conflict or a social context of deep divisions may lead some participants to completely discount arguments offered by the opposing community (or communities).

Hence, divided societies face the problem that conscientious participation and equal consideration may not be achievable because opposing communities lack enough mutual respect to actually listen to each other. They may lack enough mutual trust to think conscientious participation is worthwhile. And they may not be open to argument on such issues and are likely to think the opposing community is not open to argument as well.

There is a further condition for conscientious participation and equal consideration that has so far gone unmentioned because it is so obvious. However, in some contexts it is very much in question. In order to deliberate, participants must be able to communicate. So barriers of language clearly can affect divided societies and multinational deliberations. And this issue of mutual intelligibility (and the forms of communication available) would also apply to efforts in virtual space. Virtual deliberation has the merit that it can instantaneously cross boundaries of nationality, geography, and social division but it may also limit the kinds of mutual understanding available because it may limit the modes of communication on offer.

Divided societies: Deliberating across difference

In 2001, we collaborated with Issues Deliberation Australia on a national DP on issues affecting Aboriginals.[2] Aboriginal issues had been the subject of a wide national discussion. A 1999 referendum proposed that the Constitution add a preamble acknowledging the role of indigenous peoples in Australian history. However, this referendum proposition was defeated. There were also widespread revelations about the "stolen generation" of Aboriginals who had been taken from their parents and placed in institutions from 1869 until as recently as the 1970s. At least 100,000 children were subjected to this forced removal over the years. Courts had refused compensation to the victims focusing public discussion on the plight of the entire Aboriginal community.

In this context, a distinguished advisory board for the Deliberative Poll approved briefing documents covering the historical background to the problem and competing policy options to address it.[3] As in the Republic DP, a national sample of representative Australians was gathered to the Old Parliament House in Canberra with national broadcast of the process and its results.

The 344 participants were a good microcosm in attitudes and demographics, as compared to a larger baseline survey of 1,120. However, the Aboriginal project posed a distinctive issue. If we think of the dialogue as one that might lay the groundwork for reconciliation between two distinct communities, what was the appropriate community to sample in order to create the dialogue? Since one community, the population of Australia as a whole, is enormously larger than the community of indigenous peoples (Aboriginals and Torres Straight Islanders), how should they be represented? Indigenous people are perhaps 2.5% of the population of Australia (at least according to the 2001 Census) so a national random sample, even if it were perfectly representative, would not turn up enough Aboriginals and other indigenous people to allow for one per small group (when the sample is divided into fifteen or so in a group). And even if there is one in a group, it might be argued that such a small proportion might lead to a minority feeling distinctly outnumbered. While the DP is designed to solicit opinion at the end of the day in confidential questionnaires and to avoid the social pressure of consensus, such a lopsided representation might be intimidating, despite our best efforts to the contrary.

To explore these issues, the project recruited an oversample of indigenous people (forty-six persons in addition to the 344 from the original sample) and these were randomly assigned to some of the groups (ten out of twenty-five small groups).[4] But by randomly assigning the oversample to some of the groups, one can learn the effect of having an Aboriginal or other indigenous Australian in the group discussion. It turns out that all the groups moved in the same direction, in a direction toward greater reconciliation and support for the Aboriginals and other indigenous people. But the groups that had such members in them moved more in that direction, indicating the importance of who is in the room. Of course, a distinctive aspect of this project, as in some others focused on ethnic and national conflict, is that some of the participants embody the issue that is the topic of the DP. And in some other cases, we will see that this kind of oversampling did not seem necessary. When we turn to Bulgaria and the Roma or to Protestants and Catholics in Northern Ireland, each community has a critical mass that can be turned up by random sampling.

When the sample deliberated, their views changed significantly. The percentage believing reconciliation with Aboriginals was one of the most important issues facing the country went from 31% prior to deliberation to 63% afterward. Among supporters for the conservative-leaning governing coalition (the Liberal and National parties) the change was even greater from a lower base (from 17% to 61%). Perceptions of the disadvantaged state of the Aboriginal population increased dramatically in areas like health, housing, employment opportunities, education, life expectancy, imprisonment rates, and income.

Support for a formal acknowledgment that Australia was occupied without indigenous consent went from 68% to 81%. Support for an official apology for the "stolen generation" went from 46% to 68%, and support for compensation to those who were removed from their homes went from 39% to 61%. Support for government assistance to Aboriginals increased but particular priority was placed on education as well as health care. However, there was only a small increase in support, leaving it at less than majority, for special representatives in Parliament for indigenous people, as is the practice in New Zealand. As in other DPs the participants also became far more informed. An index of eight information questions showed a statistically significant gain averaging twenty-three points.

While the conservative government of Prime Minister John Howard resisted any action on the stolen generation issue, it is worth noting that after Labour came to power in 2007, the new Prime Minister, Kevin Rudd, offered an official apology which was approved by both houses of Parliament.

A national DP in Bulgaria in 2007 dealt with a parallel issue of the treatment of a distinct minority, in this case the Roma. The Roma in Bulgaria live in poverty, largely in ghettoes, with inadequate education, and subject to oppression by the legal system. There are about 700,000 who are identified as Roma[5] in a population of more than 7 million. With close to 10% of the population, a good sample could bring the Roma into the small group discussions without having to grapple with the oversample problem that we faced in Australia with the Aboriginals.

The Roma live in a largely separate community in dire conditions. About 400,000 live in ghettoes which typically lack sewage systems, running water, and paved streets. These living conditions lead to serious public health problems. Two-thirds of the households have a chronically ill person but about half of the Roma lack health insurance. They live in extreme poverty: 64% of the Roma live on the equivalent of only US$2 per day (the poverty line in Bulgaria) while only 24% of Turks and 9% of Bulgarians do so.

The educational system has largely failed the Roma. The percentage of the Roma who have at least completed secondary school is only 7.2% compared with 69% for the general population. There are high illiteracy rates and the separate schools for the Roma, taught in the Roma language, lack teachers and usually use a "mutual education" method where the older students teach the younger ones. In all, 70% of students drop out before the end of primary school.

The Roma are overrepresented among police suspects (by four times) and greatly overrepresented in the prison population (by eight times their share of the population). There are no Roma judges and almost none in the court system, and the Roma can rarely afford legal representation.

In this difficult situation, the Deliberative Poll gathered a national random sample of 255 to the National Palace of Culture in Sofia for a weekend of dialogue. About 10% of the sample was Roma. Broadcast extensively throughout the weekend on Bulgarian National Television, the event included Prime Minister Sergei Stanishev and other key political figures.

The deliberations focused on three policy areas: housing, crime, and education. In each area, there were arguments, on the one hand, for full integration into the broader Bulgarian society and arguments, on the other, for separate and distinct treatment of the Roma.

On housing, participants expressed far less support after deliberation for separate Roma neighborhoods but increased support for measures that would help the Roma obtain adequate and legal housing. Those who thought that "the Roma should live in separate Roma neighborhoods," declined from 43% to 21% while those who thought the government "should legalize those buildings that meet current regulations and then destroy the rest" rose from 66% to 77%. Those agreeing that "[t]he government should help people living in illegal housing to get and repay loans to build new houses" went from 47% to 55%. After deliberation, participants also placed increased value on self-reliance in approaching this issue. Those agreeing that "[t]he Roma will take better care of houses that they built with their own resources" rose from 76% to 91%.

As participants deliberated they increasingly agreed that separate Roma neighborhoods posed a problem. Those who thought "the Roma neighborhoods breed crime and disease that affect everyone" rose from 60% to 69%. And while the participants moderated somewhat in their view of what should be done, they continued to be disturbed about unpaid electricity bills in the Roma neighborhoods. For example, those believing that "power should be cut off in the neighborhoods where the residents do not pay" fell from 82% to a still very high 75%. Nevertheless, there was no support after deliberation for punitive measures such as "building a wall around the ghetto." Support for this option fell from 12% at the beginning to only 7% after deliberation.

On criminal justice, the participants moved, after deliberation, in support of employing more Roma among the police and in the courts. They also objected more strongly to police checks applied just to the Roma. The percentage agreeing that "the government should hire more Roma police officers" rose from 32% to 56%, while those agreeing that "the government should hire more Roma in the court" rose from 26% to 45%. There was also greater agreement that "more frequent police checks just of the Roma would be unfair."

On education, support rose after deliberation for integrating Roma children into the Bulgarian schools and for closing the separate Roma schools. Those agreeing that "[t]he Roma schools should be closed and *all* the children should be transported by buses to their new school" rose from 42% to 66%. Support for maintaining separate Roma schools also fell dramatically. Those believing that the "Roma schools should be preserved" fell from 46% to 24%. Participants' were also less inclined after deliberation to think that Bulgarians generally would support preserving Roma schools (49% thought before deliberation that Bulgarians would support preserving Roma schools versus only 31% after), and the same was true for their perception of support among the Roma themselves (62% before versus 48% after). The sample also thought lack of knowledge of Bulgarian language and culture was an impediment to education of the Roma. Those agreeing that this was a reason "Roma children are reluctant to attend school" rose from 38% to 59%.

In all three policy areas, the movement was generally in the direction of fuller integration and away from a separate and distinct society for the Roma—in housing, criminal justice, and the schools. The Roma in the sample moved in the same direction as the deliberators as a whole. The separate communities came very much together on a vision of a shared future as they became substantially more informed.[6]

In Northern Ireland a DP on educational issues in January 2007 shows how communities long in conflict could engage in deliberation together. Held in Omagh, the site of a notorious IRA bombing in 1998, the DP helped a scientific random sample of parents confront issues of possible educational cooperation between the communities. At the moment the schooling in Northern Ireland is largely separate among Protestants and Catholics. But with new curricular requirements coming into force at the national level and a falling population in Northern Ireland, the two communities faced the problem of deciding on forms of possible cooperation to meet the new standards or on closing or consolidating schools with lower enrollments.

This was the first Deliberative Poll in a deeply divided society with recent memories of violent conflict. Would it be possible to get a representative sample to attend? Would the two communities, largely segregated in actual life, be able to interact productively? Trust and mutual respect are usually thought to be preconditions for deliberative dialogue. If those factors were absent at the beginning would the dialogue be possible? Is it possible that the dialogue could create those conditions going forward?

First, the project gathered a representative sample of 127 parents from the Omagh area for a day's deliberation. The participants matched up well with the 600 in the initial baseline survey from which they were drawn, but they were clearly unrepresentative in one respect—gender. There was an overrepresentation of female participants inherited from the baseline survey. Apparently, women were disproportionately willing to answer a phone survey about education in Northern Ireland (or despite random selection within the household, men were disproportionately unwilling to do so). However, male and female participants changed in the same way during the deliberations so we do not believe this overrepresentation of females affected the results.[7]

Most importantly, the percentage of each community was approximately the same as in the Omagh area as a whole. Of the participants, 62.8% considered themselves to be Catholic or had a Catholic background, and according to Census figures the area is 63% Catholic (correspondingly, 33.9% considered themselves to be Protestant or had a

Protestant background). On all other socio-demographics, the participants and nonparticipants were very similar. For example, the proportions of single versus married people, of those having a university degree or postgraduate qualification, were about the same for interviewees who attended the deliberations and those who did not. The participants and nonparticpants also averaged about the same number of children.

On questions about whether the respondents were Unionist or Nationalist the baseline survey and participants were similar, but both surveys showed large percentages not answering the question or saying they were undecided. The latter is probably an indication of the degree of distrust or the degree to which people are accustomed to show discretion in what they say in such a society. On other attitudinal issues, the respondents were also a good microcosm. There were very few statistically significant differences in policy attitudes between the participants and nonparticipants, although participants began slightly more favorable about cooperation between schools.[8] The beginning knowledge level among participants and nonparticipants was essentially the same.

Even though the project was limited to a single long day of deliberation, it dramatically changed community perceptions among the participants. The percentage believing Protestants are "open to reason" increased from 36% to 52%, and the percentage believing Catholics "open to reason" increased from 40% to 56%. The percentage viewing each of the two communities as "trustworthy" showed similar increases. For Catholics, the percentage rose from 50% to 62%; for Protestants, it rose from 50% to 60%.

There were also significant changes in policy attitudes. For example, agreement that schools needing to partner to deliver the new curriculum should "be required to partner with their closest neighboring school, even if it is not of the same religious composition," increased from 60% to 72%. The increase was roughly the same for both Protestants and Catholics. And there was far greater openness to change from the current completely separate systems. Support for "[r]etaining all types of schools in the Omagh area (controlled, maintained, voluntary, special, and Irish Medium)" declined from 60% before deliberation to 43% afterward. There was also a changed perception about whether the situation was zero-sum, whether gains for one side would necessarily lead to losses by the other. Agreement that changes in the Omagh area's education system "can equally benefit both communities" increased from 40% to 51% (the alternative was that "changes that are good for one community will necessarily be bad for the other community"). The participants became dramatically more knowledgeable. The overall knowledge index increased by thirty points and some questions showed gains of more than fifty points. The project received a half hour of coverage on the BBC and was widely discussed and well received in the policy community.[9]

These results suggest a constructive answer to a fundamental question: What role might deliberation play in a deeply divided society? One position is that it is not really applicable. On this view, the preconditions for mutual trust and understanding are simply absent and the differences are so intense that dialogue is not useful or practical. This position might be applied at both the elite and mass levels. To say that there is no room for deliberation might still leave room for bargaining about power sharing and for "consociational democracy" in which carefully structured elite relations take questions of conflict off the agenda.[10] But shared deliberation on the merits about what should be done would be naive or inapplicable on this view.

A second possible position might be to limit deliberation to elite discussions on carefully restricted issues, but to abandon aspirations for deliberative democracy for the masses. Again such a position would not be an application of deliberative democracy, understood as involving the mass public in balanced and informative discussions, but it would provide a possible kind of deliberative politics. A limitation of this option is that it ignores the fact that the mass public, even in a deeply divided society may have less intense views than the organized interests that speak for them. The relative disengagement of the mass public, at least as compared to policy elites may offer an opportunity for openness to mutual dialogue under the right conditions.

A third position might sanction enclave deliberation, discussion only among the mostly like-minded in order to avoid explicit conflicts across groups. However, as Sunstein notes, enclave deliberation poses the risk of further movement to extremes. In any case, it does little for mutual understanding across deep differences and may even entrench divisions.[11]

A fourth position, the one explored in a trial version here, would foster deliberative democracy among members of the mass public, at least in a situation of well-balanced and representative deliberation. Such an effort at deliberation by a microcosm of the mass public would require that participants somehow get over the initial lack of mutual trust and respect that applies to a deeply divided society. It is an empirical question whether or not deliberation can operate so as to create its own preconditions—whether or not deliberative dialogue can, in itself, create mutual trust and mutual respect at a high enough level that people can finish the process with such views of each other even if they did not start it with them. That is the message that seems to be demonstrated in this Northern Ireland experiment. The levels of agreement with the proposition that Catholics or Protestants are "trustworthy" or "open to reason" rose dramatically following deliberation. The policy options charted a way forward for education in a shared future respecting the interests of children in both communities. The public can engage in a constructive way even when there is a legacy of violent conflict and mutual suspicion.

Virtual democracy

We have focused so far on face-to-face deliberation. Gathering a scientific microcosm physically to a single place requires resources for transportation, hotels, food, and all the logistics of a small convention. The 1996 National Issues Convention in Austin, Texas, had American Airlines as the official airline yielding some significant transportation savings. A similar arrangement with Ansett was used in Australia for the deliberation on the republic. But no matter who the partners, there are significant expenses for the transport and provision of people in real time.

In theory, if a scientific sample could deliberate online, it could save many of these costs. Virtual space instantaneously overcomes the limits of geography. There are, however, two novel issues that arise from an attempt to apply microcosmic deliberation to virtual space. First, there is the recruitment of a scientific sample. The digital divide poses a challenge. Many of the people who would normally be drawn into a random sample of the population are not online. Those who lack access tend to be poorer and less educated and to include more minority representation. If they are left out, then the microcosm will surely be unrepresentative.

A second issue is the mode of communication. Most online communication at the moment is text-based. As a result many cues that are communicated efficiently with voice and face-to-face discussion are left out. In addition, those lacking literacy may be disadvantaged. Of course, those who cannot speak or hear may be disadvantaged by verbal deliberations but there are standard ways of assisting people with handicaps and they have sometimes been used in face-to-face DPs.

We have conducted several online versions of the Deliberative Poll attempting to respond to these two challenges in various ways. In the first efforts we responded to the digital divide by providing computers to those who lacked them. We responded to the second problem, the mode of communication, by using voice rather than text, with special software that would allow moderators to convene small group discussions on a weekly basis. After several weeks, the participants took the same questionnaire as at the beginning. The changes in opinion would represent the considered judgments of the deliberative microcosm and a pre- and post-control group who did not deliberate could be easily included. This basic design has been employed several times, with the innovation that some of the projects have used recruitment with matching characteristics from a large online panel of more than a million, with random assignment to treatment and control, thus saving the expense of buying computers.

The first online Deliberative Poll was conducted in 2003 in parallel with a face-to-face DP on the same topic—American foreign policy. In the online project, a treatment sample of 280 deliberators supplied by Knowledge Networks deliberated for an hour twice a week in randomly assigned small groups for four weeks. A control group answered the same questions before and after but did not deliberate. As in the face-to-face projects, experts answered questions agreed on in the small groups. The experts were selected by the *Online Newshour* on PBS (media partner and collaborator in the project) and the answers were posted online between the weekly sessions.

As in face-to-face projects there were lots of significant changes in policy attitudes. For example, in terms of the priorities of American foreign policy, the percentages who emphasized providing food and medical help to poor countries rose from 51% to 67% and on protecting human rights in other countries rose from 49% to 61% and on protecting weaker nations from aggression from 50% to 60%. There was increased emphasis on solving global warming, and on requiring higher mileage from vehicles even if it made cars less powerful, and on requiring cleaner production of electricity even if it made it more expensive. As in the face-to-face DPs there were significant information gains and it was the people who gained information who drove the opinion changes.

At the same time there was a face-to-face DP on a national scale meeting in Philadelphia with national broadcast on PBS. The changes of opinion were generally in the same direction face-to-face and online. In both cases the changes held up in comparison to separate control groups (the online project having a pre- and post-control and the face-to-face just a posttest-only group). The face-to-face project had larger changes of opinion in the same direction. A face-to-face deliberation over an entire weekend is probably a more intense experience than a disembodied conversation twice a week for an hour at home via a computer screen. In addition the online respondents were immersed in their normal environments the rest of the time. In between the structured deliberations they would have their normal conversational partners and news sources. The face-to-face respondents were transported to a place where they interacted from dawn to dusk with the other respondents.[12]

Despite these differences, the online deliberation clearly showed that the idea of microcosmic deliberation with a scientific sample can be adapted to virtual space. Representative and informed deliberation stands in sharp contrast to the "quick votes" on media web sites where SLOPs are open to capture.

Two other online projects with MacNeil/Lehrer Productions were held in the context of elections. In the presidential primary season for 2004 a similar online DP discussed the issues in the campaign as well as candidate positions. In addition to written briefings on the issues the participants had a multimedia CD with excerpts from campaign speeches and ads. These were presented as comparably as possible in terms of time devoted to each of the nine Democrats and to President Bush. In each case the attempt was made to cover the candidate biography as well as roughly equal coverage of the candidate positions on issues.

The early stages of the primary process are a low information environment where voters cannot even use party as a cue to help choose between candidates. On what basis might voters make decisions if they had an opportunity to think and discuss more and become more informed? Some key factors are electability (which candidate has the best chance of winning the general election), candidate traits (personality characteristics such as whether the candidate is perceived to be sincere, intelligent, or "thinks like me"), and policy positions. It is well established that primary voters rely principally on candidate traits. In some ways this is a heuristic or information-simplifying device. They can assess whether they relate to someone as a person far more easily than they can examine his or her detailed policy positions. One question for the DP was whether voters would seriously take policy into account in a deliberative context. They were asked to place themselves and the candidates on four policy scales concerning trade, multilateralism, spending priorities, and taxes. The distance between candidate positions and the voter's own positions on those four issues formed the policy variable.

In the control group of voters who did not deliberate but just answered the same questions before and after, perceived traits of the candidates were by far the most powerful predictor of candidate support. Electability was a distant second and policy positions were not a factor. However, among the deliberators policy became an important factor, about as important as electability. Candidate traits were still the most important but at least the deliberators seriously weighed how close the candidates' proposed policies were to their own preferences.

In a second online DP in the 2004 presidential election, the process was applied to candidate choice in the general election. Here policy positions again became important for candidate choice, but in this case deliberation both increased the role of policy and decreased the role of personality or candidate traits. Of course, in a general election policy differences are greater among the candidates than in a primary, but in both cases the increased role of policy positions is reassuring about the possibility that ordinary citizens are capable of becoming deliberative voters.[13]

Another national online Deliberative Poll focused on possible political reforms on the eve of the 2008 primary season. Sponsored by the Colonial Williamsburg Foundation with media partner MacNeil/Lehrer Productions, the online DP engaged 301 deliberators in four one-hour sessions with a control group of 1,000.[14] The discussions focused on four aspects of the role of citizens in a democracy: political participation, exercising choice, becoming informed, and public service. In each case, there were arguments for and against the importance of the basic goal and specific policy proposals that might achieve it.

On all four topics there were statistically significant changes of opinion and large gains in information. The sample learned a lot and changed its views. In fact, thirty-nine out of fifty-six policy questions (66%) changed significantly among the deliberators from the beginning to the end of the process.[15] The project was notable because it applied the relatively modest intervention of online discussion for an hour a week to basic questions about whether or not our system should be changed in significant ways. The results show increasing interest in the fundamental democratic values at stake but a fairly nuanced view about which proposals would be worth adopting to implement them.

When citizens deliberated, they increased their sense that political participation was important, but they were selective about which proposals should encourage it. The percentage thinking "voting in elections" was "important to being a good citizen" rose from 90% to 96% and the percentage believing that "increasing political participation" was "important" rose from 88% to 93%. Support for "allowing Election Day registration" went up from 47% to 54% and support for "allowing felons to vote after they have served their sentences" went up from 52% to 62%. However, support for "making election day a national holiday" went down from 58% to 49%. Many of the respondents noted in the discussions that with early voting and absentee ballots, it was not necessary to get off from work to vote. And they realized that national holidays are expensive. There was also increased opposition to compulsory voting as in Australia. Opposition to "fining people who don't vote" increased from 68% to 78%. In general, participants supported voluntary methods for making the system more participatory and inclusive but they resisted compulsion and thought a national holiday unnecessary.

On the second topic, deliberators increased their sense that the current system did not offer voters enough choice. However they were, once again, selective about remedies. The percentage agreeing that "elections in the United States do not currently provide enough choice for voters" increased from 59% to 68%.

Support for "making it easier for 3rd party candidates to get on the ballot" increased from 70% to 79%. Participants also increased their support for a national primary. The percentage agreeing it would be "effective in increasing choice for voters" to "require all state presidential primaries to be on the same day" increased from 48% to 66%. Support for the notion that "every voter should have an equal say in selecting our presidential candidates, no matter where he or she lives" rose from 84% to 90%. Clearly, there was a sense that states outside the early primary states should have a say in presidential selection and a national primary would facilitate this goal.

However, support for term limits went down. While some experts have advocated term limits as a strategy for ending incumbency protection and increasing choice, the percentage approving term limits for members of Congress declined from 69% to 59%. Support started high and went slightly higher for the notion that "people should have the right to vote for legislators who are doing a good job no matter how long they have been in office."

On the third topic, whether or not there were ways to make voters more informed, the percentage of the deliberators believing in the "importance of discussing politics with others" increased from 67% to 81% and the percentage believing in the "importance of being informed about politics and political issues" increased from 92% to 97%. However, they were, once again, selective in the proposals they would support for enabling citizens to become better informed.

The percentage supporting a requirement that "broadcasters air more public affairs programming" increased from 51% to 69%. And the percentage supporting "free TV air time for candidates" increased from 57%

to 71%. There was also a belief that "political candidates should focus more on policy issues in their campaigns" (those agreeing increased from 88% to 97%) and comparably high agreement that political candidates now "focus too much on attacking other candidates in their campaigns."

However, support decreased sharply for subsidizing Internet access as a way of helping citizens become more informed. The percentage supporting the use of "public funds to see to it that everyone has access to the internet" went down from 44% to 33%. And there was little change in support for providing public funding for nonpartisan civic education groups to inform voters. This idea shifted from 49% to 52% (a small change that was not statistically significant).

On the last topic, public service, deliberators again increased the importance they attach to this area of citizenship but they were insistent on voluntary rather than compulsory means of achieving it. The percentage subscribing to "the importance of serving one's country through military or other public service" increased from 72% to 79%. But the deliberators emphasized the expansion of opportunities for voluntary public service rather than any form of compulsion.

The percentage who agreed with "keeping public service voluntary but expanding public service programs like AmeriCorps and Peace Corps" increased from 66% to 78%. But support for compulsory public service "in either a military or civilian program" fell from 44% to 32%.

After deliberation there was more agreement that "mandatory public service runs contrary to the idea of liberty" (agreement rose from 53% to 64%). And opposition to required military service rose from 68% to 76%. There was also increasing agreement that the all volunteer military had advantages (it "ensures that military personnel are motivated and suited to military life" according to a percentage that rose from 61% to 68%). Support fell from 47% to 44% for the notion that "having an all volunteer military shifts the burden of service on to poor people who have fewer educational and professional opportunities."

In only four hours of discussion, these deliberators offered a series of nuanced discriminations about how to achieve values in political and civic life that they subscribed to. The changes required in our institutions would be significant. And the results offer a guidepost to reforms the public could accept on reflection and those they would oppose. They would support same-day registration for voting to increase participation, but resist a national holiday. They would support free TV air time to make voters more informed, but resist subsidies for Internet access. They would support changing the Electoral College to increase choice but oppose term limits. They would support expanding public service programs but oppose making them compulsory. While the changes were numerous and significant, four hours over four weeks hardly exhausts the potential for adapting microcosmic deliberation to a virtual environment. We might imagine online deliberations that continue for months rather than weeks, capitalizing on the logistical advantage that people can participate from their homes without any need to travel to a single site. Putting the nation in a virtual room could continue for months or even years. Under these scenarios it would be hasty to conclude that online DPs, which cut the cost of a national consultation by up to 90%, are necessarily more modest in their results than face-to-face projects. It is quite possible that technology may facilitate the frequency and scope of representative and informed versions of deliberative democracy. Our first projects are only the beginning of the nascent efforts to adapt this sort of approach to an online environment.[16]

The problem of a European-wide public sphere

The problem of democratic consultation in the European Union embodies all the challenges we have been discussing up to now, plus some additional ones. To begin with, there is the widely perceived "democratic deficit" in which the policy elites are thought to be insular from the wishes of the public. But what "public"? There are twenty-seven member states and each has its own political system and its own public discussion. Yet the EU also has a Parliament, admittedly very weak in its powers to exert policy, in a confederation of states fitting in the gray area between international relations and nascent federal union. Hence the definition of the public or publics that might be consulted is the first problem. Should there be one consultation for the EU as a whole, or separate efforts in each of the member states? One consultation has the benefit of shared consideration of the different values, interests, and perspectives in a single forum where competing arguments can be considered and responded to. Separate consultations are closer to the centers of power, as each state will wish to decide on its own. To the extent that the EU is a creation of treaties between separate sovereign states, then separate consultations are warranted. But to the extent that there is a nascent federal union with ambitions for a shared public sphere, then a single consultation would be desirable.

Consider another problem. In terms of democratic theory, the development of the European Union seems caught in a fundamental and recurring dilemma, a transnational version of the dilemma we saw recurring on a more modest scale in candidate selection and policy choice. Consulting the people directly, with low levels of information, leads to a thin, plebiscitary form of politics. But consulting only elites seems undemocratic and divorced from the concerns of the people. In the Greek DP we saw how a national political party faced this issue in candidate selection. The DP offered a way out of the dilemma of whether candidates should be selected by party leaders on the one hand or by mass primaries on the other.[17] With the EU, if a decision is left to parties and Parliaments, then the people are deprived of an opportunity to signal their consent. But if the issue is brought directly to the people as in the referenda in France and the Netherlands on the proposed European Constitution in 2005, or the Irish vote on the Lisbon Treaty in 2008, then the decision may be made on grounds far afield from substantive EU concerns about which the public is usually inattentive and uninformed.

Fundamentally, this is the same problem the American Founders faced with the approval of the new US Constitution, but they avoided use of referenda (except over their protest in Rhode Island). As a result they were subject to criticism from Anti-Federalists for placing the decisions in the hands of the privileged. Just as Rhode Island voted down the US Constitution, Ireland voted down the EU "Constitution." In both cases the states were enmeshed in an existing multistate relationship, the Articles of Confederation, or the current EU regime of treaties, but in the US case, the issue was ultimately decided by threat of force of a sort that would not be acceptable within the EU.

In all these contexts, there is another option for bringing the thoughtful voice of the people into the process. The deliberative microcosm chosen by scientific sampling, not too different in basic concept from the microcosms chosen by lot in ancient Athens,[18] offers a middle ground, a third way, between mass plebiscitary consultation on the one hand and elite decision on the other, between politically equal but nondeliberative masses and politically unequal but more deliberative elites.

Because the EU has been seen as a largely elite-driven project, periodically upended by eruptions of plebiscitary democracy, there is a strategic opportunity for microcosmic deliberation to fill this middle ground. But there are additional challenges. Some are distinctive to the EU and some are recurrent versions of virtually all the problems we have faced in other contexts.

In the local, regional, and national deliberative efforts we have discussed thus far, there has been an important background condition—the existence, at least to some degree, of a "public sphere"—a shared public space where public opinion can take shape and contribute to collective will formation. Two basic questions apply to such a public sphere—how *credible* is the public opinion that takes shape within it and how *consequential* is that opinion? Credibility can be assessed in terms that we discussed earlier. Is it thoughtful? Is it informed? Is it subject to distortions from inequality and/or polarization? Whether or not it is consequential raises precisely the problem of the democratic deficit. EU policy elites are perceived as insulated and unresponsive to mass public opinion.

There is only an attenuated version of something that could be called EU public opinion. There is opinion to some degree about EU matters within the boundaries of given nation-states, public spheres of discussion segmented by national boundaries, linguistic boundaries, and their corresponding media markets. Of course, virtual discussion crosses borders to some degree but language is a continuing barrier. Generally, the French talk to the French, the Germans to the Germans, the Bulgarians to the Bulgarians, etc. Both in terms of shared discussion and collective decision, the Union is segmented largely by nation-state even though there are supranational institutions such as the European Parliament, the Commission, the European Court of Justice, the European Central Bank, and the Council of Ministers. And even at the level of the nation-state, European issues are generally of low salience and of low levels of information on the part of the mass public. European elections are famously "second order elections,"[19] decided as by-products of national politics with little discussion on their own substantive merits. If two tests for an effective public sphere are that public opinion be credible and consequential,[20] it is evident that these tests are not passed at the transnational or EU level, and that they are hardly more successfully passed even at the segmented level of the nation-state for most EU states.[21]

The first challenge facing democracy in the EU is the attenuated nature of the public sphere and its associated democratic deficit. A second challenge is that the EU encompasses deep divisions of ethnicity and nationality of the sort we have seen previously—divisions between the Roma and the majority populations in most East European states, between the Protestants and Catholics in Northern Ireland, between French and Flemish speakers in Belgium, between Greek and Turkish communities in Cyprus, and many others. Can these communities deliberate together?[22] Can they discuss a shared future? Is it perhaps easier if they are encompassed in a broader dialogue where the perceived zero-sum nature of their local discussions may not apply?

A third challenge applies to the very possibility of communication, of mutual intelligibility. There are twenty-three official languages in the EU. Language, as we have seen, is a great barrier to a shared public sphere. A microcosmic version of a European wide public sphere, if it were really representative of the people, would have to use technology to overcome the barriers of linguistic division. In this respect, an EU-wide effort is a bit like the deliberative projects in virtual space. A technology—in this case the apparatus of simultaneous interpretation with headsets—is necessary to make the dialogue possible.

A fourth challenge arises from the unique nature of the EU as a transnational entity, with some of the characteristics of a federal state and some of the characteristics of a collection of separate states with various treaty relations and different degrees of coordination in areas such as monetary policy and common borders. If public consultation is supposed to contribute to collective will formation, what is the relevant public and what are the relevant institutions that might consider its results? Who is consulted and who is the addressee of any consultation? Who is the receiver of the results, even in the best of cases? One strategy for public consultation about EU issues is to conduct it at the level of the nation-state where there is a defined population and government officials and institutions that may be addressed. There have been many referenda and countless opinion polls on EU issues at the level of the nation-state. There have even been DPs on a national level about the EU in Britain and Denmark. But such efforts do little for *European-wide* collective will formation. And problems that are EU-wide or within the growing authority of EU institutions cannot be adequately addressed within the limited boundaries of its member states.

Of course, from some perspectives the EU may develop better if left to the elites rather than to the public (or the many publics at the national level) because consultation of an uninformed public can be dangerous or irresponsible.[23] But the increasing acceptance of norms of democracy *within* the nation-state—norms that make anything more direct and more participatory seem more democratic—makes elite-only patterns of decision across nation-states seem undemocratic and unresponsive. Hence, the aspiration arises for some sort of EU-wide public consultation. If that consultation were, in itself, segmented by country, then from an EU perspective, the differences in nationality would not ever inform each other. The concerns of new Europe would not intersect with those of old Europe.

The concerns of Northern Europe, with its highly developed welfare states, would not intersect with those of Southern Europe where the pension and social welfare provisions are far less elaborate. There would be a series of "enclave deliberations" perhaps filled with misinformation about the facts applying to other countries or those who fit certain country stereotypes.

A public sphere is a deliberative communicative system. But is it necessary? On some of the theories of democracy we have discussed, it is not. The aspiration for collective will formation is not shared among all visions of democracy. Schumpeterian or merely competitive democracy makes no pretense that democracy offers the will of the people. On that view, democracy is just a competitive struggle for the people's vote that can serve the useful purpose of peacefully settling the battle of which team of elites can exercise power for a time, alternating with competing elites. This minimalistic theory of democracy also aspires to protect rights through constitutionalism and judicial decisions. Hence, we classified it earlier as emphasizing political equality through competitive electoral processes and avoiding tyranny of the majority through the protection of rights. Providing judicial guarantees and a peaceful method for alternation in power are important achievements. It should not matter from the standpoint of Competitive Democracy whether the teams compete in separate states or in a unified competition. So long as there is a competitive struggle for the people's vote and rights are protected the theory is satisfied. Any more ambitious claims about democracy would be illusory.

But by denying the meaningfulness of public will formation, Competitive Democracy keeps the mechanism of democracy without its soul. The decision-making capacity that is supposed to animate the democratic process is just the result of whatever competitive efforts, exercised in whatever way happens to win in a mostly unrestricted adversary process. So, if elections are won by manipulation or deception, by bamboozling an inattentive public, that is just the way the rough game of politics is played.

Two of our other theories of democracy also fail to emphasize deliberation by the public. Participatory Democracy, the combination of participation and political equality is concerned with whether people participate and if their votes are counted equally. It does not give a primary place to the requirement that people deliberate. While it might be nice if people thought and became informed before they voted, what matters on this view is whether or not people actually turn out.

On another of our four theories, Elite Deliberation, any public will comes via the *indirect* expression of representatives. The elites give voice to

179

what they think the public would want on reflection, or perhaps just what the elites want, on reflection. They "refine and enlarge the public views" but by passing them through elected representatives as the "chosen body of citizens." Deliberation by the mass public is not to be expected and could even be dangerous. Hence, the aspiration for citizen deliberation is on some views utopian or misguided or irresponsible. It is not, by any means, shared among all theories of democracy.

That aspiration is particularly challenged in a European-wide context. In the EU, some commentators believe the most that could be sought is a series of more developed public spheres segmented at the national level.[24] But as Nancy Fraser has pointed out, such a strategy would try to limit the application of the public sphere, essential for collective will formation, into an increasingly outmoded "Westphalian" system of separate nation-states—nation-states whose boundaries no longer comprise the effective boundaries of decisions or their effects, politically or economically, or in reflecting the movements of workers, and goods and communication processes in an increasingly mobile world of people and ideas. Somehow the European idea needs to be adapted to a transnational public sphere if democracy is to be meaningful.

Fraser outlines six areas where the idea of the public sphere, conceived at the national level, requires serious revision in the increasingly common transnational context. The European Union embodies a segmentation in these six areas to a high degree. The original Habermasian notion of the public sphere where public opinion could be filtered for collective will formation for decisions was conceived for application within a given nation-state. While Habermas has admitted the difficulties of applying the notion in a transnational context, those difficulties only reinforce the urgency of institutional experimentation to address the problems on his view. Otherwise, the encroaching powers of the EU on its nation-state members further increase the democratic deficit because those powers are exercised without democratic legitimation. If the EU were left to be "completely independent of constitutional innovations," the danger is that "this deficit expand(s) day by day because the economic and social dynamics even within the existing institutional framework perpetuate the erosion of national powers through European law." New transnational forms of legitimation are necessary but they confront the difficulties of the undeveloped European-wide public sphere and "the fragmentation of public consciousness" leaving us with "the future of a past illusion—the democratic illusion according to which societies could still determine their own destinies through political will and consciousness."[25]

Fraser nicely details the challenge facing democratic will formation beyond the nation-state and particularly in the EU context. Consider six assumptions of the traditional public sphere that clearly are violated:

a. The notion that *sovereign power* is exercised within the territorial boundaries of the nation-state. As the EU acquires more power via treaties and bureaucratic encroachments, decisions are made in Brussels, not in given nation-states.

b. The notion that the *economy* is territorially based within a nation-state. While in a globalized world this assumption is, in general, increasingly tenuous, many key economic decisions in the EU are obviously a matter not of national determination but EU-wide or in a multispeed Europe, by the centralized institutions that apply to the Eurozone, etc.

c. The notion that the democratic dialogue takes place within a *national citizenry* resident within the boundaries of a nation-state. With freedom of movement as a matter of right within EU countries and no robust EU-wide citizenship, the boundaries of the traditional nation-state are clearly transcended.

d. The notion that there would be a *national language*. With twenty-three official languages there is not a shared basis for mutual intelligibility in the same dialogue at the same time. While some societies operate with multiple languages, a state such as Switzerland made its linguistic diversity a key aspect of identity as it developed democracy over a long period. And there is a great difference between three languages and more than twenty.

e. The notion that there would be a *national literature*, culture, and shared identity. There are obviously many national literatures and only a thin recognition of shared culture and identity.

f. The notion that there would be a *shared infrastructure of communication* to permit common dialogue. Linguistic differences and national regulations of broadcast media have fragmented this possibility.

Fraser finds these factors increasingly violated even within the traditional nation-state. But of course the European context makes the challenge explicit with twenty-seven nation-states. The notorious democratic deficit of the EU has to be, in large part, the gap between elites who may or may not be deliberating, and mass publics who may not even be really aware of the issues and challenges facing EU decisions. Deliberating elites without a public sphere to support and provide input to their decisions cripples the Madisonian Elite Deliberation model. How can representatives refine and enlarge the public's views when so many publics are hardly even aware of each other and there are not even hints at the mass level of how the public would approach the viewpoints expressed by the elites from different countries in different languages and with different concerns? Elites, even when they conscientiously deliberate on the merits, may only increase the perception that they are from a different planet, and one disconnected from the concerns of the various publics they represent.

Without a European-wide public sphere Participatory Democracy will lack any basis for collective will formation. Setting aside Participatory Democracy for EU issues, we are left with three choices: we can have elites competing mostly without deliberation (which satisfies the Competitive Democracy model), or the considered judgments of elites (which satisfies the Elite Deliberation model), or we can employ the microcosmic strategy applied to Europe as a whole to engage the public in deliberative democracy. If one believes in the possibility of a European-wide public sphere, the microcosmic strategy has the merit that it would *represent* what it would be like. It brings to life the imagined European-wide community, by simulating a representative dialogue across the borders of nationality and language. Note how much farther this goes than just an effort to deepen the dialogue within nation-states. Even if one were somehow to get the mass public in each country engaged, the deliberations would take place in the silos defined by each country. But with a microcosm of the whole EU in one place, one could have a dialogue in which all the major perspectives in the mass public were brought to bear in a substantive way in the same dialogue, with arguments offered from one perspective answered from another.

As we saw earlier, J.S. Mill's Congress of Opinions offers a concrete image for how the views of a shared public can be connected to deliberations of a relatively small body in a single place. If the distribution of opinion is like the distribution of opinion in the population as a whole, then each person in the society can see his position defended as well or better than he could do so himself and answered by others in turn, as well or better than those advocates could answer it, and then any decision taken on the matter should be taken for "what are thought superior reasons" rather than "a mere act of will." The representativeness of the body ensures that all the major perspectives in the society get voiced. Gathering them to a single place ensures that they engage each other as opposed to persisting in parallel universes.

Can such a model work to bring into being the European public sphere, if only on a microcosmic level? Mill's model was proposed for a legislature in which a public sphere of shared discussion in the broader society was already presumed to exist. But with vast differences of nationality, language, and political culture, and a vast scale of population and differences in history, can deliberative democracy, even in a pilot version, be made to work?

To summarize the challenge, there are now twenty-seven countries in the EU with mass publics speaking twenty-three official languages and with communication systems that are organized and largely segmented according to the boundaries of the nation-states. Of course, new technologies such as the Internet and even satellite and cable cross these national boundaries depending on viewer interest and market incentives along with complex regulatory decisions. But the result, especially on European issues, is mostly a series of silos or segmented public spheres— all attenuated in the extent to which they realize any of the criteria mentioned above, even within their national boundaries. The capacity for public will formation even at the national level, is limited. On European issues, which are mostly low salience and often subject to misinformation and imbalanced discussion (particularly about the common agriculture policy, employment policies, etc.), there is no communicative structure and no mass basis for collective will formation. Each country and linguistic community has its own dialogue, if they talk about Europe at all. And if they do, the level of balanced discussion, information, and willingness to seriously engage the issues is low.

Putting Europe in one room

On a weekend in Brussels in October 2007, a scientific random sample of the entire European Union was gathered in microcosm to a single place—the European Parliament Building in Brussels. The Parliament is, of course, the home for elite deliberation by elected representatives. But this was the first time that a scientific microcosm of the European people gathered within its chambers to weigh public issues affecting the future of the EU.[26] The sample of 362 respondents was drawn from an initial sample of 3,500 interviewed by TNS-Sofres in all twenty-seven countries. As in other Deliberative Polls, the respondents were only invited to the event after completing a comprehensive initial questionnaire, making it possible to compare participants and nonparticipants in both attitudes and demographics.

Before the project began we faced a conceptual problem: was this a sample of twenty-seven populations or a sample of one population, a sample of twenty-seven countries or of Europe as a whole? If it were a sample of twenty-seven populations, twenty-seven distinct countries, then like the Eurobarometer we might sample a significant number for each country. The Eurobarometer typically samples 1,000 respondents per country (except for the very smallest countries such as Malta). But if we think of the relevant population to be Europe as a whole, then 3,500 is far more than adequate for an initial sample from which to draw the entire microcosm from the twenty-seven. We took the conceptual road suggested by the latter. The whole project is a contribution to exploring the possibility of a single European-wide public sphere. There has been wide speculation about whether or not such a thing could be possible.[27] Our aim was to bring it into being, in microcosm, at least for a weekend.

Once the sample was gathered a second difficulty became evident. With twenty-three official languages, how could they communicate with each other? They did so the same way elite deliberators communicate in the Parliament Building, with simultaneous interpretation and the technology of headphones. But unlike the elite deliberators, a large portion of whom speak a common language such as English or French, the ordinary citizens typically needed simultaneous interpretation in their own languages. Of the twenty-three official languages we used twenty-one because the Irish and Maltese respondents, while given the opportunity to use Gaelic or Maltese, preferred English.

All twenty-seven EU member states were represented in about the proportions of their shares of the EU population and also in about the proportions of their representation in the European Parliament. The participants were somewhat more educated than the nonparticipants but attitudinally the differences were small. There were fifty-nine policy questions and across all of them the average difference between participants and nonparticipants was only about 4% of what it could possibly have been. And on crucial questions such as enlargement they were neither more nor less in favor of admitting Turkey or of enlargement in general.[28]

The language issue helps dramatize the sense in which this deliberative microcosm was even more counterfactual than those gathered for other Deliberative Polls. Even if ordinary citizens, in their actual lives, seriously discussed European issues, they would do so only with their fellow countrymen. The plenary sessions had simultaneous interpretation in all twenty-one languages. There were small groups with simultaneous interpretation among Greeks, French, and Spanish participants, or among Poles, English, and Romanians or with Bulgarians and Germans all talking to each other face-to-face in their native languages but about shared EU concerns.

The deliberations focused on two broad areas—social policy, particularly pensions and retirement, and the EU's role in the world, particularly the potential enlargement of the EU as one of the main ways it has influenced its neighborhood.

In social policy, the participants grew more willing to make sacrifices to secure their pensions. They came to realize that the current "pay as you go" government supported pension schemes faced demographic challenges from the aging population. Fewer and fewer workers will be available to support each retiree. Between now and 2050, the *Tomorrow's Europe* briefing document noted that the number of workers for each retiree is projected to drop from four to two throughout the EU.[29] The percentage of deliberators agreeing that "keeping the retirement rules the way they are will bankrupt the retirement system" increased from 50% to 59%. But deliberators did not see privatizing the government pensions with individual accounts as the solution. The percentage that supported moving more in that direction went down sixteen points from 43% to 27%. Instead, their focus turned to increasing the retirement age and working longer in order to keep the current "pay as you go" systems. Support for "raising the retirement age" rose from 26% to 40%, and support for "making it attractive to work longer before retiring" rose from 57% to 70%.

Working until a later age is a considerable sacrifice for most people who look forward to their retirements. In fact, while there is a strong economic argument for raising the retirement age in most advanced countries, it has been resisted on political grounds.[30] The fact that such a major sacrifice would be endorsed as a way of saving a system which had other valued characteristics, such as the security of a government-run system, is an indication that the participants were really grappling with the pros and cons of difficult choices.

On the second major topic of discussion, support for enlarging the European Union diminished. The percentage agreeing that "additional countries that meet all the political and economic conditions for membership should be admitted to the EU" decreased from 65% to 60%. While support for admitting Turkey, if it met all the conditions of membership, went from 55% to 45%, support for admitting Ukraine fell by even more, from 69% to 55%. By the end of the deliberations, the Turkey issue was almost exactly balanced between support and opposition, 45% were in favor, 46% opposed with 9% neither in favor nor opposed.

While support for enlargement decreased, there was not a similar change in attitude toward the idea of admitting a Muslim country. The percentage agreeing that "adding a Muslim country to the EU would make the EU too diverse" scarcely budged (43% before, 41% after). The same was true of the percentage agreeing that "adding a Muslim country to the EU would improve the EU's relations with the Muslim world" (49% before, 47% after). However, the respondents did show an increased concern about the practicalities of EU policymaking. Those agreeing that "adding more countries to the EU would make it more difficult for the EU to make decisions" rose from 52% before deliberation to 62% after, while those agreeing that the EU is "adding too many countries too fast" rose from 46% before to 53% after.

Throughout the deliberations, there were dramatic differences between new and old member states, between the twelve countries, mostly from Eastern Europe, that have joined since 2004 (Czech Republic, Estonia, Cyprus, Latvia, Lithuania, Hungary, Malta, Poland, Slovakia, Slovenia, Romania, and Bulgaria) and the fifteen countries that were members previously (France, Germany, Italy, Belgium, The Netherlands, Luxembourg, Denmark, Ireland, United Kingdom, Greece, Spain, Portugal, Austria, Finland, and Sweden). On the pension issue, the old and new state participants moved in the same direction, but those from the new member states moved more. For example, the new member state participants started out with majority support (52%) for privatizing pensions but this dropped twenty points after deliberation to only 32%. The old member state participants started out more skeptical (39% supporting this change) but moved fourteen points down to 25% after deliberation. Generally, the participants from the new member states, who were one-third of the sample, accounted for a disproportionate share of the change. On almost every issue they moved much more sharply, often ending up, as in this case, closer to the positions of the old member participants.

On the enlargement issue, the new member state participants typically started out far more favorably disposed to enlargement. But these opinions appeared to be soft and moved far more dramatically against enlargement than did those from the old member states. On the general enlargement question, the participants from new member states went from 78% supporting admission to 63%, a drop of fifteen points while the old member state participants changed hardly at all (from 60.6% to 58.5%). On the question of admitting Turkey, the participants from new member states went from 57% to 42%, a drop of fifteen points, while the participants from the old member states dropped only from 54% to 47%. On Ukraine, the decline (and the contrast) was even more dramatic. The participants from new member states who supported admission went from 78% to 50% a dramatic decline of twenty-eight points. By contrast the participants from the old member states declined in support only from 66% to 58%.

On whether adding a Muslim country would improve the EU's relations with the Muslim world, there was no change for either new or old member states, with the participants from the old member states somewhat more favorable to that view. But on the issue of whether "adding a Muslim country to the EU would make the EU too diverse" there was a dramatic *drop* in the percentage agreeing, precisely among the new member participants, that is, the group that turned against admission of Turkey. The percentage of new member participants who agreed that a Muslim country would make the EU too diverse went down from 52% to 32% among the new member participants—a drop of twenty points. This group became more open in principle to the diversity of a Muslim member country while also lessening their support for the admission of Turkey. By contrast, among the old member state participants, the percentage believing a Muslim member would make the EU too diverse went modestly in the opposite direction, increasing from 40% to 46%.[31]

Multiple regressions revealed some of the levers of change. For example, those who came to believe that adding a Muslim country would improve the EU's relations with the Muslim world increased their support for admitting Turkey. Respondents from the new member states who were most concerned with personal economic security increased their opposition to enlargement, suggesting that the costs of enlargement and its effects on EU aid were a primary factor. The notion that adding more countries would make it too difficult for the EU to make decisions was an important factor among the participants from the old member states.[32]

Based on their answers to nine questions gauging factual knowledge, the participants learned a great deal. Those from newer and older member states learned about equally, although those from older member states started (and thus finished) at a slightly higher level. Those from new member states answered an average of 37% of the knowledge questions correctly before deliberating and 53% of them correctly after deliberating, a gain of 16%. The participants from the old member states answered an average of 40% of the knowledge questions correctly before deliberating and 56% of them correctly after deliberating, an identical gain of 16%. The knowledge question topics included the EU budget (a gain of 22%), how members of the Parliament are elected (a gain of 23%), the role of the EU in unemployment benefits (a gain of 17%), and how EU foreign aid compares with US foreign aid (a gain of 22%).[33]

We also examined the small group processes in the European-wide project. As in other projects, we grouped the policy attitudes into indices—support for EU membership of their own country, attitudes toward privatization, how to pay for pensions, attitudes toward migration/immigration/free trade, use of the military, enlargement for Turkey, general enlargement issue, levels of EU decision-making, support for a veto in EU decision-making. Using these twelve indices we were able to look at the same two key indicators of quality in deliberation that we discussed earlier—avoidance of polarization and avoidance of domination by the more privileged.

For polarization recall that the issue is whether or not Sunstein's hypothesis will hold that the groups will move out from the midpoint. His argument is that discussion will inevitably lead groups to go to extremes. If they start on one side of the midpoint they will, supposedly, go out farther from the midpoint in that same direction (starting out on the left they will move further to the left; starting out on the right they will move further to the right). In the EU project this did not happen. With twelve issue indices and eighteen small groups, there are 216 small group issue combinations. They moved away from the midpoint only 36% of the time. In this case there was a tendency, not to move to more extreme positions but in fact to move more toward the center, precisely the opposite of Sunstein's supposedly inevitable law.

As for small group domination by the more privileged, the group issue combinations moved in the direction of the initial positions of the males exactly 50% of the time (hence they also moved away from the initial positions of the males 50% of the time) and they moved in the direction of the initial positions of the more educated 60% of the time. Such a small effect in the direction of the more educated might reflect the fact that the more educated started out knowing a bit more about the EU. In any case, such a modest tendency is nothing like that envisioned in arguments about the privileged dominating the discussion, since the movements were away from the initial positions of the more educated 40% of the time.[34]

After deliberation, participants came to see themselves more as Europeans, rather than just citizens of their own countries. Overall, the percentage viewing themselves as Europeans increased from 77% to 85%, with an especially big increase from the new member states (increasing from 69% to 87%). But this move toward self-identification at the European level did not accompany any increased sense that decisions needed to be made at the European level. In one policy area after another, taxation, social policy, foreign policy, defense, only a minority (ranging from a high of 40% to a low of 25%) ended up supporting EU-level decision-making based on a large majority rather than unanimous agreement or decisions relegated primarily to the nation-state level. Identification with Europe did not produce increased support for European-level decision-making binding on the individual member states. An increased identification as Europeans did not mean any increased support for something like a United States of Europe.

Tomorrow's Europe showed that it was possible to call into being a European-wide public sphere and get a voice of the public—a unitary shared public—across the divisions of nationality and language in the twenty-seven member states. A representative microcosm in the people's house, the Parliament Building, could deliberate together, become more informed, and come to considered judgments about its priorities for its shared future. It avoided the key distortions of inequality and polarization, and weighed difficult trade-offs on pensions and enlargement. *Tomorrow's Europe* will now be followed by a second European-wide Deliberative Poll in Brussels, *EuroPolis*, in May 2009, just before the European Elections. The first European DP showed that a unitary European public sphere was possible. The second will attempt to pilot its connection to European-wide elections, providing a target audience for the public's considered judgments—the voters themselves.[35]

Implementing democratic ideals

We have considered the application of deliberative microcosms under very different conditions. Some of the cases are drawn from "normal politics" within established democracies such as the United States, Italy, Denmark, Australia, and Britain. Some are in systems without party competition—our local efforts in China. We have also looked at special challenges such as ethnic or national divisions—Northern Ireland and then Bulgaria and the problem of the Roma. We then turned to the difficulties posed by deliberation in virtual space and the transnational challenge of a European public sphere.

In all these cases, the focus has been on implementing two of our core principles simultaneously—political equality and deliberation. But the third, mass participation, has remained an aspiration, not directly much affected by the effort. To the extent we are subject to the trilemma, we will face choices about which core democratic principles to implement for what purposes.

Democratic ideals must be considered in the plural. "More democracy" does not mean any one thing. It could mean increasing the opportunities for mass participation through more referenda, primaries, or other forms of direct consultation. Or it could mean improving the degree to which the votes or preferences of everyone are considered equally through redistricting or equalizing the technology of voting or other such reforms, or it could mean increasing the extent of voter information and deliberation. In other words, it can mean more participation, or more political equality, or more deliberation. But we have found with the trilemma that these values are in conflict when pursued in any really ambitious manner.

To the extent the trilemma applies, the relation between our democratic ideals and practical steps to implement them has been rendered more complicated. The most straightforward and appealing relation between ideal theory and our actual practice is *aspirational*. We have a single coherent vision of where policy should go, a unified picture of the eventual ideal we are trying to achieve, and we move as close as possible to realizing that picture. We attempt to approximate the ideal so far as possible, with changes that clearly move in the direction of further realizing each aspect of it. For this picture to work, it should not be a contested issue—what is closer and what is farther from the ideal. Later we will see that for certain contexts, another strategy might be to *proxy* rather than *approximate* the first-best solution.

Why might it be difficult to approximate the ideal, to just attempt to move as close as possible toward realizing it? One complexity is causal and one has to do with the definition of the ideal itself. The causal issues have been worked out in the economic "theory of the second best," in which if one factor is constrained (it cannot be fully realized) then it may be less than optimal to try to achieve the maximum value of the other factors. At first it may seem counterintuitive that if we cannot maximize A, we should not still try and maximize B and C. But it may be that when A is less than its full value getting the full dose of B and C leads to an inferior result. Sometimes for example, if one is trying to make the economy more competitive, increasing competition in some industries may not be optimal if other industries are constrained not to be competitive.[36] But note that this is a causal issue. It has to do with what will best achieve the best result on an underlying dimension, which is ultimately that of utility. All other issues are instrumental ones. And there is no dispute that maximizing utility is the goal even within the ordinal intrapersonal framework of modern welfare economics.[37]

The issue of how "second-best" solutions relate to "ideal theory" was popularized by John Rawls's theory of justice. He posited his famous general and special conceptions of justice as unitary ideals to be approached, step by step, assuming the favorable conditions of only moderate scarcity and strict compliance. If conditions were so dire that people would unavoidably starve (extreme scarcity) or there was a legacy of injustice and of people not complying with the principles he proposed, then there was no presumption that his principles were the solution, But within a reasonably favorable range of conditions one needed to apply the proposed principles as far as possible.

In the more limited realm of democratic theory, the burden of our argument is that the fundamental principles of democracy do not add up to such a single, coherent ideal to be approached, step by step. Rather than a unitary ideal we are in a situation that might more plausibly be termed "ideals without an ideal." Each basic component, if emphasized substantially further, would take public policy in a different direction. Achieving political equality and participation leads to a thin, plebiscitary democracy in which deliberation is undermined. Achieving political equality and deliberation leaves out mass participation. Achieving deliberation and participation can be achieved for those unequally motivated and interested, but violates political equality. With the choices posed by the trilemma, there is not a coherent direction of movement for realizing all three principles to a high degree at the same time. We can evaluate the trade-offs in particular hard choices, perhaps coming to the conclusion that a reform is warranted, on balance, but it will remain contested whether or not that moves us closer or farther away from an ideal.

Concluding reflections: Democracy, justice, and other trilemmas

Does the pattern of conflict we have encountered with democracy mean that democratic theory is especially unsettled? Is it contested in a way that is distinctly different from other areas of political theory such as the theory of justice? In fact, I have argued that the same situation applies to distributive justice.[38] A parallel trilemma applies, for example, to the problem of equal opportunity, a key component of any theory of distributive justice. No adequate theory of justice can do without principles that specify how people are assigned to positions in the social structure: what opportunities do they have?[39]

Sometimes distribution is conceived just in terms of the overall shape of the distribution—how equal or unequal, how large the total or average share of goods. How people get and maintain positions in that structure is also crucial to the life chances of individuals. For example, think of two societies with identical structures of distribution, say of income. They have the same minimum, the same total, the same average level. But one society has a subordinate racial group because it practices some form of Apartheid, the other society has great social mobility between positions in the structure. Viewed just as abstract structures of distribution the two societies are identical. But viewed in terms of the life chances of individuals, their life histories over time moving through the structures, some have blighted prospects from the start and some are privileged. Without a theory of how people ought to get and maintain positions within the structure, a theory of equal opportunity, those two societies would be evaluated similarly in terms of distributive justice. Obviously, an account is needed to distinguish these cases for any adequate theory of justice.

Elsewhere I have argued that the equal opportunity problem is subject to a trilemma between three fundamental principles: merit, equal life chances, and the autonomy of the family. Merit is the idea that competence that is job-relevant for positions should be evaluated in an impartial way. Equality of life chances is the idea that we should not be able to predict where people should end up in the distribution based on the positions they were born into. I should not be able to predict the life chances of newborn infants based on the class background of their parents. Any society in which I could do so would be suffering from an identifiable form of injustice. Lastly, the autonomy of the family is roughly, the idea that parents should be free to be able to benefit their children. Liberty within the family sets up a conflict with equality, since parents will use their liberty to help their children prepare.

Given background conditions of inequality, of the sort that apply to every modern industrial society, the difficulty is that family autonomy becomes a zone of freedom that allows inequalities in the adult society to replicate themselves. Parents act to benefit their children by giving them every preparation possible for the coming meritocratic competition. Hence, inequalities in the adult generation tend to replicate themselves with unequal life chances. As with our democratic theory trilemma, we can get any two of the three principles, but under the assumption that there are background conditions of inequality, all three are not achievable. The upshot is that trying to improve each of these principles, or any two at the same time, will take public policy in a quite different direction. We are left with ideals without an ideal—while we can trade off conflicting principles for each marginal choice, there is no clear overall direction for us to move toward the realization of a single, coherent, and unified ideal.

Why might there be this parallel between one trilemma and another, between democratic theory and the theory of justice? It is plausible to think of the core of liberal democratic theory as a continuing dialogue about the competing roles of liberty and equality. The equality component includes a series of "process equalities" requiring equal consideration of everyone's relevant claims or interests, whether these are in meritocratic selection in the employment market, or in protection of rights in the legal system or protection of fundamental interests in the health care system or, as we saw in detail, in the consideration of one's views or votes in the political system. In all of these cases, the equality claim to equal consideration comes up against the fact that people employ their liberty to create differences, differences in the characteristics that people bring to the process of equal consideration and in their abilities to make use of the process.[40]

Consider the legal system. The core liberal democratic "process equality" would specify equality before the law. But people also have freedom to choose and employ their own legal representation. Background inequalities may lead to widely disparate treatment based on the quality of legal representation one can afford. While legal aid and pro bono work can help reduce the disparities, by leveling up somewhat at the bottom, they are virtually inevitable on a systematic basis. The well-off will always be able to afford substantially more under realistic conditions. Hence, there is a plausible trilemma between three claims: formal equality before the law, the freedom of individuals to choose and finance their own legal representation, and equality of outcomes for otherwise similar cases. The legal trilemma is closely parallel to the one applying to equal opportunity. In each case, there is a liberty claim, the claim about choosing legal representation or the claim about the freedom of families to benefit their children and a twofold equality claim—a formal claim about equal consideration and a substantive claim about the likelihood of equal outcomes for relevantly similar cases.

In our democratic theory case, the formal claim is political equality requiring equal consideration of one's views or considered judgments. The liberty claims concern the liberty to form opinions (deliberation) and the liberty to participate. As we saw earlier, under realistic conditions we can fully achieve only two out of three. We have conflicting ideals but no single ideal that drives us in an unambiguous direction for reform—if the goal is to fulfill all three simultaneously.

Of course, we can envision what a unified ideal with all three might be like. We can even imagine a plausible scenario with a transformational effort like Deliberation Day, which might simultaneously realize all three to a significant degree for at least a limited period of time—a day which precedes the election. But the splintered directionality of where we go from here marks the problem characteristic of *"ideals without an ideal."*[41] Unless we can summon the political will to make progress on all three simultaneously, it is unclear whether a given change moves us closer or farther away—precisely because, according to the trilemma, improvements in some leave us with deficits in others (at least when pushed to any substantial degree).

But there is another possible role for achieving a second-best, rather than ideal, solution. Instead of *approximating* an ideal, a second-best solution can *proxy* it. Realizing the two key principles of deliberative democracy—deliberation and political equality—for a representative microcosm offers a picture of what everyone *would* think under good conditions. In theory if everyone deliberated, the conclusions would not be much different. So the microcosm offers a proxy for the much more ambitious scenario of what would happen if everyone discussed the issues and weighed competing arguments under similarly favorable conditions.

Given that it is much more feasible to get high-quality deliberation in a manageably small, representative microcosm than it would be for the whole society, we can work out the considered judgments of the people under good conditions and insert those conclusions (and the reasons offered for them) into the policy dialogue and into the policy process. The proxy can usefully stand in for the ideal, particularly when the ideal may be far out of reach.

The ultimate pluralism of principles embodied by "ideals without an ideal"[42] provides an additional rationale for deliberative public consultation. Suppose the situation were different. Suppose we were not subject to these trilemmas. Suppose that there were an indisputable and unified ideal solution to the problems of democracy and justice, approachable in each case, step by step, without any fundamental indeterminacies applying to the direction of change. In other words, suppose there were a clear path marked out, not a splintered one. We might well be further justified in thinking that the processes of democratic choice could be put on autopilot. There would be no need for continuing public consultation because the path was clear and the instrumental questions about how best to get there could be left to experts and administrators.

However, when fundamental trade-offs of principle apply to both democratic improvements and the policy issues that they would concern, it makes sense to seek informed public input. Consulting the public's considered judgments is a bit like seeking its collective informed consent. It is the people who must bear the burdens and pay the costs and it is the people who would, hopefully, experience the benefits. When the "consent of the governed" is achieved via "top of the head" opinion, then the people would not know or much understand what they were consenting to. When panels for human subjects ask for consent before experiments, or when doctors ask for consent to medical procedures, they normally seek, whenever possible, the "informed consent" of those who would have to live or die with the risks. To the extent this can practically be sought on a collective basis, why not do the same? The benefits and burdens distributed may be just as profound.

In this book we have posited various democratic ideals—political equality, deliberation, mass participation, non-tyranny. We have also reviewed practical efforts to implement some of these ideals. In the case of deliberative democracy, our focus has been the effort to convene statistically representative microcosms of the people gathered under good conditions for deliberation. But we have also discussed other efforts to implement some of these democratic principles, ranging from ancient Athens to the American founding, where deliberation was a key ideal, to attempts by the Progressives and modern reformers where the focus shifted to participation and political equality with the spread of the mass primary and the referendum.

While democratic theory is a lively subject there is not a single dominant theory, but rather a competition among very different visions. To try and get a handle on what the different visions have in common and where they differ, we organized our discussion around their connections to core principles. The result is a rudimentary *grammar of democracy*. Each theory can most plausibly be interpreted as a commitment primarily to two of the four principles—Competitive Democracy (with its commitment to political equality in elections and non-tyranny), Participatory Democracy (with its commitment to mass participation and political equality), Elite Deliberation (with its commitment to deliberation and non-tyranny), and Deliberative Democracy (with its commitment to the combination of political equality and deliberation).

The last of these gives us the voice of the people under conditions where it would be worth listening to. If "governments derive their just powers from the consent of the governed," as Americans declared in 1776, then surely more thoughtful and meaningful consent of the governed has a place in the continuing process of doing the public's business. Reviving the Athenian ideal, with the best modern technology available, provides a practical method for bringing deliberative democracy to life.

APPENDIX

Why We Need Only Four Democratic Theories

In Chapter 2 we considered four principles that combine into four recognizable normative theories of democracy pictured below: Competitive Democracy (as outlined by Schumpeter and recently championed by Posner, Shapiro and others), Elite Deliberation (as exemplified by Madison and Mill), Participatory Democracy (as championed by the Progressives and by such modern theorists as Carole Pateman), and Deliberative Democracy. In each case, we defined the ideal type of a given position by its commitment to two of the four principles. We were agnostic about whether or not the position would accept or reject the other principles. Sometimes a theorist is silent about a principle that is not his or her focus. We even stretched to improve a position in one case by attributing political equality to the Competitive Democracy position even though its most famous proponent was notoriously not committed to it. Our rationale was that we wanted the best version of each position. A position relying on political competition that did not count votes equally would seem subject to obvious objections about the defective form of competition that was being engaged in. So we made Schumpeter's position, if not Schumpeter himself, an advocate of political equality. Of course, any effort of this kind is a bit schematic but hopefully it provides a kind of checklist of democratic possibilities and in that way helps focus discussion.

Chart III. Four democratic theories (from Chapter 3)

	Competitive democracy	Elite deliberation	Participatory democracy	Deliberative democracy
Political equality	+	?	+	+
Participation	?	?	+	?
Deliberation	?	+	?	+
Non-tyranny	+	+	?	?

If these are the four key principles, one might ask why there are just four possibilities and not sixteen. As a matter of logic there are sixteen possible combinations as detailed in Chart VII below.

Chart VII. Sixteen possible positions

	1	2	3	4	5	6	7	8	9	10	11	12	13	14	15	16
Participation	+	+	−	+	−	−	+	−	+	−	−	+	−	−	+	+
Political equality	+	+	−	−	+	−	−	−	−	+	+	+	+	−	+	−
Deliberation	+	−	+	+	−	−	−	−	−	+	+	+	−	+	−	+
Non-tyranny	+	−	+	−	+	−	−	+	+	−	+	−	−	−	+	+

Four of these are non-agnostic versions of our proposed four. They embrace the two principles that define the position in my view and instead of being ambiguous about the other two principles (symbolized by the question marks in the first chart) they reject the other two. From that perspective Position 2 is our Participatory Democracy (defined by the combination of participation and political equality), Position 3 is our Elite Deliberation (defined by the combination of deliberation and avoiding tyranny of the majority), Position 5 is our Competitive Democracy (defined by the combination of political equality and avoiding tyranny of the majority), and Position 10 is our Deliberative Democracy (defined by the combination of deliberation and political equality).

What about the remaining twelve? My explanation is that they are: (a) ruled out by the trilemma, (b) most usefully considered as variants of one of our four theories, or (c) subject to obvious objections, at least when proposed as normative theories of democracy.

Let us consider them one by one. First, Position 1 is utopian. It requires achieving all four of our principles ignoring the difficult trade-offs they pose. So this position would be nice if one could achieve it, but like any position advocating all good things at the same time, it does not make a useful contribution. Considering the trilemma, which I will assume at this point in our discussion, it involves simultaneous commitment to all three of the principles that concern institutional design (political equality, deliberation, and participation) and ignores the problem that, under realistic conditions, commitment to any two will undermine achieving the third.

We have dealt with Position 3 already. It is our Elite Deliberation theory. Position 4 requires participation and deliberation but rejects political equality and non-tyranny. There are two objections to this position as a normative theory of democracy: one based on rejecting political equality and the other based on rejecting non-tyranny. Mass participation without political equality is possible. It is indeed one of the options in our trilemma. However, it does not, by definition, give voice to the deliberative views of "we the people." It gives a distorted picture of informed opinion. We saw that it might in fact be useful as a strategy for civic education probably among the more privileged and motivated. However, as a contribution to Deliberative Democracy, it is defective because it includes no requirement that the people be equally represented. Also by rejecting the principle of non-tyranny it explicitly rules out any basis for objecting if and when the people do bad things.

Position 5 is our Competitive Democracy position. It is focused on competitive elections and then protecting against tyranny of the majority through rights and constitutional guarantees.

Position 6 is obviously inadequate as a normative theory of democracy since it rejects all four of our principles.

Position 7 embraces participation but rejects political equality, deliberation, and non-tyranny. This position is inadequate, provided we are correct that the other principles have merit. As we have seen, it is possible to combine participation with other principles, so why stop short? We can view this as a defective version of the Participatory Democracy position. It advocates mass participation but without equal counting (and without valuing improvements in the other principles).

Similarly Position 8 is committed to only one of our principles, non-tyranny, but explicitly rejects political equality, deliberation, and participation. Since deliberation can be combined with other principles, why stop at one? The argument here is like that for Position 7. This position is probably most plausibly viewed as a defective version of Competitive Democracy. It wants to protect against the excesses of democracy but is not even committed to equal counting. In fact, this is reminiscent of the actual Schumpeterian position.

Position 9 embraces participation and non-tyranny but rejects political equality and deliberation. As we have seen, participation without political equality does not equally count people's preferences and thus leads to distortions opening it to obvious objections. This position is probably best viewed as a defective version of Participatory Democracy.

Position 10 offers the core commitments of our Deliberative Democracy position, combining political equality and deliberation. It thus counts people's views equally under conditions where they can think about the judgments that are being counted.

Position 11 offers those same core commitments but also embraces non-tyranny as a requirement. If the political psychology posited by Madison and Mill is correct, that people will likely embrace the public interest when they deliberate and "cool reason" is unlikely to commit tyranny of the majority (see our discussion of *Federalist* No. 10), then this extension of the agnostic version of Deliberative Democracy (agnostic about non-tyranny) is entirely realizable. However, we defined the core of Deliberative Democracy as the combination of political equality and deliberation and left it an empirical question whether deliberation would in fact work this way. Position 11 is more ambitious than Position 10 and both are variants of Deliberative Democracy (which is defined as explicitly affirming political equality and deliberation but agnostic about participation and non-tyranny).

Position 12 falls under the same objection as Position 1. It posits all three of the principles concerned with democratic design (political equality, participation, and deliberation). It only differs from Position 1 in failing to add non-tyranny as well. But if we are correct in the trilemma, this position is less than useful as a democratic theory because it requires achieving all good things at the same time.

Position 13 is committed just to political equality but rejects participation, deliberation, and non-tyranny. As we have seen, political equality can be combined with other principles, so why stop at only one and reject the other three? This position could be seen as a defective version of Competitive Democracy or even Deliberative Democracy.

Position 14 is committed just to deliberation but rejects political equality, participation, and non-tyranny. As we have seen, political deliberation can be combined with other principles, so why stop at only one and reject the other three? This position might be seen as a defective version of Deliberative Democracy, defective because it lacks any concern for political equality.

Position 15 is committed to participation, political equality, and non-tyranny. It is best seen as a variant of Competitive Democracy but one that adds a concern for mass participation. As we saw earlier, some of the advocates of Competitive Democracy, like Schumpeter and Posner, are worried about the dangers of mass participation. But this variant of Competitive Democracy is a reasonable alternative for anyone concerned with competitive elections.

Position 16 is committed to participation, deliberation, and non-tyranny but rejects political equality. As we have seen, participation without political equality leads to distorted counting of votes. And deliberation without political equality leads to a distorted, if considered, public voice. The requirement of non-tyranny, probably achievable to some degree via rights and judicial protections, is an attractive protection. But as a normative theory of democracy this position seems subject to clear objections.

Notes

Chapter 1

1. For a now classic account of how new technologies can be deployed to mobilize demonstrations see Howard Reingold (2002), *Smart Mobs: The Next Social Revolution*, New York: Basic Books.
2. See the argument of Lawrence R. Jacobs and Robert Y. Shapiro (2000), *Politicians Don't Pander: Political Manipulation and the Loss of Democratic Responsiveness*, Chicago: University of Chicago Press.
3. This position, famously advocated by Joseph A. Schumpeter (1942), *Capitalism, Socialism and Democracy*, New York: Harper & Row, has recently undergone a resurgence. See especially Richard A. Posner (2003), *Law, Pragmatism and Democracy*, Cambridge, MA: Harvard University Press, and Ian Shapiro (2002), *The Moral Foundations of Politics*, New Haven, CT: Yale University Press.
4. This term was famously coined by Anthony Downs (1957), *An Economic Theory of Democracy*, New York: Harper & Row. For some important subtleties see Russell Hardin (2002), "The Street Level Epistemology of Democratic Participation" in *Journal of Political Philosophy*, 10/2, pp. 212–29. For the implications of low information levels among the mass public see Michael delli Carpini and Scott Keeter (1996), *What Americans Know About Politics and Why It Matters*, New Haven, CT: Yale University Press, and Scott Althaus (2003), *Collective Preferences in Democratic Politics: Opinion Surveys and the Will of the People*. New York: Cambridge University Press.
5. See George F. Bishop (2005), *The Illusion of Public Opinion: Fact and Artifact in American Public Opinion*, Lanham, MD: Rowman & Littlefield, pp. 27–30.
6. For comparisons of exposure to disagreement interpersonally and through the media see Diana C. Mutz and Paul S. Martin (2001), "Facilitating Communication across Lines of Political Difference: The Role of Mass Media" in *American Political Science Review*, 95/1 (March).
7. In *Hearing the Other Side*, Mutz argues that deliberation may suppress further political participation but her measure of deliberation is mere exposure, under any conditions, to someone with a different point of view. Without efforts to create a safe public space or civil discourse, exposure to strong partisan differences may well depress participation. See Diana C. Mutz (2002), *Hearing the Other Side: Deliberative Versus*

Participatory Democracy, Cambridge: Cambridge University Press. One could argue that bare exposure is not deliberation and that real deliberation may enhance future participation, as we find below.

8. John Stuart Mill (1869), *On Liberty*, London: Longman. For an account of how Mill's notion of "individuality" amounts to a theory of "autonomy" see John Gray (1983), *Mill On Liberty: A Defence*, London: Routledge. For an argument that we are exercising freedom of association to cluster with the like-minded see Bill Bishop (2008), *The Big Sort: Why the Clustering of Like-Minded America is Tearing us Apart*, New York: Houghton Mifflin.

9. The issue has proved controversial. For competing views see the symposium in the *Boston Review*: "Is the Internet Bad for Democracy?" ⟨http://www.bostonreview.net/BR26.3/contents.html⟩. For experimental confirmation of partisan selectivity, particularly with respect to Fox News even for nonpolitical issues, see Shanto Iyengar and Kyu S. Hahn "Red Media, Blue Media: Evidence of Ideological Selectivity in Media Use" in *Journal of Communication* (forthcoming). Available at ⟨http://pcl. stanford.edu/research/2008/iyengar-redmedia.pdf⟩.

10. For the advertising campaign see Fred Pearce (2008), "Time to Bury the 'Clean Coal' Myth" in *The Guardian*, October 30, ⟨http://www.guardian. co.uk/environment/2008/oct/30/fossilfuels-carbonemissions⟩. We return to this issue in Chapter 5 in the context of a series of Deliberative Polls about energy choices.

11. See Shanto Iyengar and Donald Kinder (1987), *News That Matters*, Chicago: University of Chicago Press, and also John Zaller and Stanley Feldman (1992), "A Simple Theory of the Survey Response" in *American Journal of Political Science*, 36, pp. 579–616.

12. See Kathleen Hall Jamieson (1993), *Dirty Politics: Deception, Distraction and Democracy*, New York: Oxford University Press, for the best account of manipulation in a campaign context.

13. In 2008, presidential candidate John Edwards was supported in advertising by a 527 run by a key aide. See ⟨http://www.politico.com/blogs/ bensmith/1207/A_527_twofer.html⟩. In the general election, pro McCain ads were run by 527s in part by his own campaign chairmen. See, for example, Mark Silva "McCain Advisors on '527' Attacking Obama", ⟨http://www.swamppolitics.com/news/politics/blog/2008/05/mccain_ advisers_on_527_attacki.html⟩.

14. ⟨http://campaignsilo.firedoglake.com/2008/11/04/dirty-tricks-text-messages-tell-obama-voters-to-vote-wednesday/⟩

15. See ⟨http://www.politico.com/news/stories/0108/8109.html⟩, "Email Smear Taxes Obama Campaign," accessed January 26, 2008.

16. Manipulation is sometimes used more broadly but I am focusing here on its objectionable forms.

17. The term "selective incentives" comes from the classic discussion by Mancur Olson (1965), *The Logic of Collective Action*, Cambridge, MA: Harvard University Press.

18. We have experimented with civic education modeled on the Deliberative Poll in a fully controlled experiment in a school setting with some significant results. See Robert C. Luskin, James S. Fishkin, Neil Malhotra, and Alice Siu (2007), "Deliberation in the Schools: A Way of Enhancing Civic Engagement?" Paper presented at the biennial General Conference of the European Consortium for Political Research, Pisa, Italy, September 6–9. Available at ⟨http://cdd.stanford.edu/research/papers/2007/civic-education.pdf⟩.

19. Russell Hardin (2003), "The Street Level Eipistemology of Political Participation" in James S. Fishkin and Peter Laslett, eds., *Debating Deliberative Democracy: Philosophy, Politics and Society*, vol. 7, Oxford: Basil Blackwell.

20. See, for example, Arthur R. Lupia (1994), "Shortcuts Versus Encyclopedias: Information and Voting Behavior in California Insurance Election Reforms" in *American Political Science Review*, 88/1 (March), pp. 63–76. The key information cues in Lupia's argument, that Ralph Nader or the insurance industry had endorsed particular referendum propositions, were known by only about half the respondents. See table B-1. Another influential statement of the same general position can be found in Samuel Popkin (1991), *The Reasoning Voter: Communication and Persuasion in Presidential Campaigns*, Chicago: University of Chicago Press.

21. For the Australian referendum case see Robert C. Luskin, James S. Fishkin, Ian McAllister, John Higley, and Pamela Ryan (2000), "Deliberation and Referendum Voting." Paper presented at the meetings of the American Political Science Association, Washington, DC. Available at ⟨http://cdd.stanford.edu/research/papers/2005/referendum-voting.pdf⟩. For the British case see Robert C. Luskin, James S. Fishkin, Roger Jowell, and Alison Park (1999), "Learning and Voting in Britain: Insights from the Deliberative Poll." Paper presented at the meetings of the American Political Science Association Atlanta, GA. Available at ⟨http://cdd.stanford.edu/research/papers/2000/general_election_paper.pdf⟩.

22. Robert A. Dahl (1956), *A Preface to Democratic Theory*, Chicago: University of Chicago Press. See Chapter 5.

23. For an argument that the idea of issue publics actually solves "the problem of democratic accountability" see Vincent L. Hutchings (2003), *Public Opinion and Democratic Accountability: How Citizens Learn about Politics*, Princeton, NJ: Princeton University Press. The book begins with a dramatic case that weighs against the argument—Eugene McCarthy surprising Lyndon Johnson in the New Hampshire primary with the issue public concerned about the Vietnam war being mobilized—but believing wrongly that McCarthy wanted to escalate. Issue publics are not always more informed and they are certainly not representative.

24. Deliberative Polling is a trademark of James S. Fishkin. Any fees from the trademark are used to support research at the Center for Deliberative Democracy at Stanford.

25. This project was led by Professor John Panaretos of the Athens University of Economics and Business with the collaboration of Evdokia Xekalaki,

Robert C. Luskin, and myself. We are grateful to George Papandreou for his vision and support.

26. George A. Papandreou (2006), "Picking candidates by the numbers" in *International Herald Tribune*, June 7. Available at ⟨http://cdd.stanford.edu/press/2006/iht-picking.pdf⟩.

27. John Lloyd (2006), "The Periclean Primary" in *La Repubblica*, October 6 (translation made available by the author). Available at ⟨http://cdd.stanford.edu/press/2006/mar-pericle-eng.pdf⟩.

28. See James S. Fishkin, Robert C. Luskin, John Panaretos, Alice Siu, and Evdokia Xekalaki (2008), "Returning Deliberative Democracy to Athens: Deliberative Polling for Candidate Selection." Paper presented at the annual meeting of the American Political Science Association, August. Available at ⟨http://cdd.stanford.edu⟩.

29. Candidate choice in primaries is often driven by reactions to candidate personality traits. However, two American cases show that deliberation can make policy more consequential in candidate choice. See Shanto Iyengar, Robert C. Luskin, and James S. Fishkin, "Deliberative Preferences in the Presidential Nomination Campaign: Evidence from an Online Deliberative Poll." Working Paper under submission. Previously presented at the annual meeting of the American Political Science Association, 2005. Available at ⟨http://cdd.stanford.edu/research/papers/2005/presidential-nomination.pdf⟩, and Robert C. Luskin, Kyu S. Hahn, James S. Fishkin, and Shanto Iyengar (2006), "The Deliberative Voter." Working Paper, Center for Deliberative Democracy. Available at ⟨http://cdd.stanford.edu/research/papers/2006/deliberative-voter.pdf⟩. The first concerns a Deliberative Poll during the primary season and the second a DP during the general election.

30. "Papandreou hails procedure for naming PASOK candidate" Athens News Agency (June 6, 2006). Available at ⟨http://www.hri.org/news/greek/ana/2006/06-06-05.ana.html⟩.

31. For a detailed account of the working and structure of these Athenian institutions see Mogens Herman Hansen (1991), *The Athenian Democracy in the Age of Demosthenes*, Oxford: Blackwell, and Josiah Ober (1991), *Mass and Elite in Democratic Athens*, Princeton, NJ: Princeton University Press.

32. See Robert A. Dahl (1989), *Democracy and Its Critics*, New Haven and London: Yale University Press, pp. 16–19 for a discussion of size in Athenian democracy. James Madison in *Federalist* No. 10 simply assumed that a "pure" or direct democracy would have to be small enough for everyone to administer it in person. James Madison, Alexander Hamilton, and John Jay (1987), *The Federalist Papers*, New York: Penguin, p. 126.

33. See Hansen, p. 53 for the estimate that there were 60,000 adult male citizens in fifth-century Athens.

34. See Hansen, p. 131. For the population trend from the fifth century down to perhaps 30,000 in the fourth century see Josiah Ober (2008), *Democracy and Knowledge: Learning and Innovation in Classical Athens*, Princeton, NJ: Princeton University Press, p. 74, figure 2.5.

35. See I.F. Stone (1989), *The Trial of Socrates*, New York: Anchor Books.
36. For a stimulating overview see Bernard Manin (1996), *The Principles of Representative Government*, Cambridge: Cambridge University Press.
37. The flowering of interest in deliberative democracy is remarkable. For some indications of the breadth of the dialogue see edited volumes such as James Bohman and William Rehg, eds. (1997), *Deliberative Democracy*, Cambridge, MA: MIT Press, Jon Elster, ed. (1998), *Deliberative Democracy*, Cambridge: Cambridge University Press, and James Fishkin and Peter Laslett, eds. *Debating Deliberative Democracy: Philosophy, Politics and Society*, vol. 7.
38. For more on mass democracy and its contrast with deliberative institutions, see James Fishkin (1991), *Democracy and Deliberation: New Directions for Democratic Reform*, New Haven and London: Yale University Press.
39. George Gallup (1938), "Public Opinion in a Democracy," Princeton, NJ: The Stafford Little Lectures.
40. James Madison (1987), *Notes of Debates in the Federal Convention of 1787*. Reported by James Madison with an Introduction by Adrienne Koch, New York: Norton, p. 40.
41. See the section "Deliberation" in Chapter 2 for a more detailed discussion.
42. Jack N. Rakove (1997), "The Mirror of Representation" in *Original Meanings: Politics and Ideas in the Making of the Constitution*, New York: Vintage Books, p. 203.
43. Herbert Storing, ed. (1981), *The Complete Anti-Federalist*, Chicago: University of Chicago Press, vol. II, p. 265.
44. "Rhode Island's Assembly Refuses to Call a Convention and Submits the Constitution Directly to the People" in Bernard Bailyn, ed. (1993), *The Debate on the Constitution* Part II, New York: The Library of America, p. 271.
45. "The Freemen of Providence Submit Eight Reasons for Calling a Convention" in Bailyn, ed., *The Debate*, p. 280.
46. "Is this the Man of the Century?" in *The Guardian*, October 30, 1997, p. 1.
47. See ⟨http://vmajorityrights.com/index.php/weblog/comments/ron_paul_demolishes_other_republicans_in_online_polls/⟩ (accessed January 2, 2007).
48. He received 41% compared to 25% for Huckabee and 14% for John McCain, in Facebook's self-selected poll, ⟨http://www.facebook.com/politics/debate.php?id=7067904614⟩ (accessed January 5, 2008).
49. "Lycurgus" in *Plutarch on Sparta*, New York: Penguin, 1988, p. 38.
50. For a good overview of these activities and the vision behind them see David Mathews (1994), *Politics for People*, Chicago: University of Illinois Press.
51. We return to this question in our section "Deliberation" in Chapter 2.

52. For the latter see Roger Jowell et al. (1993), "The 1992 British General Election: The Failure of the Polls" in *Public Opinion Quarterly*, 57, pp. 238–63.

53. The small numbers defeat statistical evaluation. In addition, these research designs do not permit evaluation of how those agreeing to participate compare to those who do not.

54. George Gallup (1938), "Public Opinion in a Democracy," Princeton, NJ: The Stafford Little Lectures, p. 15.

55. Actual town meetings are imperfect by our criteria for both inclusion and deliberation. For a landmark study focused on one town see Jane J. Mansbridge (1980), *Beyond Adversary Democracy*, New York: Basic Books. For a study analyzing a large number of cases linking size of town with participation see Frank M. Bryan (2004), *Real Democracy: The New England Town Meeting and How It Works*, Chicago: University of Chicago Press.

56. For an overview see James S. Fishkin (1997), *The Voice of the People: Public Opinion and Democracy*, New Haven and London: Yale University Press, expanded paperback edition. See also Robert C. Luskin, James Fishkin, and Roger Jowell (2002), "Considered Opinions: Deliberative Polling in Britain" in *British Journal of Political Science*, 32, pp. 455–87.

57. Rawls's original position is of course the famous idea of choosing first principles for a just society behind a veil of ignorance in which one has no specific knowledge about one's self or one's society that might permit tailoring the principles to one's own advantage. Persons in actual life can imagine what they would choose under these perfected conditions and see the moral relevance of some considerations compared to others. By contrast, Deliberative Polling is not a thought experiment but rather, at its best, a real experiment. However, it is a step in the same direction—of showing what people would think under somewhat perfected conditions. Of course it differs in being an embodiment of democratic ideas rather than moral choice per se. But in both cases there is a normative claim. A key difference is the fact that the participants in the Deliberative Polling (DP) decision procedure do not abstract from their actual lives and preferences. In this respect, the DP decision procedure is more in the spirit of the early Rawls, who offered far more modest and realistic procedures that would go a certain distance toward perfecting judgment. See Rawls (1951), "Outline of a Decision Procedure for Ethics" in *Philosophical Review*, 60/2 (April), pp. 177–97.

58. See Donald Campbell and Julian Stanley (1963), *Experimental and Quasi-Experimental Designs for Research*, Chicago: Rand-McNally.

59. A detailed account of this proposal and how it could practically be implemented can be found in Bruce Ackerman and James S. Fishkin (2004), *Deliberation Day*, New Haven and London: Yale University Press.

60. Bruce Ackerman (1991), *We the People, vol. I: Foundations*, Cambridge, MA: Harvard University Press, and (1998), *We the People, vol. II: Transformations*, Cambridge, MA: Harvard University Press.

Chapter 2

1. J.S. Mill argued that public voting rather than secret ballot would encourage voters to think about their votes. See J.S. Mill (1991), *Considerations on Representative Government*, New York: Prometheus Books, originally published 1862, chapter X. For a contemporary elaboration of this position see Geoffrey Brennan and Philip Pettit (1990), "Unveiling the Vote" in *British Journal of Political Science*, 20/3 (July), pp. 311–33.

2. For an example where one precinct elects a single delegate and another elects twelve see ⟨http://blogs.britannica.com/blog/main/2007/11/the-iowa-caucuses-are-like-the-electoral-college-at-least-for-democrats/⟩ (accessed on January 2, 2008).

3. For reflections on the plasticity of modern "mandates" see Robert A. Dahl, "The Pseudo-democratization of the American Presidency" The Tanner Lectures on Human Values. Available at ⟨http://www.tannerlectures.utah.edu/lectures/documents/dahl89.pdf⟩.

4. See Luskin, Fishkin, and Jowell "Considered Opinions."

5. See, for example, Anne Philips (1995), *The Politics of Presence: The Political Representation of Gender, Ethnicity and Race*, Oxford: Oxford University Press; and Jane Mansbridge (1999), "Should Blacks Represent Blacks and Women Represent Women?" in *Journal of Politics*, pp. 628–57.

6. These considerations add weight to the argument that a deliberative microcosm should be both attitudinally and demographically representative—and demonstrably so. Strangely, most deliberative forums have designs that make it difficult or impossible to evaluate attitudinal representativeness making it impossible to know if they offer a microcosm of the population's perspectives on the issues being discussed. A good example of the blindness to the need for building an evaluation of attitudinal representativeness into the design of deliberative forums can be found in Archon Fung's claim that the Deliberative Poll is equivalent to self-selected forums such as *America Speaks* in representativeness. See Archon Fung (2003), "Recipes for Public Spheres: Eight Institutional Design Choices and Their Consequences" in *Journal of Political Philosophy*, 11/3, pp. 338–67. Fung only evaluates representativeness demographically and says that it is equivalent to supplement self-selected participations with others recruited to fill the same demographic categories without any data about attitudes on the issue. See the discussion of SLOPs below for more of the limitations of this approach.

7. I take the term "audience democracy" from Bernard Manin who uses it to characterize the conditions of the mass public in plebiscitary processes. See Bernard Manin (1997) *Principles of Representative Government*, pp. 218–35.

8. Australia Deliberates: Reconciliation—Where From Here? Final Report Tabled in the Federal Parliament of Australia, September 25, 2001, pp. 47–9. Report available at ⟨http://ida.org.au/UserFiles/File/Australia%20Deliberates_Reconciliation_FINAL%20REPORT.pdf⟩.

9. In other cases, where the topic of deliberation concerns policy toward a given minority group, the issue can be avoided if the group is more numerous. This was the case in the Deliberative Poll we conducted on the condition of the Roma in Bulgaria. The Roma were 10% of the sample. In a population approaching 8 million, the Roma are estimated to comprise up to 800,000 although self-identification in census questions leads to lower numbers. See *Briefing Material: National Deliberative Poll: Policies Toward the Roma in Bulgaria*, p. 5. Available at ⟨http://cdd.stanford.edu/docs/2007/bulgaria-roma-2007.pdf⟩.

10. A phrase Habermas applied to the ideal speech situation and to his conception of deliberation. It is essentially the same as the phrase J.S. Mill applied to the Congress of Opinions. For Habermas see, for example, Jurgen Habermas (1999), "Introduction" in *Ratio Juris*, 12/4, pp. 329–35, especially p. 332 and Habermas (1996), *Between Facts and Norms: Contributions to a Discourse Theory of Law and Democracy*, Cambridge, MA: MIT Press, chapter 7.

11. One could certainly imagine a useful line of experimentation devoted to this question.

12. Our British collaborator Roger Jowell collected these data. For more on the British election project see Robert C. Luskin, James S. Fishkin, Roger Jowell, and Alison Park (1999), "Learning and Voting in Britain: Insights from the Deliberative Poll." Paper presented at the meetings of the American Political Science Association, Atlanta, Ga. Available at ⟨http://cdd.stanford.edu/research/papers/2000/general_election_paper.pdf⟩.

13. See "From Athens to Athens" in Chapter 1. The random sampling was instituted by lottery among those who were willing to put their names on a list.

14. See, for example, L. S. Shapley and M. Shubik (1954), "A Method for Evaluating the Distribution of Power in a Committee System" in *American Political Science Review*, 48, pp. 787–92. For a slightly different variant see John H. Banzhaff III (1965), "Weighted Voting Doesn't Work: A Mathematical Analysis" in *Rutgers Law Review*, 19/2, pp. 317–43.

15. In *Democracy and Deliberation* (New Haven: Yale University Press, 1991) I treated some of the issues that I will treat here under deliberation within political equality itself. While I think one could set this up either way, this strategy helps clarify the trilemma I will explore below.

16. See Sidney Verba, Kay Lehman Schlozman, and Henry Brady (1995), *Voice and Equality: Civic Voluntarism in American Politics*, Cambridge, MA: Harvard University Press, pp. 38–40, who also define political participation in such a way that it excludes media consumption and discussion when it is not aimed, directly or indirectly, at influencing government officials or policies.

17. See my earlier presentation of this trilemma in Bruce Ackerman and James S. Fishkin (2004), *Deliberation Day*, New Haven and London: Yale University Press, pp. 201–4. For a trilemma in a different sphere see James S. Fishkin (1984), *Justice, Equal Opportunity and the Family*, New Haven and London: Yale University Press. For parallels and the general problem

of liberal "process equalities" see the discussion of other trilemmas in the concluding section of Chapter 6 below. For additional discussion of the trilemma of democratic reform, see Anthony McGann (2006), *The Logic of Democracy: Reconciling Equality, Deliberation and Minority Protection*, Cambridge: Cambridge University Press, pp. 126–9.

18. See previous discussion which situates Deliberation Day within a range of reform proposals.
19. See Deliberation Day, Chapter 6.
20. See Ackerman, *We the People*, vol. I (1991) for the concept and vol. II (1998) for historical evidence.
21. For an overview see Alexander Keyssar (2000), *The Right to Vote: The Contested History of Democracy in the United States*, New York: Basic Books.
22. The classic discussion is Mancur Olson (1965), *The Logic of Collective Action*, Cambridge, MA: Harvard University Press. See also Russell Hardin (1982), *Collective Action*, Washington, DC: RFF Press.
23. Verba, Schlozman, and Brady, p. 15.
24. See David Glass, Peveril Squire, and Raymond Wolfinger (1984), "Voter Turnout: An International Comparison" in *Public Opinion*, December–January, pp. 49–55, for a classic statement of this argument. In 2008 there were about 150 million registered voters out of an eligible population of 207 million (taking into account age, citizenship, non-felon status, etc.), leading to a percentage of something like 72% of the eligible population being registered. The percentage of eligible voters who turned out in 2008 was about 62% (129 million out of about 207), while the percentage of registered voters who turned out was 86% (129 million out of 150). Just as when Glass, Squire, and Wolfinger wrote, the international comparisons are entirely different depending on whether one considers percentage of eligible or registered. Putting the entire burden of registration on the individual voter differentiates the United States from most other countries.
25. Sidney Verba, Kay Lehman Schlozman, and Henry Brady (1995), *Voice and Equality: Civic Voluntarism in American Politics*, Cambridge, MA: Harvard University Press, p. 11.
26. Morris P. Fiorina (1999), "Extreme Voices: The Dark Side of Civic Engagement" in Theda Skocpol and Morris P. Fiorina, eds., *Civic Engagement in American Democracy*, Washington, DC: Brookings Institution Press, and New York: Russell Sage Foundation, pp. 395–425.
27. See Verba, Schlozman and Brady, pp. 178–82.
28. Part of the argument in E.J. Dionne (2004), *Why Americans Hate Politics*, New York: Simon & Schuster. Diana Mutz also argues that cross-cutting exposure (which she calls deliberation) will suppress political participation partly by putting social relations at risk and partly by creating ambivalence. See D. Mutz (2004), *Hearing the Other Side: Deliberative versus Participatory Democracy*, Cambridge: Cambridge University Press. "People entrenched in politically heterogeneous social networks retreat from political activity mainly out of a desire to avoid putting their social relations at risk," p. 123.

29. Raymond Wolfinger and Steven Rosenstone (1980), *Who Votes?* New Haven and London: Yale University Press.

30. Study Circles has recently changed its name to Everyday Democracy. For a good overview of the rationale behind the National Issues Forums see David Mathews (1994), *Politics for People: Finding a Responsible Public Voice*, Urbana, IL: University of Illinois Press.

31. Cass R. Sunstein (2007), *Republic.com 2.0*, Princeton, NJ: Princeton University Press, pp. 77–80.

32. For an overview see John Gastil (2008), *Political Communciation and Deliberation*, Thousand Oaks, CA: Sage Publications. See also John Gastil (2004), "Adult Civic Education Through the National Issues Forums" in *Adult Education* Quarterly, 54/4 (August), pp. 308–28.

33. J.S. Mill, *Considerations on Representative Government*, p. 116.

34. For an overview see Anna Coote and Jo Lenaghan (1997), *Citizens Juries: Theory into Practice*, London: Institute for Public Policy Research.

35. See the coverage of the well-known Citizens Jury conducted by the Jefferson Center on the Clinton health care plan. For example, Julie Rovner (1994), "President Clinton's Health Care Plan on Trial Last Year," NPR, September 30.

36. A key limitation is that attitudinal data are only collected on arrival, not on first contact. Hence there is no basis for evaluating whether the participants are representative in terms of their viewpoints. The design would also be strengthened with control groups so one could know what changes are due to changes in the world (what Campbell and Stanley call "history) and what changes are due to the deliberations themselves. See D.T. Campbell and J.C. Stanley (1966), *Experimental and Quasi-Experimental Designs for Research*, New York: Rand MacNally. The vulnerability in this case is increased because of the length of time required for all the different deliberations to accumulate to a significant number.

37. See Christa Daryl Slaton (1992), *Televote*, New York: Praeger.

38. See Peter Neijens (1987), *The Choice Questionnaire. Design and Evaluation of an Instrument for Collecting Informed Opinions of a Population*, Amsterdam: Free University Press.

39. For an interesting experiment in viewing the first Deliberative Poll televised in the United States see Kenneth A. Rasinski, Norman M. Bradburn, and Douglas Lauen (1999), "Effects of NIC Media Coverage Among the Public" in Max McCombs and Amy Reynolds, eds., *The Poll with a Human Face: The National Issues Convention Experiment in Political Communication*, Mahwah, NJ: Lawrence Erlbaum Associates.

40. Joseph A. Schumpeter (1942), *Capitalism, Socialism and Democracy*, New York: Harper & Row, p. 242.

41. This account has obviously been influenced by Robert Dahl's discussion of Madison and the problem of tyranny in democratic theory in Robert Dahl (1956), *A Preface to Democratic Theory*, Chicago: University of Chicago Press. The rest of my argument has also benefited greatly from Dahl's discussion of the problem of achieving "enlightened

understanding" in *Democracy and Its Critics*, New Haven, CT: Yale University Press.

42. See James S. Fishkin (1979), *Tyranny and Legitimacy: A Critique of Political Theories*, Baltimore, MD: Johns Hopkins University Press.

43. When decision-makers are in a blind alley situation such that no matter which option they choose, terrible consequences will result for at least some people, it hardly seems appropriate to use such a severe term as "tyranny." Rather, they are in a situation that might better be characterized as "tragic choice."

Chapter 3

1. See Richard Posner, *Law, Pragmatism and Democracy*, and Ian Shapiro, *The Moral Foundations of Politics*.

2. For a critique of Schumpeter's views on the issue of inclusion see Robert A. Dahl, *Democracy and its Critics*, pp. 121–2.

3. For elaborations on the democratic limitations of the US Constitution, see Robert A. Dahl (2003), *How Democratic is the American Constitution?* New Haven and London: Yale University Press, and Sanford Levinson (2006), *Our Undemocratic Constitution*, New York: Oxford University Press.

4. For an argument that the parties will rarely, if ever differ on the big issues, however much they try to accentuate the appearance of differences, see Charles E. Lindblom (1977), *Politics and Markets*, New York: Basic Books.

5. Instead of one alternative to Schumpeterian competitive democracy, we will consider fifteen and then argue that it is useful to boil it down to a total of four basic democratic theories. See Chapter 3 and then the Appendix.

6. Richard A. Posner, *Law, Pragmatism and Democracy*, p. 163.

7. Other examples include the embedding of experiments within survey research, such as the choice questionnaire and the vast literature on mock juries.

8. If one accepts the argument of our trilemma, embracing both would be unrealistic. In any case, it would not then be distinctive about competition but just a claim that we should have all good things at the same time.

9. Note that we will treat Madison as a proponent of elite deliberation, not competitive democracy. But the two positions share a concern for avoiding tyranny of the majority and avoid embracing mass participation for that reason.

10. Donald Green and Ian Shapiro (1996), *Pathologies of Rational Choice Theory*, New Haven and London: Yale University Press, especially chapter 4.

11. See, for example, William Riker and Peter Ordeshook (1968), "A Theory of the Calculus of Voting," in *American Political Science Review*, 62/1, pp. 25–42. See also Donald Green and Ian Shapiro, *Pathologies of Rational Choice Theory*, for a discussion of how much of this approach has avoided empirical investigation.

12. For my own account of these issues see James S. Fishkin (1982), *Limits of Obligation*, New Haven and London: Yale University Press, which applies issues of obligation to large numbers of actors, including voters.

13. This reading has much in common with the valuable book by Joseph Bessette (1994), *The Mild Voice of Reason*, Chicago: University of Chicago Press. See, for example, his claim that the Framers "did not see their system as simply displacing citizen deliberation with those of the wise and virtuous. . . . Representatives according to Madison would pronounce the 'public voice' not their own enlightened judgments" (p. 45). Curiously, when Bessette goes on to study deliberation in Congress, he defines it simply as "reasoning on the merits of public policy" and drops all reference to refinement of the public views and whether members are sensitive to what they think their constituents would think if the latter were better informed.

14. See Edmund S. Morgan (1986), "Safety in Numbers: Madison, Hume and the Tenth Federalist" in *Huntington Library Quarterly*, pp. 95–112. See p. 105. Even this premise seems to assume that it is the politicians who will be offering rather than receiving the bribes or inducements. No one in Madison's time could have envisaged our use of television and the enormous appetites for campaign funding that it creates, rendering politicians who wish to be re-elected in need of so much financial support that the collection of campaign money comes perilously close to bribery, offered by factions and interests.

15. However, for an account of the transformation of the New Hampshire primary from retail politics to "wholesale" campaigning see Gary R. Orren and Nelson W. Polsby (1987), *Media and Momentum: The New Hampshire Primary and Nomination Politics*, Chatham, NJ: Chatham House.

16. For a classic statement of the dilemma see Hanna Pitkin (1967), *The Concept of Representation*, Berkeley, CA: University of California Press, chapter 7. Pitkin does not consider the middle ground position sketched here, but is (in my view) unduly dismissive of the Madisonian "filter" later in the book (pp. 194–5). Interestingly, she later offered a rereading of Locke on obligation in terms of hypothetical consent—what citizens would agree to, if they were more informed. See Pitkin (1974), "Obligation and Consent" in Peter Laslett, W.G. Runciman, and Quentin Skinner, eds., *Philosophy, Politics and Society*, Fourth Series, Oxford: Basil Blackwell.

17. Testimony of Samuel H. Beer before the House Judiciary Committee, December 8, 1998.

18. See, for example, then Representative Lindsey Graham discussing the public's views on impeachment: "they have an impression about this case from just tons and tons and tons and tons of talk, tons and tons and tons of spin; and that one in five, they tell me, are paying close attention to this. The question you must ask: If every American were required to do what I have done, is sit silently, listen to the evidence, would it be different?" CNN transcript, January 16, 1999.

19. A famous argument along these lines was offered by Robert Paul Wolff (1968), *In Defence of Anarchism*, New York: Harper & Row.

20. See Stephen Ansolabehere and Shanto Iyengar (1995), *Going Negative: How Political Advertisements Shrink and Polarize the Electorate*, New York: Free Press.

21. For a narrative with compelling cases see Spencer Overton (2006), *Stealing Democracy: the New Politics of Voter Suppression*, New York: Norton.

22. For a somewhat utopian proposal along these lines see John Burnheim (1985), *Is Democracy Possible?* Berkeley, CA: University of California Press.

23. See Carole Pateman (1970), *Participation and Democratic Theory*, Cambridge: Cambridge University Press, chapters 4 and 5. For an influential modern example of worker democracy, see Jaques Kaswan and Ruth Kaswan (1989), "The Mondragon Cooperatives – in Spain" in *Whole Earth Review*, Spring. Available at ⟨http://findarticles.com/p/articles/mi_m1510/is_n62/ai_7422455⟩. Some other important statements of participatory democracy include Benjamin R. Barber (1984), *Strong Democracy: Participatory Politics for a New Age*, Berkeley, CA: University of California Press, and Loïc Blondiaux (2008), *Le Nouvel Esprit de la Democratie*, Paris: Editions du Scuil.

24. See Bruce Ackerman and James S. Fishkin, *Deliberation Day*, New Haven: Yale University Press, for one effort to devise such a strategy—combining participation and deliberation in many decentralized sites for discussion on a human scale before national elections.

25. For the effectiveness of voter handbooks see David Magleby (1984), *Direct Legislation: Voting on Ballot Propositions*, Baltimore, MD: Johns Hopkins University Press, pp. 137–9. For experiments with the effectiveness of high technology voter handbooks see Shanto Iyengar and Simon Jackman, "Can Information Technology Energize Voters? Experimental Evidence from the 2000 and 2002 Campaigns." Available at ⟨http://pcl.stanford.edu/common/docs/research/iyengar/2003/energize.pdf⟩. Iyengar and Jackman look at effects of CD-based handbooks on voter interest and turnout.

26. The near-circus atmosphere of the California gubernatorial recall election provides a disquieting counterpart to the serious democratic expectations of Hiram Johnson and the Progressive reformers who designed it.

27. One hopeful sign is that some modest educative effects have been found in referenda. But these clearly fall short of the aspirations of the participatory theory. They are not like the effects that a Rousseau or a Mill would have aspired to, but worth noting nevertheless. A particularly interesting case can be found in Denmark where there have been seven national referenda on Europe. The Danes are consistently at the top in knowledge of Europe and the successive referenda campaigns are a likely explanation. But few polities would want to devote the time and resources to having referenda, over and over, on variants of the same topic. For US evidence see Daniel A. Smith and Caroline Tolbert (2004), *Educated by Initiative: The Effects of Direct Democracy on Citizens and Political Organizations*

in the American States, Ann Arbor, MI: University of Michigan Press.

28. See Frank Bryan (2003), *Real Democracy: The New England Town Meeting and How it Works*, Chicago: University of Chicago Press, for a detailed assessment of town meetings showing how the amount of participation varies with the size of the town.

29. We have conducted some of these online Deliberative Polls with random sampling (for which we had to supply computers for those who did not have them). We have also conducted them by recruiting a sample from a large online panel with a matching technology and then randomly assigned between treatment and control. In this case, the point was to compare a microcosm that deliberated with one that did not. See the section "Virtual Democracy" in Chapter 6.

30. See Aristophanes's satire on the courts in *The Wasps* in which the jurors are both unrepresentative and irresponsible, in Jeffrey Henderson, ed. (1998), *Aristophanes: Clouds, Wasps and Peace*, translated by Jeffrey Henderson, Cambridge, MA: Harvard University Press.

31. More travel appears to be an incentive so that the national and international events tend to get better samples participating.

32. See Chapter 5.

33. John Rawls (1971), *A Theory of Justice*, Cambridge, MA: Harvard University Press, p. 48. I am indebted to Dan Brock for suggesting this parallel.

34. See Henry E. Brady, James S. Fishkin, and Robert C. Luskin (2003), "Informed public opinion about foreign policy" in *The Brookings Review*, 21/3 (Summer); ABI/INFORM Global p. 16. Available at ⟨http:// cdd.stanford. edu/research/papers/2003/informed.pdf⟩. Also Robert C. Luskin, James Fishkin, and Shanto Iyengar, (2006), "Considered Opinions on U.S. Foreign Policy: Evidence from Online and Face-to-Face Deliberative Polling." Available at ⟨http://cdd.stanford.edu/research/papers/ 2006/foreign-policy.pdf⟩.

35. Iris Marion Young (2002), *Inclusion and Democracy*, Oxford: Oxford University Press, and Lynn M. Sanders (1997), "Against Deliberation," in *Political Theory*, 25/3, pp. 347–76.

36. By contrast, note that on the view offered here there is no privileged position for consensus.

37. Posner, *Law Pragmatism and Democracy*, and Shapiro, *Moral Foundations*, for spirited defenses of this position. But it is not only aggregative/ competitive theorists who accept the distinction, it is also common among deliberative theorists. See Iris Marion Young, "Two Models of Democracy" (section I.1) in *Inclusion and Democracy* where she endorses the deliberative model despite interrogating it from a feminist perspective.

38. See James S. Fishkin (1991), *Democracy and Deliberation: New Directions for Democratic Reform*, New Haven and London: Yale University Press, and Fishkin (1995), *The Voice of the People: Public Opinion and Democracy*, New Haven and London: Yale University Press.

39. See, for example, Joshua Cohen (1997), "Procedure and Substance in Deliberative Democracy," in James Bohman and William Rehg, eds., *Deliberative Democracy: Essays on Reason and Politics*, Cambridge, MA: MIT Press, and Amy Gutmann and Dennis Thompson (1996), *Democracy and Disagreement*, Cambridge, MA: Harvard University Press.

40. See Douglas W. Rae, "The Limits of Consensual Decision" for an elegant exposition of these issues.

41. See note to Cohen, and Gutmann and Thompson above.

42. Criteria for quality in deliberation are discussed in the section "Deliberation" in Chapter 2 and also in Bruce Ackerman and James S. Fishkin (2004), *Deliberation Day*, New Haven and London: Yale University Press, pp. 180–4.

43. In theory, this objection applies to both Categories III and IV because both employ raw preferences without any requirements for how preferences are formed. However, it is especially apt for Category IV because that approach depends on the legitimacy of consensus and brainwashing would provide a plausible basis for undermining that claim.

44. See Chapter 3 and the Appendix for discussions of the range of alternative theories.

45. This chart was also presented in Deliberation Day where it was used to make a different argument.

46. For accounts of how mass participation, whether deliberative or not, can serve to some degree as a proxy for consent see Bernard Manin, *The Principles of Representative Government*, chapter two and Ian Budge (1996), *The New Challenge of Direct Democracy*, Cambridge: Polity Press, chapter one.

47. Following Robert Goodin's suggestion that individuals in isolation might engage in "deliberation within" we might imagine that each individual might deliberate without discussion in a recognizable sense, but with some appropriate stimulus. Such a scenario would not require small groups and could be scaled to any size, depending on cost and other practical factors. However, if the individuals did not interact, then the process would be canned and prepackaged. One might imagine ways in which digests of the arguments of others would be presented and updated to each individual, reduced to a manageable format. With the right technology such a process might be possible. It would focus on facilitating deliberation without discussion in a recognizable sense (the updating of digests of the arguments of others would still be a form of communication). Clearly, technology to adapt deliberative processes that effectively motivate large numbers to really weigh competing arguments is an important area. Nevertheless, it seems unlikely that such developments would render large-scale deliberation reliably continuous (most people doing it all the time) rather than episodic as in the crisis of a constitutional moment. See Robert E. Goodin, "Deliberation Within," in Fishkin and Laslett, *Debating Deliberative Democracy*.

48. See Ackerman, *We the People*, vols. I and II.

49. Posner has charged deliberative democracy with elitism, in enshrining the views of a select few as the voice of the people. It is worth considering that whether or not the position is elitest should turn on how they are selected. A random and representative sample of the people has more resources to defend against charges of elitism than would, say, members of the Senate. See Posner, *Law, Pragmatism and Democracy*, section entitled "Democracy and Condescension," pp. 155–8.

50. See Jacobs and Shapiro, *Politicans Don't Pander* for an account of how political actors attempt to mold public opinion in support of predetermined policy goals. See pp. 45–56 for the basic rationale.

51. The Democratic-Republican party which he cofounded with Jefferson was a precursor of the modern Democratic Party.

Chapter 4

1. This timeline gives a sense of the variety of possible applications. More details on most of the projects are available at the Center for Deliberative Democracy web site ⟨http://cdd.stanford.edu⟩. My thanks to Nuri Kim for her work on this timeline. It does not include important DP projects conducted by two other entities: the Southwestern Pennsylvania Program for Deliberative Democracy led by Robert Cavalier at Carnegie Mellon, and Issues Deliberation Australia, under the leadership of Pam Ryan, which has conducted local and regional DPs in addition to the national projects referred to here. The ASSCU projects in the timeline are part of two years of training we have conducted for the American Democracy Project and those trainings have led to numerous other DPs in campuses around the country (for details see tab on American Democracy on the CDD web site). While this timeline is far from complete it shows the DPs we have been directly involved in as of this writing.

2. See section "Changes in Policy" in Chapter 5.

3. Note that inclusion in the selection process does not guarantee all aspects of inclusion. One could turn up in the random sample but be systematically ignored in the discussions. More on making the dialogue as well as the selection inclusive can be found below in sections "Avoiding Distortions: the Problem of Domination" in Chapter 4 and "Domination?" in Chapter 5.

4. One difference stems from geography. If people gathered in their local communities for deliberation, then their discussions would lack, by national standards, geographical diversity. In *Deliberation Day* we even envisage Internet-based universal deliberation that overcomes this limitation, rendering the scenario even more ambitious. However, see Luskin, Fishkin, and Iyengar, "Considered Opinions on US Foreign Policy" for an account of online deliberation compared to face-to-face.

5. See Fiorina, "Extreme Voices: The Dark Side of Civic Engagement."

6. See Nancy Fraser's valuable (1993), "Rethinking the Public Sphere: A Contribution to the Critique of Actually Existing Democracy" in Bruce

Robbins, ed., *The Phantom Public Sphere*, Minneapolis, MN: University of Minnesota Press, pp. 1–32, especially pp. 10–11.

7. See John Brehm for the threat of nonresponse to the validity of surveys. The problem has only gotten worse since he wrote, given the spread of cell phones, the disappearance of landlines, and the tumbling of response rates. John Brehm (1993), *The Phantom Respondents: Opinion Surveys and Political Representation*, Ann Arbor, MI: University of Michigan Press.

8. Iris Marion Young, *Inclusion and Democracy*, pp. 52–7.

9. See, for example, Cass R. Sunstein (2003), "The Law of Group Polarization" in James S. Fishkin and Peter Laslett, eds., *Debating Deliberative Democracy*, Oxford: Blackwell, pp. 80–101. Sunstein has sometimes granted an exception for the DP but he has recently seemed to take it back. See the discussion in our sections on polarization below: "Avoiding Distortions: Polarization and Groupthink" in Chapter 4 and "Movement to Extremes?" in Chapter 5.

10. Irving L. Janis (1972), *Victims of Groupthink*, Boston, MA: Houghton Mifflin.

11. The punch line of a Deliberative Poll is a change in policy attitudes. For some purposes it is worth distinguishing other kinds of opinion items. First, there are values. However, we do not expect deliberation to affect fundamental values. So I have not distinguished them in the list above. Value questions are, however, useful in explaining opinion change and most DPs include them. In addition, there are other attitude items that serve a useful explanatory purpose. In particular, there is a group of items we call empirical premises. There are many contested causal connections in the public mind that provide a rationale (when, indeed, these connections are subject to thought) for the connections between a person's beliefs and values and his or her policy attitudes. Will lowering taxes of a given sort increase or decrease revenue over the long term? Will increasing the rate of imprisonment decrease crime? But at what cost? In attempting to explain, and ultimately understand, changes in policy attitudes it is often key to also understand whether those changes are connected to empirical premises. I have not included them in the list above because our interest in them is primarily as explanatory variables not as dependent variables. As with fundamental values we use them primarily to explain changes in policy attitudes or voting intention.

12. The term is from Duncan Black (1963), *The Theory of Committees and Elections*, Cambridge: Cambridge University Press.

Chapter 5

1. To take an influential example, Dahl advocated deliberative microcosms as part of his "Sketches for An Advanced Democratic Country" in Robert A. Dahl (1989), *Democracy and Its Critics*, New Haven and London: Yale University Press, chapter 23.

2. See James S. Fishkin, Baogang He, and Alice Siu (2006), "Public Consultation Through Deliberation in China: The First Chinese Deliberative Poll"

in Ethan Lieb and Baogang He, eds., *The Search for Deliberative Democracy in China*, New York: Palgrave Macmillan, pp. 229–44.

3. See James S. Fishkin, Baogang He, Robert C. Luskin, and Alice Siu (2006), "Deliberative Democracy in an Unlikely Place" in *British Journal of Political Science* (forthcoming). Available at ⟨http://cdd.stanford.edu/research/papers/2006/china-unlikely.pdf⟩.

4. See Luskin, Fishkin, and Jowell, "Considered opinions" for the information-driven model. See "Deliberative Democracy in an Unlikely Place" for the China application.

5. See "Deliberative Democracy in an Unlikely Place." These proportions are the proportions of the policy indices that move toward or away from the time 1 positions. The more economically advantaged were the entrepreneurs in employment classification as the questionnaire did not ask about income directly.

6. See "Deliberative Democracy in an Unlikely Place" for more details.

7. Because some of these projects were less expensive it was possible to do twelve rather than ten as initially expected.

8. See Joel McCormick (2006), "It's Their Call" in *Stanford Magazine* January/February. Available at ⟨http://cdd.stanford.edu/press/2006/stanfordmag-call.pdf⟩.

9. Howard W. French (2005), "China's New Frontiers: Tests of Democracy and Dissent" in *The New York Times*, June 19.

10. "Participatory budgeting" is of course a term made famous in Porto Alegre, Brazil, but it is conducted there without scientific samples. At this writing, plans are at an advanced stage for Porto Alegre's first Deliberative Poll, to be conducted in 2009.

11. Amy Gutmann and Dennis Thompson (1996), *Democracy and Disagreement*, Cambridge, MA: Harvard University Press, pp. 143–4 and Amy Gutmann and Dennis Thompson (2004), *Why Deliberative Democracy?* Princeton, NJ: Princeton University Press, pp. 17–19. Shapiro critiques this case on the grounds that self-selection led to an unrepresentative process in which the key people affected were left out. In addition, "it is hard to find a relationship between the final rankings and the results of the deliberative process." Given that the binding character of the results is one of the criteria they propose for a process to be considered deliberative democracy, this is a serious criticism. Ian Shapiro (1999), "Enough of Deliberation" in Stephen Macedo, ed., *Deliberative Politics: Essays on Democracy and Disagreement*, Oxford: Oxford University Press, pp. 28–38; quotation from p. 33.

12. Gutmann and Thompson, *Why Deliberative Democracy?* See p. 11.

13. Gutmann and Thompson, *Why Deliberative Democracy?* See p. 5: a "characteristic of deliberative democracy is that its process aims at producing a decision that is *binding* for some period of time" (italics in original). In the same section they add caveats about how decisions taken can be revised in the future and how discussion must be intended to influence decisions (without necessarily determining them, now or in the future).

14. Essentially the same methodology was applied in California on an even larger scale in a health care deliberation called *CaliforniaSpeaks*, in which 120,000 people were initially solicited. An eventual 3,500 participated but only 60% were from this process. About 40% were "indirectly recruited" (friends or family who came along to the event were 21% and persons recruited by interest groups or grass-roots organizations were 19%). See Archon Fung and Taiku Lee (2008), "The Difference Deliberation Makes: A Report on the CaliforniaSpeaks Statewide Conversations on Healthcare Reform," October. Fung and Lee note that in comparison to a separate survey of the general public from the Public Policy Institute of California, the participants are politically different (only 18% self-identified as conservative as opposed to 37% of the California general public), demographically different (only 13% Latino compared to 36% of the California public) and much more interested in politics (61% very interested in politics compared to 21% of the general public).

15. See Technical Report, pp. 35ff. Available at ⟨http://www.citizensassembly.bc.ca/resources/TechReport(full).pdf⟩.

16. For an optimistic and theoretically rich account see Mark E. Warren and Hilary Pearse, eds. (2008), *Designing Deliberative Democracy: The British Columbia Citizens Assembly*, Cambridge: Cambridge University Press. Apart from discussing quotas for certain groups (such as Aboriginals), the contributions basically treat the effort as equivalent to other methods of "random sampling" and fail to address the issue of attitudinal representativeness.

17. See section in Chapter 6, "Putting Europe in One Room."

18. See, for example, Dieter Rucht (2008), "Deliberative Democracy in Global Justice Movements." Paper presented at International Workshop-Conference: Democratic Innovations—Theoretical and Practical Challenges of Evaluation, WZB, Berlin, February 7 9. Rucht offers an interesting case of activists who attempted to deliberate for whom the rules and agenda were such a subject of discussion that on his analysis the deliberation failed.

19. See Luskin, Fishkin, and Jowell, "Considered Opinions."

20. As Luskin and Fishkin note in a paper on the National Issues Convention: "Though statistically significant, most of these differences are relatively narrow. The widest no doubt is for age. Participants average six and a half years younger than non-participants. They also, not coincidentally, average roughly two thirds of a point higher on an eight point education scale. More typically, the differences are on the order of the following examples: the participants average between one sixth and one half a point higher on four point scales gauging political interest, discussion and campaign activity; a quarter of a point more agreement on the four point scale that politics is too complicated to understand; and a quarter of a point more liberal (though still to the conservative side of the mid point) on the seven point liberal-conservative scale." See Robert C. Luskin and James S. Fishkin, "Deliberative Polling, Public Opinion and Democracy." Available at ⟨http://cdd.stanford.edu⟩.

21. John R. Hibbing and Elizabeth Thiess-Morse (2002), *Stealth Democracy: Americans' Beliefs about How Government Should Work*, Cambridge: Cambridge University Press.
22. This conclusion seems to hold except for issues in which there is massive public discussion at the time of the DP. For such highly salient issues the preparatory period can also produce significant attitude change. For one of the experiments embedded within a DP see Cynthia Farrar, James Fishkin, Don Green, Christian List, Robert C. Luskin, and Elizabeth Levy Paluck (2006), "Disaggregating Deliberations' Effects: An Experiment Within a Deliberative Poll" in *British Journal of Political Science* (forthcoming). Available at ⟨http://cdd.stanford.edu/research/papers/2006/nh-disaggregating.pdf⟩.
23. See Robert C. Luskin, James S. Fishkin, and Kyu Hahn (2007), "Deliberation and Net Attitude Change." Paper presented at the ECPR General Conference, Pisa, Italy, September 6–8. Available at ⟨http://cdd.stanford.edu/research/papers/2007/deliberation-net-change.pdf⟩.
24. "Considered Opinions," p. 475.
25. These questions are taken from an index of seven questions. See James Fishkin, Tony Gallagher, Robert Luskin, Jennifer McGrady, Ian O'Flynn, and David Russell (2007), "A Deliberative Poll on Education: What Provision Do Informed Parents in Northern Ireland Want?" Final Report. Available at ⟨http://cdd.stanford.edu/polls/nireland/2007/omagh-report.pdf⟩, p. 32.
26. We have conducted other such efforts in Nebraska (with Alan Tomkins), in Turin (with Pierangelo Isernia), and in Bulgaria (with the Centre for Liberal Strategies). These will be reported in separate collaborative papers.
27. Cynthia Farrar, James S. Fishkin, Donald P. Green, Christian List, Robert C. Luskin, and Elizabeth Levy Paluck, "Disaggregating Deliberation's Effects." Our thanks to Don Green for suggesting the split half design.
28. The expectation of participating in a discussion with others may be a big factor in motivating people to become informed. See Chaffee for the notion of "communication utility" in Steven H. Chaffee (1972), "The Interpersonal Context of Mass Communication" in G. Gerald Kline and Philip J. Tichenor, eds., *Current Perspectives in Mass Communication Research*, Beverly Hills, CA: Sage, pp. 95–120. See p. 98.
29. These projects were a collaboration with Dennis Thomas, a former chair of the Texas Public Utility Commission, Robert Luskin, my Texas colleague, and Will Guild who runs a Texas survey research firm, the Guild Group.
30. See "Installed Wind Capacity" on the site of State Energy Conservation Office ⟨http://www.seco.cpa.state.tx.us/re_wind.htm⟩.
31. The Danish Deliberative Poll, conducted in August 2000, was a collaboration with a team of Danish political scientists led by Kasper M. Hansen and Vibeke Normann Andersen, and sponsored by the Danish publication *Monday Morning* as well as the Danish Broadcasting Corporation.

32. See, for example, James S. Fishkin (1997), *The Voice of the People: Public Opinion and Democracy*, New Haven and London: Yale University Press, 2nd edition, appendix E, p. 221. See also Robert C. Luskin and James S. Fishkin (2005), "Deliberative Polling, Public Opinion, and Democracy: The Case of the National Issues Convention." Available at ⟨http://cdd.stanford.edu/research/papers/2005/issues-convention.pdf⟩.

33. See Shanto Iyengar, Robert C. Luskin, and James S. Fishkin (2004), "Deliberative Preferences in the Presidential Nomination Campaign: Evidence from an Online Deliberative Poll." Paper presented at the annual meeting of the American Political Science Association, Chicago. Available at ⟨http://cdd.stanford.edu/research/papers/2005/presidential-nomination.pdf⟩. See also Robert C. Luskin, Kyu S. Hahn, James S. Fishkin, and Shanto Iyengar (2006), "The Deliberative Voter." Paper presented at the annual meeting of the American Political Science Association Philadelphia. Available at ⟨http://cdd.stanford.edu/research/papers/2006/deliberative-voter.pdf⟩.

34. Alice Siu (2008), "Look Who's Talking: Examining Social Influence, Opinion Change and Argument Quality in Deliberation." Ph.D. dissertation, Department of Communication, Stanford University, December.

35. Despite the strategic incentives for policy elites, it is worth noting that there is in fact some high quality deliberation among elected representatives. See the innovative work on the "discourse quality index" applied to members of parliament in four countries by Jürg Steiner, André Bächtiger, Markus Spörndli, and Marco R. Steenbergen (2005), *Deliberative Politics in Action: Analyzing Parliamentary Discourse*, Cambridge: Cambridge University Press.

36. Alice Siu, "Look Who's Talking," chapter 2.

37. Siu found that the small groups moved toward the initial position of the males 51% of the time, toward the initial positions of the more educated 54% of the time, toward the initial positions of those with higher income 52% of the time, and toward the initial positions of the white participants 48% of the time. This strategy for analyzing the issue of domination by the more advantaged was suggested by Robert Luskin.

38. While Sunstein has treated the DP as a possible exception to his law, he has since been asserting that the law is general and applies to DP-like processes. See Cass R. Sunstein (2006), *Infotopia: How Many Minds Produce Knowledge*, Oxford: Oxford University Press, especially chapter two, and David Schkade, Cass R. Sunstein, and Reid Hastie (2007), "What Happened on Deliberation Day?" in *California Law Review*, 95/3, pp. 915–40. The latter, most recent experiment uses a jury-like process and a deliberation limited to only fifteen minutes. It is difficult to generalize from such an experiment to either the Deliberation Day proposal (which is meant for a whole day without an agreed verdict) or the DP which also involves moderated discussion, no agreed consensus, and at least a whole day of deliberation.

39. Robert C. Luskin, James S. Fishkin, and Kyu Hahn (2007), "Consensus and Polarization in Small Group Deliberations." Paper Presented

at meetings of the American Political Science Association, Chicago. Available at ⟨http://cdd.stanford.edu/research/papers/2007/consensus-polarization.pdf⟩.

40. Luskin, Fishkin, and Hahn, "Consensus and Polarization."

41. Luskin, et al. find that the mean absolute net change, on a 0–1 scale to which the indices were normed, is 0.096. See Luskin, Fishkin, and Hahn, "Net Attitude Change."

42. Across the nine DPs the correlation between the time 1 mean knowledge score and the mean absolute net change is −0.583. See Luskin, Fishkin, and Hahn, "Net Attitude Change."

43. Popkin, "The Reasoning Voter," and Lupia, "Shortcuts Versus Encyclopedias."

44. At the time, the Centre was called Social and Community Planning Research (SCPR) and its Director, Roger Jowell, was a central collaborator in this project and in all our British projects. Our thanks to David Lloyd, then Commissioning Editor for News and Public Affairs at Channel Four, for making this project possible.

45. This plan was devised by our collaborator Roger Jowell and achieved the aim of focusing expert discussion and allowing arguments offered to be answered in a balanced and substantive way.

46. Robert C. Luskin, James S. Fishkin, Roger Jowell, and Alison Park (1999), "Learning and Voting in Britain: Insights from the Deliberative Poll." Paper presented at the meetings of the American Political Science Association, Atlanta. Available at ⟨http://cdd.stanford.edu/research/papers/2000/general_election_paper.pdf⟩.

47. The project team was led by our Danish collaborators Kasper Moeller Hansen and Vibeke N. Andersen, and the project was sponsored by the publication *Monday Morning* with a broad coalition of civil society groups.

48. See Kasper M. Hansen (2004), *Deliberative Democracy and Opinion Formation*, Odense: University Press of Southern Denmark, p. 144.

49. Hansen, p. 135.

50. See Robert C. Luskin (2001), "True Versus Measured Information Gain." Working Paper. Available at ⟨http://cdd.stanford.edu/research/papers/2001/true-infogain.pdf⟩.

51. Luskin and Fishkin, "Deliberative Polling, Public Opinion and Democracy."

52. See, for example, Luskin et al., "Considered Opinions;" Fishkin et al., "Deliberative Democracy in an Unlikely Place;" Farrar et al., "Disaggregating Deliberation's Effects."

53. See Robert C. Luskin and James S. Fishkin, "Deliberation and Better Citizens." Available at ⟨http://cdd.stanford.edu/research/papers/2002/bettercitizens.pdf⟩.

54. J.S. Mill, *Considerations on Representative Government*, p. 79.

55. We begin to examine that empirical question below. The issue has a long history. See Jane J. Mansbridge (1999), "On the Idea that Participation Makes Better Citizens" in Stephen L. Elkin and Karol Soltan, eds., *Citizen*

Competence and Democratic Institutions, University Park, PA: Pennsylvania State University Press, pp. 291–328. Mansbridge frames the issue about participation in general but many of her cases are discursive participation. J.S. Mill was heavily influenced by Toqueville and the two long reviews he wrote of *Democracy in America* were a precursor to his discussions of the issue in *Representative Government*. They are reprinted as introductions to each edition in Alexis de Tocqueville, (1961), *Democracy in America*, vols. I and II, New York: Schocken Books. For public spiritedness in the China case see Fishkin, He, Luskin, and Siu, "Deliberative Democracy in an Unlikely Place."

56. Farrar et al., "Disaggregating Deliberation's Effects."
57. Luskin and Fishkin, "Deliberative Polling, Public Opinion and Democracy," and Luskin and Fishkin, "Deliberation and Better Citizens."
58. Luskin and Fishkin, "Deliberation and Better Citizens."
59. See, for example, Posner *Law, Pragmatism and Democracy*, pp. 190–1.
60. See Luskin, Fishkin, Malhotra, and Siu, "Deliberation in the Schools." For the rationale behind NIFs see David Mathews, *Politics for People*.
61. See Gerry Mackie (2003), *Democracy Defended*, Cambridge: Cambridge University Press, for an argument that cycles are vanishingly rare, even in the key cases discussed in the literature.
62. See Christian List, Robert C. Luskin, James S. Fishkin, and Iain McLean, "Deliberation, Single-Peakedness, and the Possibility of Meaningful Democracy: Evidence from Deliberative Polls." Working Paper under submission. Earlier version presented at the American Political Science Association, Washington, DC, 2000. Available at ⟨http://cdd. stanford.edu/research/papers/2007/meaningful-democracy.pdf⟩. For earlier work on the idea that one might measure degrees of single peakedness or preference structuration, see R.G; Niemi (1969), "Majority Decision-Making with Partial Unidimensionality" in *American Political Science Review*, 63 (June 2), pp. 488–97.
63. See David Miller for discussion of the hypothesis that discussion will increase proximity to single-peakedness. David Miller (2003), "Deliberative Democracy and Social Choice," in James S. Fishkin and Peter Laslett, eds., *Debating Deliberative Democracy*, pp. 182–99.
64. See List et al., "Deliberation, Single Peakedness," and also Farrar et al., "Disaggregating Deliberation's Effects."
65. Michael Tackett (1996), "Conference Elicits Anxiety Over Economy: Citizens Air Common Concerns in Texas" in *Chicago Tribune*, January 21, p.1.
66. See "Powerful Reasons Help Explain Unease of Workers Over Lost Jobs Amid Prosperity" in *Buffalo News*, October 5, 1996, p. 2C.
67. Rosen's group and its reflections are recounted in Jay Rosen (1999), *What Are Journalists for?*, New Haven and London: Yale University Press, pp. 9–16.
68. See "Textbook Example of How to Lose the Argument: Lessons For Britain" in *The Independent*, September 30, 2000. Available at ⟨http://www.independent.co.uk/news/uk/politics/textbook-example-of-how-to-lose-the-argument-698994.html⟩.

69. See Mike Steketee (1999), "Yes Surges, But No Still Ahead" in *The Australian*, November 9: "Voters have swung back to the republic in the last week of the referendum campaign but a further shift would be needed to carry today's historic ballot."

70. The Deliberative Poll was held by Regione Lazio – Assessorato a Bilancio, programmazione economico finanziaria e partecipazione (Department of Budgeting, Financial Planning and Participation). It was promoted and carried out by the magazine *Reset* with the support of Ispo (Istituto per gli Studi sulla Pubblica Opinione – Institute for Studies on Public Opinion) directed by Renato Mannheimer. The survey and the final event were sponsored by the bank Dexia, Lega Coop (the Italian association of cooperative societies), and the newspaper, *E-polis*. Since then the Associazione per la Democrazia Informata has been created to promote Deliberative Polling in Italy.

71. One exception was that the sample was somewhat more left leaning. However, when we weighted the results by ideology the main results remained unchanged. See ⟨http://cdd.stanford.edu/polls/italy/2007/lazio-pressrelease.pdf⟩. One reason for the lower than normal turnout may have been the state government's reluctance to pay a cash incentive for participation.

72. Mauro Buonocore (2007), "The First Time in Italy" in *Reset*, 101, May–June (English translation provided by the author). Available at ⟨http://cdd.stanford.edu/press/2007/reset-firstitaly-eng.pdf⟩.

73. In November 1995 there were no commercially viable wind projects in Texas. See Testimony of Mike Sloan, Managing Consultant, The Wind Coalition, before the House Select Committee on Energy Independence and Global Warming, Hearing on "Renewable Electricity Standards: Lighting the Way", September 20, 2007. Available at ⟨http://globalwarming. house.gov/tools/assets/files/0038.doc⟩.

74. The first of this series was hosted by Central Power and Light (CPL) in Corpus Christi, Texas, in May 1996 followed by West Texas Utilities (WTU) in Abilene; Southwestern Electric Power Company (SWEPCO) in Shreveport, Louisiana; El Paso Electric (EPE) in El Paso; Houston Light and Power (HLP) in Houston, Entergy in Beaumont, Southwestern Public Service Company (SPS) in Amarillo, and then Texas Utilities in Dallas.

75. Testimony of Mike Sloan.

76. Russel Smith (2001), "That's Right, I Said A Texas Wind Boom" in *Whole Earth*, Summer, p. 1. Available at ⟨http://findarticles.com/p/articles/mi_m0GER/is_/ai_76896168⟩.

77. See Rebecca Smith (2004), "States Lead Renewable-Energy Push; As Federal Efforts Stall, Debate Over Foreign Oil Has Intensified Locally" in *Wall Street Journal*, Eastern Edition, New York, September 22, p. A.8. Available at ⟨http://cdd.stanford.edu/press/2004/wsjenergy/index.html⟩.

78. See Nebraska Public Power District Customer Meeting on Energy Alternatives Summary of Results August 19, 2003, prepared by The Public Decision Partnership: Will Guild, Ron Lehr, and Dennis Thomas. Available at ⟨http://cdd.stanford.edu/polls/energy/2003/nppdresults.pdf⟩.

79. See "NPPD Board Approves State's Largest Wind Farm." Available at ⟨http://www.nppd.com/Newsroom/NewsRelease.asp?NewsReleaseID=159⟩.

80. Nova Scotia Power Customer Energy Forum: Summary of Results November 19–20, 2004. Available at ⟨http://cdd.stanford.edu/polls/energy/2004/ns-results-summary.pdf⟩.

81. See the company report at ⟨http://www.canelect.ca/en/pdf_Review_05/RA05_NScotia_P_eng.pdf⟩.

82. See Report on the Deliberative Poll on "Vermont's Energy Future," Center for Deliberative Opinion Research University of Texas at Austin. Report prepared by Robert C. Luskin, David B. Crow, James S. Fishkin, Will Guild, and Dennis Thomas. Available at ⟨http://cdd.stanford.edu/polls/energy/2008/vermont-results.pdf⟩.

83. See ⟨http://publicservice.vermont.gov/planning/CEP%20%20WEB%20DRAFT%20FINAL%206-4-08.pdf⟩.

84. The same process was repeated in February 2009, with similar receptiveness by the LPC, and a commitment by the town and the LPC to continue the pattern on an annual basis.

85. See ⟨http://www.tekno.dk/subpage.php3?article=468&toppic=kategori12&language=uk⟩.

Chapter 6

1. I take the term "normal politics" from Ackerman's *We the People*, vol. 1, where it is applied to standard conditions of party competition outside the kind of national crisis that might lead to a period of constitutional change.

2. Dr. Pam Ryan conceived and created the project. Two distinguished Australian political leaders, Ian Sinclair and Barry Jones, presided over the sessions. For details on the whole initiative, see Reconciliation, Final Report ⟨http://ida.org.au/UserFiles/File/Australia% 20Deliberates_Reconciliation_ FINAL%20REPORT.pdf⟩.

3. The Advisory Committee included former Prime Minister Bob Hawke; former National Party Leader and Speaker of the House, Ian Sinclair; former MP and ALP Federal President, Barry Jones; Democrat Senator Aden Ridgeway; the Chair of the Aboriginal and Torres Strait Islander Commission, Geoff Clark; Liberal Members of Parliament Sharman Stone (also Member of the Council for Aboriginal Reconciliation) and Warren Entsch; Liberal Senator Jeannie Ferris; Labor Shadow Minister Bob McMullan; former Chair of the Council for Aboriginal Reconciliation Evelyn Scott; former High Court Judge and author of a major study of the "stolen generation" *Bringing Them Home*, Sir Ronald Wilson; former Liberal Minister Fred Chaney; and independent film maker Rachel Perkins. For more details, including the involvement of government ministers, see Reconciliation, Final Report ⟨http://ida.org.au/UserFiles/File/Australia%20Deliberates_Reconciliation_FINAL%20REPORT.pdf⟩.

4. The "before and after" results reported in what follows are of the random sample and not the additional oversample of indigenous Australians.

5. See page 7 of the project's briefing document. Despite the estimates of more than 700,000, only 300,000 identified themselves as Roma in the Census. See ⟨http://cdd.stanford.edu/docs/2007/bulgaria-roma-2007.pdf⟩.

6. See Executive Summary: National Deliberative Poll—Policies Toward the Roma in Bulgaria. Available at ⟨http://cdd.stanford.edu/polls/bulgaria/2007/bulgaria-results.pdf⟩.

7. The participants were 76% female. Male and female respondents changed in the same way on thirty-seven out of thirty-nine of the policy issues in the study. See "Northern Ireland's First 'Deliberative Poll' Shows Views of Informed Parents." Available at ⟨http://cdd.stanford.edu/polls/nireland/2007/omagh-results.pdf⟩.

8. See James S. Fishkin, Robert C. Luskin, Ian O'Flynn, and David Russell, "Deliberating Across Deep Divides." Working Paper, Center for Deliberative Democracy. Available at ⟨http://cdd.stanford.edu⟩. See appendix.

9. See ⟨http://cdd.stanford.edu/polls/nireland/2007/omagh-video.html⟩ for the BBC program.

10. For arguments both for and against the application of "consociational democracy" to divided societies see the excellent collection Ian O'Flynn and David Russell, eds. (2005), *Power Sharing: New Challenges for Divided Societies*, London: Pluto Press.

11. The fact that our DPs do not confirm Sunstein's law of group polarization under the controlled conditions of balanced discussion with representative samples does not undermine the case Sunstein makes for polarization outside these special conditions (unrepresentative groups without balanced discussion). For some useful but different perspectives on the problem of deliberation in divided societies see Ian O'Flynn (2007), "Divided Societies and Deliberative Democracy" in *British Journal of Political Science*, 37/4, pp. 731–51 and John S. Dryzek (2005), "Deliberative Democracy in Divided Societies: Alternatives to Agonism and Analgesia" in *Political Theory*, 33, pp. 218–42.

12. Robert C. Luskin, James S. Fishkin, and Shanto Iyengar "Considered Opinions on U.S. Foreign Policy: Evidence from Online and Face-to-Face Deliberative Polling." Available at ⟨http://cdd.stanford.edu/research/papers/2006/foreign-policy.pdf⟩.

13. See Luskin et al., "The Deliberative Voter."

14. The sample was recruited by YouGov/Polimetrix from an existing panel of more than one million with matching on a variety of socio-demographic factors and randomly assigned between treatment and control.

15. These changes held up in comparison to the pre/post control group.

16. See, for example, Joseph Cappella, Vincent Price, and Lilach Nir (2002), "Argument Quality as a Reliable and Valid Measure of Opinion Quality: Electronic Dialogue During Campaign 2000" in *Political Communication*, 19, pp. 73–93 for a related effort to apply online deliberation and study its quality.

17. Papandreou, "Picking Candidates by the Numbers."
18. Key differences, of course, were the limited number of citizens in the total population and the fact that citizens had to put their names on a list to be part of the lottery for participation. See Hansen, *The Athenian Democracy*, p. 181.
19. See Hermann Schmitt (2005), "The European Parliament Elections of June 2004: Still Second Order?" in *West European Politics*, 28/3, pp. 650–79. The "Second Order Elections" thesis continues to apply to the old member states but less to the new ones.
20. See Fraser, "Rethinking the Public Sphere," for a persuasive summary of the case for these two tests.
21. Knowledge levels about EU issues are notoriously low in most EU states, with the notable exception of Denmark which has had seven referendum campaigns on EU issues.
22. Some of these conflicts arose in the dialogue at the EU-wide Deliberative Poll. See the plenary discussion in "Europe in One Room" in which the conflict between Greece and Turkey in Cyprus was the subject of discussion from the floor and in which the conflict in Northern Ireland was the subject of discussion by the panelists.
23. For a good expression of this Posnerian position on EU issues, see Andrew Moravscik "Another Angle." Available at ⟨http://www.princeton.edu/~amoravcs/library/E!Sharp.pdf⟩.
24. See, for example, Andrew Moravcsik, "What Can We Learn from the Collapse of the European Constitutional Project?" Available at ⟨http://www.princeton.edu/~amoravcs/library/PVS04.pdf⟩.
25. Jürgen Habermas (1995), "Remarks on Dieter Grimm's 'Does Europe Need a Constitution?'" in *European Law Journal*, 1/3 (November), pp. 303–7, especially p. 305.
26. The project was called Tomorrow's Europe and it was led by Stephen Boucher and Henri Monceau of Notre Europe with an advisory group of twenty-two partner organizations and a balanced reading committee of MEPs representing competing points of view. Details can be found at ⟨http://cdd.stanford.edu/polls/eu/and also at: http://www.tomorrowseurope.eu/⟩.
27. See Philip Schlesinger and Deirdre Kevin, "Can the European Union become a sphere of Publics?" and Erik Oddvar Eriksen and John Erik Fossum (2000), "Conclusion: Legitimation through Deliberation" in Erik Oddvar Eriksen and John Erik Fossum, eds., *Democracy in the European Union: Integration through Deliberation*? London: Routledge. See also Samantha Besson (2006), "Deliberative Democracy in the European Union: Towards the Deterritorialization of Democracy" in Samantha Besson and Jose Luis Marti, eds., *Deliberative Democracy and its Discontents*, London: Ashgate, pp. 181–214.
28. They did, however, begin more in favor of admitting Ukraine, a position which changed with deliberation. See Robert C. Luskin, James S. Fishkin, Stephen Boucher, and Henri Monceau, (2008), "Considered Opinions on Further EU Enlargement: Evidence from an EU-Wide

Deliberative Poll." Working Paper Center for Deliberative Democracy, presented at the annual meeting of the International Society of Political Psychology, Paris, France, July 9–12. Available at 〈http://cdd.stanford.edu/research/papers/2008/EU-enlargement.pdf〉. See also "Opinion Changes: Before and After Deliberation." Available at 〈http://cdd.stanford.edu/polls/eu/2007/eu-dpoll-allopinionchange.pdf〉.

29. See 〈http://cdd.stanford.edu/docs/2007/eu/eu-dpoll-ENG.pdf〉, p. 14.

30. For a good summary of demographic arguments in favor of raising the retirement age and the political difficulties which count against it see Heather Jerbi (2006), "Where Policy Meets Politics" in *Contingencies: American Academy of Actuaries*, March/April. Available at 〈http://www.contingencies.org/marapr06/policy_briefing_0306.asp〉.

31. "New Member States vs. Old Member States." Available at 〈http://cdd.stanford.edu/polls/eu/2007/eu-dpoll-new-old.pdf〉.

32. See Luskin, Fishkin, Boucher, and Monceau, "Considered Opinions on Further EU Enlargement."

33. "Knowledge Gains: Before and After Deliberation." Available at 〈http://cdd.stanford.edu/polls/eu/2007/eu-dpoll-knowledge.pdf〉.

34. See Luskin, Fishkin, Boucher, and Monceau, "Considered Opinions on Further EU Enlargement."

35. Results from Europolis will be available on the CDD web site http://cdd.stanford.edu after the event May 29–31, 2009.

36. R.G. Lipsey and Kelvin Lancaster (1956/7), "The General Theory of Second Best" in *The Review of Economic Studies*, 24/1, pp. 11–32.

37. If a Paretian, ordinalistic framework is applied, then at least there is no clearly better, or Pareto-superior, alternative.

38. I believe the problem is not limited to political theory and social choice. There are parallels with personal morality. See Fishkin, *Limits of Obligation* for an argument about the intractable conflict between our notions of general obligation and personal liberty once the problem of social scale is taken into account. See James S. Fishkin (1982), *The Limits of Obligation*, New Haven and London: Yale University Press.

39. See James S. Fishkin (1984), *Justice, Equal Opportunity and the Family*, New Haven and London: Yale University Press.

40. See James S. Fishkin (1992), *Dialogue of Justice*, New Haven and London: Yale University Press, pp. 180–6.

41. Fishkin, *Justice, Equal Opportunity*, chapter 1.

42. A related position can be found in Isaiah Berlin (1969), *Four Essays on Liberty*, Oxford: Oxford University Press, pp. 170–1 and William A. Galston (2005), *The Practice of Liberal Pluralism*, Cambridge: Cambridge University Press, part I.

Index

Page numbers in *italics* indicate the entry is in the appendix.

Made in the USA
Lexington, KY
02 June 2013